THE MOST
EVIL
SECRET SOCIETIES
IN HISTORY

THE MOST
EVIL
SECRET SOCIETIES
IN HISTORY

SHELLEY KLEIN

MICHAEL O'MARA BOOKS LIMITED

First published in Great Britain in 2005 by
Michael O'Mara Books Limited
9 Lion Yard
Tremadoc Road
London SW4 7NQ

A CIP catalogue record for this book is available from the British Library

ISBN 1-84317-167-8

1 3 5 7 9 10 8 6 4 2

www.mombooks.com

Designed and typeset by Design 23

Printed in Singapore by Tien Wah Press

CONTENTS

INTRODUCTION

For as long as man has been able to communicate with his fellow man, to create social hierarchies and organize mutually beneficial gatherings, he has also, or so it seems, been fascinated by the creation and presence of secret societies. Most of these are (and have always been) harmless organizations, groups of like-minded individuals with a common aim in mind. Men's dining clubs would fall into this category, or university fraternities, societies that at worst appeal to those interested in the advancement of mildly elitist views or strangely arcane beliefs. Some organizations, however, far from being innocent, instead harbor more sinister agendas, requiring blood oaths, total surrender of one's personal life or subjugation to a despotic leader. This collection is an attempt to gather a few of these secretive, shadowy groups together – societies that have operated throughout the world in countries as diverse as Japan, America, Kenya, Germany, England, Switzerland and Italy.

Often, when talking of secret societies, it becomes immediately apparent that the organizations under discussion fall into recognizably different categories. So it is with the groups examined here. There is a marked difference between those societies harboring a political agenda (such as the Socialist Patients Collective, the Mau Mau, Odessa and the Hashishim) and those 'Doomsday' organizations such as Aum Shinrikyo or the Order of the Solar Temple. Similarly, the Ku Klux Klan, whose main purpose was, and sadly still is, the advancement of highly racist views can, to some extent, be grouped with the Thule Society (with both groups' belief in a perfect race) while the Tong and the Camorra belong under a general heading of 'organized crime.' But what of such groups as the Hell Fire Club? How do they fit into the picture, and under which category do they fall?

In many respects the Hell Fire Club stands out in this collection by being the 'least' evil. Formed in the eighteenth century by a group of highly influential men who liked to dabble in politics but whose main purpose in life was pure debauchery, they were, when compared to just about every other secret society in this collection, a relatively harmless group. That said, what the Hell Fire Club illustrated beautifully is man's seemingly insatiable desire to create an 'us-versus-them' scenario by forming a group to which only a small number of chosen individuals can belong. This is clearly a central tenet of any secret society.

Argenteum Astrum – Aleister Crowley's secretive organization – is another prime example of this. Vaguely distasteful, unashamedly elitist and bordering on the insane, what Argenteum Astrum really signified was the desire of some individuals to be thought of as 'special,' set apart from the majority, better than the rest. To satisfy this desire, the more impenetrable a group's teachings appear, and the more obscure or bizarre the initiation rites, the more attractive the group becomes. This rationale may go some way to explain why cults such as Aum Shinrikyo (whose initiation rituals were bizarre in the extreme) or the Order of the Solar Temple attracted such large numbers of followers. The teachings of these respective groups become a religion to their disciples, a means by which they will ultimately achieve immortality.

The Hashishim were no strangers to this notion, for they were convinced that by carrying out their role as assassin they would be rewarded with the eternal delights of paradise. Certain parallels can be drawn between this ancient cult and present-day suicide bombers although, whereas the former went to great lengths to kill only their desired target and not harm innocent bystanders, the same cannot be said of the modern-day terrorists. The Thugs in India, whose whole cult was built (initially at least) around the idea of achieving eternal glory by sacrificing innocent wayfarers to the goddess Kali, also eventually ceased the religious aspect of their teachings in favor of more self-serving ideals – those of theft for personal gain.

Personal gain becomes something of a recurring theme when studying secret societies, whether it takes the form of enjoying of messiah-like status (as was the case with Aleister Crowley) or whether the cachet is fundamentally monetary, as with Aum Shinrikyo's leader, Shoku Asahara. The Odessa organization might also fall into this category, having been set up primarily to aid Nazi war criminals after the end of World War II and, although it didn't operate perhaps quite so 'romantically' as the novelist Frederick Forsyth suggests in *The Odessa File*, it was nonetheless a highly successful outfit, and one that enabled several high-ranking Nazi officers to escape the hangman's noose. There can be few better or more self-serving reasons to form a secret society than self-preservation, but when studying these organizations it quickly becomes apparent that the huge interest in groups such as Odessa exists for quite another reason – that of pandering to our obsession with conspiracy theories. If Odessa existed, after all, surely other secret societies and their evil machinations could yet be influencing world politics?

In this respect there can be no secret society on earth that holds such fascination as the Illuminati. Unknown to most people until the publication of Dan Brown's novel *Angels and Demons* in 2000, since the book hit the shops the public's appetite for information on this highly esoteric organization has reached monumental proportions. But why should this be, and what is it about this particular group that has caused such a global reaction?

The answer lies with the fact that Dan Brown is a marvellous weaver of stories and in *Angels and Demons* he has created the type of scenario beloved by so many of us – a small group of people battling against a much larger, incredibly powerful organization, in this case the Catholic Church. This type of 'David and Goliath' plot is as old as time itself; indeed it seems fundamental to mankind's psyche and so perhaps Dan Brown has released an emotional trigger within us all. But more than this, Brown has also tapped into the public's often deep-seated belief that 'all is not as it seems'; that, behind the scenes, evil conspiracies are afoot; that the public is constantly being duped, lied to, lulled into a false sense of security and fed anything but the truth. Take, for instance, Hitler's suicide at the end of World War II or the first landing of man on the moon. Both events have had millions of words written about them asserting that neither episode took place. Hitler, or so many right-wing conspiracy theorists would have us believe, is alive and kicking somewhere in South America – while the first moon landing, according to many people, actually took place in a TV studio after America was forced to abort the real flight due to technical problems. Wild, woolly and way-out conspiracy theories can be found around every corner.

The Illuminati are simply an extension of this idea, for although a sect of that name did exist back in eighteenth-century Bavaria, and although that sect did espouse the overthrowing of established religion in favor of a New World Order, there is absolutely no evidence to suggest that they have reformed or that they have any way succeeded in this plan.

Instead, it is terrorist organizations such as the Socialist Patients Collective (who were sympathetic to a whole raft of other terrorist groups – the Red Army Faction, the American Weather Underground Organization and the Black Panther party, to name but a few,) and those who actively try to change the face of politics in their respective countries that we should be wary of. However idealistic their aims initially may have been, the fact that they resorted to violence in order to make their case heard ultimately negates any positive outcome they might have achieved. Similarly, the Mau Mau, who it could be argued had a legitimate reason for forming a clandestine outfit in opposition to Kenya's British administration, in taking up arms and slaughtering not only their white 'masters' but also vast numbers of their black countrymen lost any semblance of political validity, becoming simply violent criminals.

Similarly, organizations such as the Thule or the Ku Klux Klan, present a far greater threat than the James Bond-type societies hellbent on ruling the world. After all, both the Thule and the KKK were (and, in the case of the latter group, still are) truly insidious organizations whose teachings, without any shadow of doubt, have affected millions of people all over the world.

To a lesser extent the Tong and the Camorra have also, through their individual operations, brought misery to thousands of people, although they do not preach a religion of hatred or racial superiority. Nevertheless, both the Tong and the Camorra, because they have both created an aura of mystery around their operations, fascinate the general public to an extent where they have been dangerously romanticized. In this they are similar to the Mafia, whose secret operations have produced a plethora of books, films and documentaries all pandering to our deep-seated desire to know something we shouldn't. In other words, part of our fascination with secret societies stems from an overwhelming need to find out what lies behind Bluebeard's locked door. This may also help to explain why there are always plenty of people willing to join up to some of the more bizarre secret societies out there. While it is easy to understand why racists would want to belong to the Ku Klux Klan, or why left-wing guerrillas would eagerly sign up to the Socialist Patients Collective, it is perhaps beyond our comprehension why anyone would wish to enrol with a group as odd as the Order of the Solar Temple.

Naturally, we may assume such individuals are psychiatrically disturbed, lost souls looking for something to live by, or easily manipulated into giving away their life's savings, but, while such assumptions may have some basis in truth, for certain people curiosity plays no small part in their decision-making processes. They want to know what it is like on the other side of the door, are the promises of a sweet hereafter true, and will their lives suddenly blossom? Of course, once they have taken that first step over the threshold, it is often (given the powerful personalities of the leaders, and brainwashing techniques they sometimes employed) impossible to extricate themselves from the group. Those that do attempt to leave may face the threat of death or, in the case of the Solar Temple, prompt a doomsday scenario leading to the deaths of many others, too. After the Solar Temple's mass 'suicides,' the Swiss government set up an information center on religious cults so that the general public could be better informed about the dangers of joining such organizations.

What then can be done to dissuade people from joining up to such evil, warped and, in many cases, murderous operations? The answer is very little. Wherever man congregates, at some time or another, a secret society is bound to be formed or, put another way, just as city of London residents are never more than a few feet away from an unseen rat, so the chances are that wherever you live in the world there is some kind of secret society in operation, either plotting the downfall of a sworn enemy or planning some equally bizarre and evil act.

Shelley Klein

THE ILLUMINATI – FOUNDERS OF A NEW WORLD ORDER

> As Weishaupt lived under the tyranny of a despot and priests, he
> knew that caution was necessary even in spreading information,
> and the principles of pure morality. This has given an air of
> mystery to his views, was the foundation of his banishment [...] If
> Weishaupt had written here, where no secrecy is necessary in our
> endeavors to render men wise and virtuous, he would not have
> thought of any secret machinery for that purpose.
>
> THOMAS JEFFERSON

Ever since Dan Brown wrote his bestselling novel, *Angels and Demons*, the Illuminati has been the subject of intense speculation among both the general public and the media alike. In his novel, Brown presents an intriguing scenario, one in which a highly secretive society that has been presumed extinct for several centuries establishes itself once again in order to continue its bloody feud against the Catholic church. But how much of the Brown plotline is based on fact? Did such a group ever exist and if so is it still functioning today?

When attempting to study the nature and activities of secret societies, it quickly becomes very difficult (occasionally well-nigh impossible) to separate fact from fiction, reality from centuries-old fabrication, the truth from downright lies. The case of the Illuminati is no exception and it is, in fact, even more difficult to distil the truth from all of the available information about this group owing to the huge public interest in new world orders, global conspiracy theories and shadowy organizations who supposedly control world affairs. Over the centuries, several groups have laid claim to the name Illuminati, boasting their possession of Gnostic texts or of other even more arcane information not otherwise available to the general public. The first known record of the name Illuminati comes in the second century AD when a self-styled prophet by the name of Montanus, who had previously belonged to the cult of Cybele, converted to Christianity. He then set up a group in direct opposition to the institutionalized church. Alongside the prophetesses, Prisca (or Priscilla) and Maxilla, Montanus's most famous convert to the cause was the Catholic apologist Tertullian. But it is the fourth-century historian, Eusebius, who best illustrates Montanus's extraordinary gifts, describing how converts underwent all manner of religious experiences including 'speaking in tongues' and receiving apocalyptic visions.

> Their opposition and their recent heresy which has separated them from
> the Church arose on the following account [...] a recent convert,

Montanus by name, through his unquenchable desire for leadership, gave the adversary opportunity against him. And he became beside himself […] in a sort of frenzy and ecstasy, he raved and began to babble and utter strange things, prophesying in a manner contrary to the custom of the Church handed down by tradition from the beginning.[1]

Aside from these reveries however, what lay at the heart of Montanus's teachings was a type of 'end-of-the-world' scenario so beloved of almost all the sects studied in this book. To help his followers come to terms with his apocalyptic vision, Montanus laid down a strict moral code for them to follow, one that would purify the Christian soul and deter disciples from coveting material goods. This form of illuminism flourished for several centuries, particularly in Asia Minor, before gradually diminishing until, in the ninth century, it died out altogether.

Nothing was then heard of the Illuminati in any shape or form until, in fifteenth- and sixteenth-century Spain, a group calling themselves the Alumbrado (which roughly translates as 'Illuminati') appeared. The Alumbrado claimed to be in direct communion with the Holy Spirit and stated that all outward forms of religious adherence, such as the observance of the liturgy, were unnecessary. One of their earliest leaders, who wholeheartedly embraced these teachings, was a laborer's daughter from Salamanca known as La Beata de Piedrahita. She declared that she held long conversations with both Jesus and the Virgin Mary, claims that quite naturally brought her to the attention of the Inquisition. Miraculously, she escaped death at the hands of her interogators, although others weren't quite as lucky. In Toledo, adherents to the Alumbrado were subjected to severe beatings and imprisonment while the Inquisition served no less than three separate edicts against the group, issued in 1568, 1574 and 1623.

It was also in 1623 that a movement known as the Illuminés was established in France (some say having traveled up from Seville in Spain). Quite rapidly this movement attained a strong following in the Picardy region although very little documentation remains as to the nature of the group, its beliefs or practices. What is generally agreed upon is that Pierce Guérin, the curé of Saint-Georges de Roye, who founded his own group called the Gurinets, joined the Illuminés in 1634.

Over a century later, in 1772, yet another group called the Illuminés came to light in the south of France, but while little is known about the Picardy sect, even less is known about this second organization. Finally, we arrive at perhaps the best known of all the Illuminati-style societies, which started in eighteenth-century Bavaria.

Adam Weishaupt was born on 6 February 1748 in Ingolstadt and as a young boy was educated by Jesuit priests who instilled in him not only discretion, but also respect for the hierarchic obedience of the Society of Jesus (or Jesuits). Yet despite his early allegiance to the order, his appointment as Professor of Natural and Canon Law at the University of Ingolstadt in 1775 angered his teachers for not only did he grow to espouse seriously liberal, cosmopolitan views, but he also 'condemned bigotry and superstitious Priests.'[2] Not everyone was against him however, for soon Weishaupt had earned a good reputation amongst both students and professors alike and even those at neighboring universities were impressed by his teachings. Perhaps this support afforded Weishaupt confidence, and no doubt this in turn led to the suggestion that he should become the leader of a more influential group.

On 1 May 1776, with the help of Baron Adolph von Knigge, Weishaupt formed the 'Order of Perfectibilists', which later became known as the Illuminati. Interestingly, some historians have since claimed that this founding date marks the origin of the Communist May Day observance, although there is little evidence to support the theory. What is certain is that in 1777, Weishaupt was invited to join a Freemasonry Lodge, the Theodor zum guten Rath (Lodge Theodor), in Munich. He accepted the invitation even though most of his energies were still devoted to the Illuminati, whose doctrine was a curious mixture of Islamic mysticism, Jesuit mental discipline and some of Freemasonry's own teachings, many of which also cherished the idea of 'illumination'. Nonetheless, Weishaupt's group was a law unto itself with its own agenda and initiatives. Its declared mission was an adherence to a strict code of morality in order to create a society of men strong enough to oppose the forces of evil.

Yet, despite being completely separate from the Freemasons, an apocryphal story has grown up around the conception of the Illuminati, a story that relates how a courier by the name of Lanz, who had recently joined the Illuminati, was struck down by a bolt of lightning whilst carrying a bundle of Weishaupt's most important papers. Lanz died, but when his body was discovered by the authorities, so too were Weishaupt's documents which were said to reveal a direct link between his group and that of Freemasonry. Perhaps this is why, in Dan Brown's novel, a basic premise of the story is that in the sixteenth century the Illuminati (who Robert Langdon believes had already established themselves in Italy), having been banished from Rome, were taken in by the Bavarian Freemasons after which they set about using the latter as a front for their

Adam Weishaupt was Professor of Natural and Canon Law at the University of Ingolstadt in 1775, but was sacked from his post nine years later after forming a group called the Order of Perfectibilists, later known as the Illuminati.

activities, effectively forming a secret society within a secret society. They then set their sights on the United States, once again using the Freemasons as a front in order to attain a foothold on American soil. 'The Illuminati,' says Langdon, 'took advantage of the infiltration and helped found banks, universities, and industry to finance their ultimate quest [. . .] The creation of a single unified world state – a kind of secular New World Order.'[3]

This is a wonderful idea, and one that illustrates how clever Brown is when it comes to weaving good yarns, but there is little evidence to support his plotline and as for the story of Lanz, there is also little doubt in most historians' minds that the anecdote was an invention by anti-Masonic writers and Jesuit groups opposed to Weishaupt and his new order. There was, after all, little in Weishaupt's teachings that mainstream religion could warm to. Take for example this early nineteenth-century analysis of Weishaupt's methods and underlying agenda:

> His scheme appears to be calculated, not so much for uniting persons of similar sentiments in one society, as for seducing those of opposite inclinations, and by a most artful and detestable process, gradually obliterating from their minds every moral and religious sentiment. It is in this view principally that this plan of seduction calls for the attention of mankind, as it develops the secret, insidious policy by which the agents of faction and infidelity lead on their disciples, still concealing their real designs, until the mind is involved in a maze of error, or entangled in snares from which there is no retreat.'[4]

By 1780, the Illuminati had grown in strength, with its co-founder, Knigge, recording how the group had enrolled approximately two thousand members throughout Europe. Weishaupt was delighted. His mission of 'illuminating' his disciples' minds through reasoned argument was working and seemed to complement the oncoming Enlightenment when radical free thinkers such as Voltaire and Jean Jacques Rousseau were at work espousing, amongst other theories, the concept that religion should be 'reasonable' and consequently result in the highest moral behavior of its adherents.

But this was Bavaria in the mid-eighteenth century – a highly conservative, inward-looking state dominated by the Roman Catholic church who did not take kindly to Weishaupt's type of radical rationalism, nor his arguments that nations and religions should be swept away alongside such institutionalized ideas as property and marriage. As a result, the Illuminati was labeled seditious and in 1784 the Bavarian government banned the Society. Weishaupt subsequently lost his position at Ingolstadt University and fled Bavaria to sanctuary in Gotha.

Despite the apparent collapse of the Illuminati, the flood of anti-Illuminati literature written by those opposed to the group's beliefs means that, ironically, we know more about the group today than we would ever otherwise have done. Two books in particular stand out: *Proofs of a Conspiracy Against All the Religions and Governments of Europe* and which was published in Ireland in 1797, written by John

Robison, a professor at Edinburgh University, and a work by Abbé Augustin Barruel, *Memoirs Illustrating the History of Jacobinism* (also published in 1797), a four-volume tome that contains several vivid conspiracy theories involving not only the Illuminati but also the Freemasons, the Knights Templar and the Rosicrucians. Each of these sects, according to the author, were aiming to overthrow not only religion but also all political institutions and governments.

Of the four volumes of Barruél's book, the first two were dedicated to exposing the campaign against Christianity by French and European philosophers such as Voltaire, Diderot and Rousseau. The third volume concerns the Illuminati – in particular, how Weishaupt recruited several French, German and other European Freemasonry leaders to join his new society, thus gathering together all the different factions under the Illuminati's overall control. In the fourth volume Barruél accuses the Illuminati of being the true cause behind the French Revolution (1789), an episode from which, he claims, France never truly recovered.

Both Barruel's book and that of Robison had a tremendous effect when they were first published and even after several decades their accusations were being read by eminent statesmen. For example, George Washington in America was said to have drawn the conclusion that every government was in danger from Illuminists trying to overthrow them by bringing revolutionary Jacobinism into play. Nor was Washington alone in his fears. Other prominent Americans (indeed, nearly everyone except Washington's own Secretary of State, Thomas Jefferson) feared the Illuminists and added to Barruel's and Robison's theories by producing books of their own. One of these was Seth Payson who wrote *Proof of the Illuminati*, which was first published in 1802. Among numerous accusations to be found in its pages is the printing of a letter which was supposed to have been sent by Weishaupt (under the pseudonym 'Spartacus') to Hertel Canon of Munich (under the pseudonym 'Marius') giving details of how he has made his sister-in-law pregnant. 'We have already made several attempts to destroy the child,' wrote Spartacus, '[. . .] Could I depend on Celse's secrecy (Professor Buder at Munich), he could be of great service to me; he had promised me his aid three years ago. Mention it to him if you think it proper.'[5]

Whether the letter is real or not, the obvious conclusion to be drawn from its inclusion in Payson's book is that every attempt was being made by the religious establishment to blacken Weishaupt's reputation. Not that the abortion claim was the worst of the mud being slung in his direction, for Payson also accuses Weishaupt of brainwashing his devotees and of seducing them so that they would act out his every wish.

Nevertheless, books such as those by Robison, Barruel and Payson do give us – even if only a fraction of what they write is true – a fascinating insight into Weishaupt's secret order. Robison is a pains to point out that, although Weishaupt himself preferred to remain a shadowy figure within the society, other members of his order were more prominent so that they could actively recruit new members. 'These are the Minervals,' states Robison. 'They are the only visible members of the

Illuminati and in order for a candidate to be admitted to the group, he has to make himself known to a Minerval who in turn reports the request to the council. After this, a certain amount of time passes during which the candidate is secretly observed. If he is deemed unfit, nothing more is made of his request; if on the other hand he is successful, he receives an invitation to attend a secret conference where he is admitted as a Novitiate.'

'But,' wrote Payson in true conspiratorial style, 'the Insinuators are the principal agents for propagating the order. These are invisible spies, seeking whom they may devour, who enter on their tablets, with which they are always to be furnished, the names of such as they judge would be useful to the order, with the reasons for or against their admission.'[6]

By employing such emotive language, it is little wonder that the Illuminati's reputation was one to be feared. But the abuse didn't stop there for Payson goes on to explain how the Insinuators, once they have chosen a target, return to 'seduce' these unwilling victims until, having been brainwashed, they become a pupil of the Illuminati.

In many ways this methodology mirrors the current-day practices of cults when recruiting new members; the gradual initiation of intended victims by group members who have been specially trained for such a task. However, once the candidate had become a fully fledged member of the Illuminati they would have had very little in common with their modern-day counterparts, for under the tutelage of an instructor their first task was to learn that 'silence and secrecy are the very soul of the order.'[7] To this end, each member of the Illuminati was given a new name – indeed the only name by which he would be known to others within the group (thus

Weishaupt was known as Spartacus, Knigge as Philo etc.) – while even place names were given codenames (for instance Bavaria was Achaia, Munich was Athens, Vienna was Rome, Austria was Egypt and so on). Having digested all

The symbol of Yale University's Skull and Bones Society. The society was formed in 1832 and its members have numbered several American presidents, the list of whom is said to include George W. Bush and his father, George Bush Senior.

of this information, the novitiate would then be required to learn the statutes of the society, the most vital being that a knowledge of mankind was the most important tenet, and to acquire it the new member was commissioned to observe the world at all times and note down all these observations. The novitiate also had to present his superiors with a written account of his life, noting down details such as his place of birth, his enemies, his friends, his likes and dislikes, secret writings and all manner of personal information. These revelations were then assessed with a view to either accepting or rejecting the candidate. If accepted, the novitiate was then required to undergo an initiation ceremony.

At dead of night he was led into a small, dimly lit room where he was questioned as to his readiness to devote himself to the order. According to several sources a solemn oath then had to be taken at sword point, which include swearing to eternal silence and complete obedience to the order on pain of death. The novice was then afforded the title of 'Minerval'. It was at this point, or so Payson states, that the Illuminati and Freemasonry converged. That said, apart from telling us that Minervals enter a lodge (a term commonly used by Freemasons), Payson fails to furnish us with any further evidence of a connection.

Minervals usually met in groups under the tutelage of a more illuminated superior. During these gatherings they were encouraged to discuss illuminism in great detail, including its laws and those acts which were acceptable or not acceptable within the order. For instance, under certain circumstances suicide was sanctioned. The same was also the case for theft and murder, both of which could be practiced for the good of the group. As always, during these discussions the novitiates or Minervals would be watched carefully by their superiors who were constantly judging their suitability to progress onto the next rung of the Illuminati ladder.

After the position of Minerval came that of the Illuminatus Minor. At this point it was the instructor's duty to remove any trace of political and religious prejudice the novitiate might harbor. In addition, the novitiate was also required to study the Illuminati's secret arts – such as the art of mind control and of concealing one's true feelings from others. Having passed this stage in their training the Illuminatus Minor now proceeds to the title of Illuminatus Major, or Scotch Novice. Once again Payson was at pains to point out just how close the process through which the novitiates progressed came to brainwashing. 'It is impossible,' he wrote, '[. . .] to give a full view of the slow, artful, and insidious process by which the mind is powerfully, though insensibly, drawn from the possession of its former principles, and fired with a fanciful idea of soon attaining the regions of sublime wisdom.'[8]

At this stage the Scotch Novice, with guidance from his new counselor, was required to acquaint himself with all of mankind's many miseries, miseries which the Illuminati blamed on the pressure citizens of every nation had to endure from both church and state. Once the novitiate had completed this term of study he then moved on to the title of Scotch Knight, the last stage before he reached a state of full illuminism. This stage differed radically in tone from those that went before because, instead of being confined to dark chambers and secrecy, a Scotch Knight was privileged to enter a new lodge whose splendor was second to none. As well as studying further rules and regulations, a Scotch Knight was also tasked with converting every opportunity that came his way to the advantage of the Illuminati.

Having passed these tests it was now time for the novitiate to become acquainted with the Illuminati's 'lesser mysteries', revelations that required him to take on the title of 'Priest' or 'Edopt.' In this role he was taught that there was no religion, and no government on earth which answered to the needs of mankind, but instead the only effective means by which to remedy the situation was through those societies privileged enough to know the secret of Jesus.

On this occasion, it is safe to say that both the Illuminati's and the Freemasons' creeds united to the extent that the secret of Jesus was revealed to be the reinstatement of mankind to his original liberty and equality. In Freemasonry, one of the symbols employed is that of a rough-hewn stone representing the primitive nature of man, savage but ultimately free. The split stone represents the fallen nature of humanity, divided by state and religion. (In Dan Brown's *Angels and Demons*, his protagonist Robert Langdon claims that the Order of the Freemasons was used as a means of shielding the Illuminati from the inevitable fall-out from the Catholic Church – not a wholly ludicrous theory given both the political and religious climate of eighteenth-century Europe.)

The Edopt was also entitled to don a white tunic with a broad scarlet belt, with scarlet ribbons tied to one sleeve. After the position of Edopt was achieved, the novitiate was allowed to move on to the role of Regent, a position that required him to be led to his lodge dressed as a slave tied with chains, a condition meant to represent the miserable position of mankind bowed down by society and government. A voice from within the lodge then denies him entrance, declaring that only freemen may enter, after which the novitiate's guide replies that the Edopt's desire is to be free; that he has reached illumination; that he flies from all tyrants and seeks refuge only among freemen.

By 1784, both church and state saw to it that Weishaupt's activities were significantly restricted. Payson (basing his evidence on Barruél and Robison's findings) declared this turn of events was brought about by the discovery of dangerous publications – several of which were traced back to the lodge Theodore of which Weishaupt was, of course, a member. The Elector of Bavaria instructed the lodge to curtail their activities. When he was ignored, he had no option but to order a judicial inquiry, only to discover that several other Masonic lodges were also associated with a group called the Illuminati. Four professors were arrested: Utschneider, Cosandey, Renner, and Grunberger, all of whom later gave testimony to the evil goings-on within their respective groups – activities that ranged from illicit sexual practices to suicide. It was at this point that Weishaupt was sacked from his job at the university and banished from Bavaria. Various documents are then said to have come to light illustrating the truly pernicious nature of the Illuminati society. Barruél, in his book on Jacobinism, claims that the following extract is a direct quotation from one of Weishaupt's private letters:

> It is very proper to make your inferiors believe, without telling them the real state of the case, that all other secret societies, particularly that of Free Masonry, are secretly directed by us. Or else, and it is really the fact in some states, that potent monarchs are governed by our order. When any thing remarkable or important comes to pass, hint that it originated with our order. Should any person by his merit acquire a great reputation, let it be generally understood that he is one of us.[9]

Despite these fighting words however, once banished there was little Weishaupt could do to keep the Illuminati going. At this point the entire society appears to have faded gently from view.[10] That is, until recently, when a handful of contemporary researchers have claimed that the Bavarian Illuminati is up and running again, still aiming to establish a New World Order. Their evidence appears to lie with the emergence of several organizations as varied as the Yale Skull and Bones Society and the Bilderberg Group.

The former is an elite club that includes some of the most powerful men of the twentieth century including several American presidents. Established in 1832, not long after the abolition of the Bavarian Illuminati, it is said that the Skull and Bones was none other than a new-world version of the type of societies so rife in Germany during the mid-nineteenth century. No wonder then, that outsiders claim this group to be a hotbed of Illuminati plottings and conspiracies. Several critics continue to demand the club's termination, much as detractors did back in the eighteenth century. One such is Ron Rosenbaum, a columnist for the *New York Observer*. 'I think,' says Rosenbaum, 'there is a deep and legitimate distrust in America for power and privilege that are cloaked in secrecy. It's not supposed to be the way we do things. We're supposed to do things out in the open in America. And so that any society or institution that hints that there is something hidden is, I think, a legitimate subject for investigation.'[11]

Another good reason for investigating the club is that several American presidents, including the present incumbent of the White House, George W. Bush, as well as his father George Bush Senior, and his grandfather, are alleged to have belonged to this group and have been said to have invited other Skull and Bones members to join them in government.

But the Skull and Bones is not the only secretive organization potentially at work in the upper echelons of government. The Bilderberg Group, an elite coterie of power brokers, bankers, economists and world leaders who meet in secret to discuss world affairs was formed shortly after the end of World War II. In 1954, the Bilderberg's agenda was to promote transatlantic cooperation so that future wars could be averted. Meeting in secret, usually in Holland, where the group held its first meeting at the Bilderberg Hotel, not a word of what is discussed ever reaches the general public. Is it any wonder that conspiracy theorists have linked this organization with shady goings-on, not to mention the establishment of a New World Order second only to that espoused by the Illuminati? Both the Oklahoma City bomber, Timothy McVeigh, and international terrorist Osama Bin Laden, are said to have believed in the theory 'that Bilderberg pulls the strings with which national governments dance.'[12] In response to this assumption, the former Chancellor of the Exchequer in Britain, Denis Healey, who was one of the founding members of Bilderberg, vehemently denies the group exerts any sinister influence on world affairs. 'There's absolutely nothing in it,' he said. 'We never sought to reach a consensus on the big issues at Bilderberg. It's simply a place for discussion.'[13]

Similarly, a group calling itself the Trilateral Commission, formed in 1973 by private citizens from Japan, Europe and North America, insist that their group's sole function is not to act as a screen shielding the evil machinations of the Illuminati, but as a think-tank established to foster greater cooperation amongst the democratic, industrialized countries of the world. The European Union has also been accused of being involved in Illuminati-managed decisions, as has the UN and the Council on Foreign Relations. This latter group, which was founded in 1921, is yet another independent, non-partisan organization for scholars dedicated to promoting a better understanding of the world and the foreign policies adopted by the United States and other governments. That is what the CFR professes to be. On the other hand, conspiracy theorists are more inclined to believe that it is the promotional wing of the ruling elite in America who use its members (all of whom are influential politicians, academics or economists) to further the cause of the New World Order and surreptitiously transplant its doctrines into mainstream American life. The conspiracy theorists' websites use quotes by any number of influential persons to support their ideas. The following, for instance, was written on February 23, 1945 by President Roosevelt: 'The real truth of the matter is, as you and I know, that a financial element in the large centers has owned the government ever since the days of Andrew Jackson.' Or how about this from Felix Frankfurter, Justice of the Supreme Court in America (1939–62): 'The real rulers in Washington are invisible and exercise power from behind the scenes.' Neither quote is a shattering exposé of anything even remotely underhand, yet time and again what these people say is presented to us as concrete evidence that a secret society is at work, attempting to dominate the world. Be it the EU, the Commonwealth Institute or any other multi-national gathering – whether political or economic, conspiracy theorists continue to insist that the Illuminati (amongst others) are involved. They also point to acts of terrorism such as 9/11, assassinations such as John F. Kennedy's and all manner of other world-shattering events as having been orchestrated by the Illuminati.

David Icke, a British ex-footballer turned author, states in an article which appears on a website called appropriately enough, www.propagandamatrix.com, that 'It was clear that something of enormous magnitude was being orchestrated that would so devastate the collective human mind with fear, horror, and insecurity, that "solutions" could be offered that would advance the agenda in a colossal leap almost overnight. This is what we saw in America on the ritually-significant eleventh day of the ninth month – 911 is the number for emergencies in the United States. Ritual and esoteric codes are at the heart of everything the Illuminati undertakes.'[14]

So does such a society really exist and if it does, is it really attempting, as Robert Langdon would have us believe, to control world freedom? The idea of a secret organization attempting to rule the world seems a deep-seated one in the psyche of modern-day man. After all, this is the premise, give or take a few plotlines, behind all of the James Bond movies, not to mention thousands of other books and films that would have us believe in such hidden agendas.

There is scant evidence, however, to back up such speculation but, given the freedom of speech we have in most democratic countries, conspiracy theorists will always be able to point at men of power and influence and accuse them of pursuing a hidden agenda. Perhaps this is evidence in itself that mankind has a deep-rooted need for conspiracy theories; we want to blame the problems of the world on a faceless organization more than any thing else; we want there to exist a sinister secret organization, the eradication of which would solve all our problems overnight. The Illuminati fits the bill and, even if it no longer exists as a covert group, it will live on in the minds of many as a convenient scapegoat for all the world's ills.

[1] *Ecclesiastical History*, Eusebius, Bishop of Caesarea (*c.* AD 264–340).

[2] *An Encyclopedia of Freemasonry and its Kindred Sciences*, Albert G. Mackey, Macoy Publishing and Masonic Supply Co., 1900.

[3] *Angels and Demons*, Dan Brown, Transworld, 2000.

[4] *Proof of the Illuminati*, Seth Payson and Benedict Williamson. Originally printed by Samuel Etheridge, 1802; Invisible Press, 2003.

[5] Ibid.

[6] Ibid.

[7] Ibid.

[8] Ibid.

[9] *Memoirs Illustrating the History of Jacobinism*, Volume III, Abbé Augustin Barruel, 1797.

[10] Although the Illuminati dropped off the political map at this point, Payson is at pains to point out that yet another secret society, this time calling itself the German Union, picked up where the Illuminati left off.

[11] 'Skull and Bones,' www.CBSNews.com, June 13, 2004.

[12] 'Bilderberg: The ultimate conspiracy theory,' Jonathan Duffy, BBC News Online Magazine, www.news.bbc.co.uk, June 3, 2004.

[13] Ibid.

[14] 'Problem, Reaction, Solution,' David Icke, www.propagandamatrix.com.

ARGENTEUM ASTRUM – ORGIES IN SICILY

I took an immediate dislike to him [Crowley], but he interested
and amused me. He was a great talker and he talked
uncommonly well. In early youth, I was told, he was extremely
handsome, but when I knew him he had put on weight, and his
hair was thinning [. . .] He was a fake, but not entirely a fake. [. . .]
He was a liar and unbecomingly boastful, but the odd thing was
that he had actually done some of the things he boasted of.

W. SOMERSET MAUGHAM, Introduction to the
1986 edition of *The Magician*

The story of Argenteum Astrum is really the story of one man: Aleister
Crowley, also known amongst other things as 'The Great Beast' and 'The
Wickedest Man on Earth'. Both soubriquets were earned through his
involvement not only with Satanism and illicit drugs, but also with a sinister type of
'magick' whose central credo was best summed up in one of Crowley's own
teachings, 'Do what thou wilt shall be the whole of the law.' Indeed Crowley saw
himself as the Prophet of a New Aeon, a man whose wisdom would supplant that of
the Christian era and reveal a new, more libertarian dawn. No wonder that he cast
such a dark shadow over the early twentieth century or that he has since been
presented as one of the most vile cult leaders of all time, the type of character who
caught the eye of the writer Somerset Maugham, said to have based his novel, *The
Magician* (1906) on The Great Beast.

Born in Leamington, in Warwickshire, England on October 12, 1875, Crowley
was named Edward Alexander by his doting parents, Emily and Edward Snr. His was
a relatively wealthy family and the youngster enjoyed a comfortable Victorian
childhood, if not a typical one, as both parents belonged to a strict branch of the
Quakers, also known as the Plymouth Brethren.

Religion played an important role in Crowley's formative years, although as time
went on he grew to despise the faith his parents so obviously adored. In his book *The
Confessions of Aleister Crowley*, he wrote that the repressive atmosphere he experienced
at home made him, 'prepared to go out of my way to perform any act which might
serve as a magical affirmation of my revolt'.[1] Even more bizarrely, it was Crowley's
mother, Emily, who seemingly first implanted the idea into her son's mind that he
was some type of antichrist, one whom she hoped would soon see the light and be
redeemed but who instead began to revel in his role as Beast.

In 1895, at the age of twenty, Crowley entered Trinity College, Cambridge where he spent the next three years enjoying his newly acquired freedom. These were good years where he read widely (if somewhat esoterically) and dabbled with the idea of eventually joining the diplomatic service. This was, however, only one of several career plans that never quite reached fruition. Instead, at the age of twenty-three, Crowley decided to join an occult secret society known as The Hermetic Order of the Golden Dawn, a relatively new group founded in 1887 by William Wynn Westcott and Samuel Liddell MacGregor Mathers and which boasted among its members such luminaries as the Irish poet, W. B. Yeats. The Golden Dawn was a highly influential society, one that claimed to synthesize several branches of religion and magic such as the Kabbalah, alchemy, tarot, astrology, divination, numerology, Masonic symbolism and ritual magic into one cohesive, logical whole.

Adopting the magical name of 'Perdurabo', which in Latin means 'I will endure', Crowley was eager to submerse himself in study and spent many hours poring over various of the society's core tomes. The reward for this hard work was that he rapidly rose through the Golden Dawn's ranks, but his presence wasn't always seen as beneficial and soon enough Crowley had managed to fragment the group to the extent that barely two years after he had first joined, he was expelled. Understandably angry, he decided to travel to Mexico to continue his magical studies. He also decided to form what would become the first in a long line of societies, the Lamp of the Invisible Light, albeit that this was still affiliated to the Golden Dawn. Better known by the abbreviation LIL, according to Crowley it was begun with the full knowledge and encouragement of Samuel Mathers, although LIL never seems to have numbered more than two members. The first was Crowley and the second was someone known as Don Jesus Medina (undoubtedly a pseudonym). Having established the society, Crowley quickly grew bored of it, preferring instead to pursue his own studies and fulful his wish to learn how to render oneself invisible. 'I reached a point,' wrote Crowley, 'where my physical reflection in a mirror became faint and flickering. It gave very much the effect of the interrupted images of the cinematograph in its early days.'[2] Whether this reveals early signs of psychological disturbance has been debated over many years, but what these words do illustrate is Crowley's unremitting sense of himself, his own abilities and power.

After Mexico, the great magician then moved on to India and a little later to France, only returning to England in 1903. He then met and married a woman by the name of Rose Kelly. The following year, the couple traveled to Egypt and it was here, according to Crowley, that he had the most formative experience of his entire career.

For quite some time, Crowley had been attempting to call up his Holy Guardian Angel, something he believed everyone possessed, though few were fortunate enough to experience. His experiments had met with little success until his stay in Egypt where he tried to summon up sylphs for Rose's enjoyment. Suddenly, Rose said she began to experience some type of psychic message from the Egyptian god, Horus. At first, Crowley was sceptical. Rose, after all, had never displayed any type of psychic

Aleister Crowley began his life as an occultist at the age of twenty-three when he joined an organization known as the Hermetic Order of the Golden Dawn, but was expelled from the order after only two years for causing turmoil within its ranks.

or clairvoyant gift before but, following several days of intensive questioning, Crowley became convinced that his wife had indeed become the conduit for messages between himself and the god. For three days, Crowley took dictation from an emissary of the god, a 'personage' by the name Aiwass, dictation that resulted in a text, *Liber Al vel Legis*, which is now commonly referred to as *The Book of the Law*. In it Crowley (or Aiwass) lays down three basic philosophies, the first being 'Do What Thou Wilt Shall Be The Whole of the Law,' the second, 'Love Is The Law, Love Under Will' and the third, 'Every Man And Every Woman Is A Star.'

The book also names Crowley as the prophet of a New Aeon and, therefore, the supreme magical authority, over-ruling all others. Given Crowley's megalomaniac tendencies, it wasn't long before he gleefully reported this 'promotion' to his one-time friend and Golden Dawn founder, Samuel Mathers. The result was instant warfare; a kind of magical duel in which it is said the two men cast spells over each other. Mathers was supposed to have sent an evil force to attack Crowley's hunting dogs, which he kept back in England, causing them to die as well as making Crowley's servants fall seriously ill. In retaliation, Crowley summoned the help of Beelzebub and his forty-nine servitor spirits, after which Mathers' attacks ceased and peace was restored.

By this time Rose had fallen pregnant and, on July 28, 1904, having returned to England, she gave birth to a daughter whom Crowley named Nuit Ma Ahathoor Hecate Sappho Jezebel Lilith. To explain himself Crowley wrote the following note:

> Nuit was given in honor of our Lady of the Stars; Ma, goddess of justice, because the sign of Libra was rising; Ahathoor, goddess of Love and Beauty, because Venus rules Libra; I'm not sure about the name Hecate, but it may have been a compliment to the infernal gods; a poet could hardly do less than commemorate the only lady who ever wrote poetry, Sappho; Jezebel still held her place as my favorite character in Scripture; and Lilith, of course, holds undisputed possession of my affections in the realm of demons.

Perhaps due to the birth of his daughter, Crowley grew less and less interested in the realms of magic and in 1905 he decided to take part in a climbing expedition to Kanchenjunga in the Himalayas. The climb was to prove fatal for several members of the team but, seemingly unperturbed by these deaths, Crowley continued his travels through India then on to Japan and China, from where he went to North America before sailing back to England. It was not until his return that he learned of his daughter's death. Rose and Nuit had followed Crowley out to India for the first leg of his tour, but the little girl had contracted typhoid in Rangoon (now Yangon) and, although hospitalized, had died shortly afterwards.

Grieving the death of his daughter and increasingly estranged from Rose, who had begun to drink heavily, Crowley renewed a 'magical collaboration' with an old friend of his from his time with the Golden Dawn, a man called George Cecil Jones. The two friends decided to form a new magical order, one whose driving force and leadership would be left in Crowley's capable hands and whose name was to be Argenteum Astrum or the A.'.A.'.

In many respects the A.'.A.'. was a continuation of the Golden Dawn. Crowley and Jones reintroduced the Golden Dawn Neophyte Ritual, the purpose of which was 'to transform the consciousness of the "Candidate" by severing the continuity of his life and directing him upon the hitherto invisible spiritual path.'³ Robed and blindfolded, the new recruit was led into a consecrated temple. He would then choose a motto, just as Crowley chose 'Perdurabo' at his initiation, after which the candidate took an oath swearing that he would keep secret all the mysteries of the group. He was made to listen to various chants and instructions, before being asked to kneel. The blindfold was then removed and the candidate welcomed into the order.

One of the first men to undergo this ritual was Captain John Frederick Charles Fuller who joined the A.'.A.'. in 1906, taking the magical name of Per Ardua Ad Astra, 'through effort to the stars.'

Meanwhile, Rose, having fallen pregnant for a second time, gave birth to another daughter, this time named Lola Zaza. Due to Rose's heavy drinking, Crowley had all but left the family home and set himself up in a bachelor flat where he entertained several lovers, two of whom, Ada Leverson and Vera Snepp, were written about extensively in his poetry. But Crowley's verses weren't the only writing he produced during this period for, in 1907, what later became known as the Holy Books began to be 'received' much as had happened with *The Book of the Law*. Crowley claimed to write the texts as though they were dictated from another dimension through a type of unconscious channeling of ideas. At the same time, he also produced what he considered one of his finest works, a satirical drama called *The World's Tragedy*, in the preface to which he expounded some of his more outrageous theories. It included a defence of sodomy in the context that 'there seems no better way to avoid the contamination of woman and the morose pleasures of solitary vice. (Not that women themselves are unclean. It is the worship of them as ideals that rots the soul).'⁴ The preface also contains a reference to the seduction of young boys (Crowley had always been attracted to men as well as to women and through his life conducted several homosexual affairs), indeed one of his main goals during this period was the recruitment of such into the A.'.A.'. Both he and Fuller traveled to Oxford and Cambridge Universities with the intention of signing up new members, one of whom Crowley immediately fell in love with, a man by the name of Victor Neuberg (whose chosen A.'.A.'. soubriquet was Omnia Vincam meaning 'I shall conquer all'.) The hapless Neuberg thereafter followed Crowley to Paris (where the latter was living temporarily), where a bizarre type of sexual initiation took place.

Neuberg had confessed to Crowley that he was a virgin, a confession that prompted Crowley to devise a devious plan, ensuring that ever afterward he, Crowley, would be Neuberg's sexual master. The plan involved a woman with whom Crowley had been conducting an affair, Euphemia Lamb (wife of the artist Henry Lamb.) Crowley encouraged his young student to fall in love with Euphemia and

The design of this ceremonial seal was commissioned by Aleister Crowley for use in rituals performed by members of his Argenteum Astrum, or Silver Star, secret society.

eventually propose to her after which Crowley persuaded Neuberg that he had to visit a prostitute so that he at least knew the rudiments of sex. After this was accomplished, Crowley, pretending that he knew nothing of Neuberg and Euphemia's engagement, advised the student to tell Euphemia of his sexual infidelity, a confession which prompted the 'wronged' Euphemia to reject her suitor outright. Neuberg was understandably distraught, but three days later Crowley engineered an even worse turn of events for he had Neuberg visit his bedroom where the young man witnessed Euphemia in a state of complete undress sitting on Crowley's bed. Naturally, his vision of the purity of womanhood was shattered forever, and Crowley had proved himself Neuberg's sexual superior. It was a tough lesson, but it was only the first in a long line of brutalities Neuberg was to suffer.

Over the following few months, Crowley forced Neuberg to follow a course of vigils and fasts after which he insisted that he and his student should travel through Spain and Morocco on foot. Neuberg then took a Vow of Holy Obedience to Crowley. One can only imagine how arduous this journey was, both mentally and physically, but during this time Crowley and Neuberg, master and student, began a sexual relationship.

It was also during these long, unbroken walks that Crowley decided to set up a magazine whose central aim was the promotion of Argenteum Astrum. Called *The Equinox*, and published twice yearly at the spring and winter equinoxes, the magazine was devoted to 'magic, yoga and other mystical disciplines'[6] with most of the articles penned by Crowley while Captain Fuller, as Crowley's trusted second-in-command, contributed many of the illustrations.

Crowley also channeled his energies into a recruitment drive, much of which centered around Cambridge University. As well as persuading Victor Neuberg to become his disciple, he also recruited two other students into the order, Kenneth Ward and Norman Mudd. The Senior Dean of Trinity College, the Reverend R. St. J. Parry, however, was furious at what he saw as Crowley's poaching of his pupils, not to mention the content of Crowley's teachings which he regarded as highly contentious. Parry banned Crowley from entering the college and demanded that Mudd and Ward sever all ties with their 'spiritual' leader.

Never one to be cowed by figures of authority, Crowley instead concentrated his efforts on Neuberg, retiring with him to his house in Scotland, Boleskin, where he lived with Rose, but where he now set Neuberg further tasks and tests. Most of these involved solitary confinement within his bedroom, the only interruptions being the serving of meals brought by Crowley himself. Understandably, many commentators have condemned the abusive, ultimately sadomasochistic nature of such a relationship, with Crowley quite literally in control of Neuberg's life. Critics have also pointed out that Crowley and his student no doubt had sexual relations during this period, and it is also probable that Neuberg's final test as a Probationer wanting to attain full membership of Argenteum Astrum was the performance of a sacred sexual act with his teacher. Whatever the case, there is evidence that Neuberg at times found Crowley's methods unnecessarily vicious. On more than one occasion he scourged Neuberg on his back and buttocks with a gorse switch and also a bunch of nettles.

My worthy Guru is quite unnecessarily rude and brutal, I know not why. Probably he does not know himself. He is apparently brutal merely to amuse himself and to pass the time away. Anyhow I won't stick it any more.

It seems to me unnecessary and brutal rudeness is the prerogative of a cad of the lowest type [. . .] It is ungenerous also to abuse one's position as a Guru:

It is like striking an inferior who will be ruined if he dares to retaliate.[7]

At the end of Neuberg's first period of solitary confinement, far from allowing his student any respite, his Guru announced a further ten days' physical discomfort during which Neuberg was to stay naked in his room with only a bed of gorse to sleep on.

With all this happening, it is hard to believe Crowley had time to concentrate on other matters but it was also during this period that he divorced Rose, whose alcoholism had grown out of all control. Rose was later committed to an asylum, although once out of Crowley's clutches she did recover and, on her release, remarried.

Meanwhile, Crowley and his main disciple, Neuberg, took a trip to Northern Africa where they continued their master/servant relationship while studying and writing together. On their return, Crowley continued working on *The Equinox* whose offices at 124 Victoria Street in London also served as a meeting place for the A.'.A.'., where everyone would gather together to talk, drink and experiment with drugs. Perhaps as a rebuttal of his homosexual affair with Neuberg, Crowley also took several female lovers, most of whom were members of the group and, therefore, open to much the same types of abuse as Neuberg had been.

Unconcerned about the growing criticism of his activities, Crowley now determined to stage a play, *The Rites of Eleusis*, whose main aim was the merging of poetry, dance, magic ritual and music into a vehicle that would heighten the consciousness of all those involved. A second reason for staging *The Rites* was to expand the membership of the A.'.A.'., for in recent months numbers had dropped and Crowley's personal finances were looking somewhat unhealthy. Nevertheless, by staging the play in public and in full view of the British press, Crowley was opening himself not only to ridicule, but to outrage. One tabloid newspaper published four articles attacking both the play and its producer. The *Looking Glass* was a racing paper, edited by West De Wend Fenton who made it his duty to expose Crowley, warts and all.

> Remember the doctrine which we have endeavored faintly to outline,
> remember the long periods of complete darkness – remember the dances
> and the heavily scented atmosphere, the avowed object of which is to
> produce what Crowley terms an 'ecstasy' – and then say if it is fitting and
> right that young girls and married women should be allowed to attend
> such performances under the guise of the cult of a new religion.[8]

If this review was scathing, those that followed were even worse, for in part three of his exposé Fenton, referring back to Crowley's days with the Golden Dawn sect, accused him of engaging in 'unmentionable immoralities' with Allan Bennett (Crowley's one-time mentor and friend). Another Golden Dawn member mentioned in the same paragraph was George Cecil Jones, a married man with four children who was employed as an analytical chemist by a highly respectable company. Naturally the implication was that Jones was also a homosexual, engaged in 'unmentionable immoralities,' and indeed it was Jones who eventually decided to sue the *Looking Glass* for defamation of character.

The trial was held in April 1911 but the outcome pleased no one save Fenton for, although the jury established that Jones had been defamed by implication, they also concurred that the defamation was essentially true. During the trial, much of the evidence submitted centered on Aleister Crowley with one of the chief witnesses being his old adversary, Samuel Liddell MacGregor Mathers. Suddenly it seemed as if their 'magical duel' had begun all over again, only this time Mathers had the upper hand.

The fall-out from the trial hit Crowley hard. His most trusted second-in-command, Captain Fuller, announced that he could no longer be acquainted with the group for fear of damaging his career and several other members now decided to leave.

In contrast, one new member of the group was a married woman by the name of Mary Desti who, perhaps due to her striking good looks or to her exceptional gifts, was destined to become Crowley's new partner. Soon after Crowley had initiated her into the Argentum Astrum as a probationer (with the chosen name Virakam – a combination of the Sanskrit words for 'man' and 'lust'), they traveled to Switzerland and afterwards settled, along with her young son, Preston, in Italy. The ensuing weeks were not idyllic, Preston quickly growing to loathe Crowley, particularly the way in which he treated his mother.

> [Crowley's] repugnant reaction each time my poor mother had so far forgotten his teachings as to utter in his hearing a singular personal pronoun like 'I' or 'me' or 'mine.' The instant his ears were so assaulted, he solemnly withdrew an open penknife from his robe, raised his arm so the loose sleeve of his robe fell back to expose his bare forearm, and then with the penknife slashed a small fresh slice under the ladder of slices he had already incised into his forearm [. . .] Reading about some of his subsequent exploits, I realize that my mother and I were lucky to escape with our lives.[9]

Although shortly after arriving in Italy Desti had filed for divorce from her husband, Solomon Sturges, eventually she and Crowley parted ways leaving her free to marry a Turkish man called Veli Bey.

Single again, Crowley traveled extensively during this period and continued to write and explore his own particular brand of 'erotomagick.' But bad press followed him wherever he went and in 1912 yet another grim episode occurred involving a young woman by the name of Joan Hayes. Employed by Crowley to perform in a re-run of *The Rites of Eleusis* for which she had to dance on stage with Crowley's ex-lover Victor Neuberg, the two began an affair. Crowley was far from happy with this, believing that it interfered with his protégé's work, but the affair continued even after Hayes married another man, Wilfred Merton. The marriage was doomed to failure and six months after it had begun, the two separated, shortly after which, in August 1912, Hayes shot herself through the heart. It was a grisly turn of events, but one made all the more dreadful by Neuberg's assertion that Crowley had somehow murdered her through a combination of psychological bullying and black magick. Nor was Crowley averse to admitting (however obliquely) to this crime.

An adept known to The Master Therion [Crowley] once found it
necessary to slay a Circe who was bewitching brethren. He merely
walked to the door of her room, and drew an Astral T (the symbol of
Saturn) with an astral dagger. Within 48 hours she shot herself.[10]

Obviously the above statement cannot be proved, nor is there any doubt that it is
anything other than the self-satisfied posturing of a highly egotistical man, but as with
other previous examples, it does illustrate the nature of this vain and vile individual.
Who else, after all would claim responsibility for killing a harmless woman? Neuberg
obviously agreed for save from a brief sojourn with his mentor in Paris, by 1914 he
had grown completely disillusioned with Crowley to the extent that he broke off all
communications with him. Interestingly, rather like Crowley's wife, Rose, Neuberg
then went on to suffer a complete breakdown, but afterwards recovered enough to
marry and later raise a family and run a successful publishing business. Once out of
Crowley's clutches, or so it seemed, everyone stood a good chance of success.

Argenteum Astrum, by way of contrast, was falling apart. Disillusioned by the bad
press he had received after the Jones v. The *Looking Glass* trial and never quite
regaining the membership numbers he lost as a result of the court action, Crowley
began channeling his energies into other areas. Not that the didn't continue, but
without the support of people such as Captain Fuller and Victor Neuberg, Crowley
lost interest and maybe even impetus in his new world order.

Instead he acquainted himself with a German, Rosicrucian magical sect known as
the Ordo Templi Orientis (OTO) – or the Order of the Temple of the Orient –
becoming the head of the English-speaking branch some time afterwards. Later, he
sat out the majority of World War I in the United States, writing vast amounts of what
amounted to anti-British propaganda, while experimenting with drugs such as
cocaine, opium and heroin to which he rapidly grew addicted. It was during his
American stay that Crowley also met Leah Hirsig – the woman with whom he was to
return to England and who was also to give him his third child, Anne Léa –
nicknamed Poupée. The couple returned to London separately, but in the early part
of 1920 decided to retreat abroad, this time to Italy where they rented the Villa Santa
Barbara – a place Crowley soon renamed the Abbey of Thelema – his new religious
order. In fact the teachings of Thelema were nothing more than an extension of those
of the argenteum Astrum, i.e. its main principle was the founding of a New Aeon
although such worthy aims were somewhat undermined by the Abbey's soon-to-be
adopted nickname – the 'horsel' (a bowdlerized version of 'whore's cell'.) Once more
Crowley was in his element, presiding over rituals, practicing his particular brand of
erotomagick and indulging in acts of sadomasochism. Hirsig joined him in the latter,
and if the following account is true, seemingly enjoyed her role of torturer.

She held a lighted cigarette against my breast. I shrank back and
moaned. She spat her scorn, and puffed at it and put it back. I shrank
and moaned. She made me fold my arms, sucked at the paper till the
tobacco crackled with the fierceness of its burning; she put it back for

the third time. I braced myself; I tightened lip and thrust my breast against it.[11]

New members showed up at the Abbey every week hoping for Crowley's guidance, but although on the surface things appeared to be going well, the reality was that Crowley had acute financial problems, added to which the seemingly idyllic Villa Santa Barbra was nothing short of an unsanitary slum. Crowley was taking increasing amounts of cocaine and heroine to feed his growing habit – the subject of which became central to a novel written during this period, *Diary of a Drug Fiend*, in which the central theme is that of a young couple struggling to free themselves from drug addiction. Sadly fiction did not reflect fact, for Crowley never attempted to free himself from his addiction. Instead, he sank into further acts of depravity, at one time creating what he termed the 'Seth ceremony' which not only called for a chosen member of his group to have intercourse with a goat but afterwards for the goat to be slaughtered and its blood drunk. With all this afoot and bearing in mind the unsanitary conditions in the abbey, it is hardly surprising that a death knell began to ring. Poupée died on October 14, 1920 at a hospital in Palermo and barely six days later Hirsig, who was pregnant again, suffered a miscarriage. The loss of two children in such quick succession must have been devastating and perhaps it was this that drove Crowley to write his *Diary of Drug Fiend*. Certainly he was in need of money, but just as when he staged *The Rites of Eleusis*, the press ripped the novel apart. In particular a critic by the name of James Douglas who worked for the *Sunday Express* wrote an article entitled 'A Book for Burning' in which he said, 'Although there is an attempt to pretend that the book is merely a study of the deprivation caused by cocaine, in reality it is an ecstatic eulogy of the drug and of its effects upon the body and the mind.'[12]

Following on from this article, press coverage of Crowley and the fun and games at the villa grew even worse. The *Sunday Express* printed another article entitled, 'Aleister Crowley's Orgies in Sicily' with the subtitle, 'The Beast 666.' With all the bad publicity, one might have thought, new disciples would have been sparse on the ground, but nothing was further from the truth. One of them, Frederick Charles Loveday (better known as Raoul) showed up at the villa with his wife, May, in late 1922. May was never happy in Crowley's company and constantly begged her husband to leave, particularly when Crowley gave them both razors with which to cut themselves every time they lapsed into using the word 'I' – a pronoun only Crowley was allowed to utter.

By 1923 things had grown even worse, with Raoul falling seriously ill. May put this event down to a combination of factors amongst which was the large quantity of drugs that her husband had begun to take at Crowley's instigation, alongside the drinking of a cat's blood as part of a ritual over which Crowley presided. Despite these two health-defying acts however, it was almost certainly the consumption of contaminated water that caused Raoul's illness. He died on February 16, 1923, three days after which May returned to England where she gave an interview to the *Sunday*

Aleister Crowley had many articles, essays and books published, both fictional novels and supposedly non-fiction books about 'magick' and the occult but his first published work was a poem, Aceldama, *in 1898.*

Express who promptly labeled Crowley a 'drug fiend' and 'the spreader of obscene practices.'

Back in Italy, Crowley was handed an expulsion order, an event which prompted him to spend many years wandering the world, forever plagued by his reputation as 'the wickedest man in the world.' These were desperate times, with Crowley constantly trying to feed his heroine habit, whilst at the same time in search of more money and disciples. The heydays of the Golden Dawn and Argenteum Astrum were over, and now all that lay ahead were years of isolation without even a publisher willing to print his work.

Aleister Crowley died on December 1, 1947 from myocardial degeneration combined with acute bronchitis. He was seventy-two-years old. There are various accounts of his last words – a Mr. Rowe recorded that they were 'Sometimes I hate myself', whilst someone else insisted that, 'I am perplexed,' was the last thing he uttered. The truth is however, that at the time of Crowley's passing, no one else was present in the room, therefore whatever it was he said before he died, fittingly remains secret.

[1] Interestingly, Crowley was not alone in his rebellion against the Plymouth Brethren as a young child, for another famous deserter was the literary critic and writer Sir Edmund Gosse (1849-1928), who wrote a wonderful memoir of his experiences called *Father and Son* (1907).

[2] *The Confessions of Aleister Crowley*, Jonathan Cape, 1969.

[3] *The Confessions of Aleister Crowley*, op. cit.

[4] *Do What Thou Wilt: A Life of Aleister Crowley*, Lawrence Sutin, St Martin's Press, 2002.

[5] *The World's Tragedy*, Aleister Crowley (1910), Falcon Press (AZ), 1985.

[6] *Do What Thou Wilt: A Life of Aleister Crowley*, op. cit.

[7] 1909 Diary (typescript), Victor Neuberg, OTO (Order of the Temple of the Orient) Archives.

[8] *The Looking Glass*, October 29, 1910.

[9] *Preston Sturges*, Preston Sturges, ed. Sandy Sturges, Simon & Schuster, 1990.

[10] *Magick in Theory and Practice*, Aleister Crowley, 1930; various subsequent reprints.

[11] *Do What Thou Wilt: A Life of Aleister Crowley*, op. cit.

[12] 'A Book for Burning,' *Sunday Express*, November 19, 1922.

THE THULE SOCIETY – NAZISM'S PRECURSORS

> The Thule people died as the first sacrifices for the Swastika.
> The Thule people were those to whom Hitler first came, and the
> Thule People were those with whom Hitler first allied himself.
> RUDOLF VON SEBOTTENDORFF, *Before Hitler Came*, 1933

World War I was supposed to be the 'war to end all wars'. Millions of men, women and children had died during its progress, but while the soldiers who limped home to Britain were at least safe in the knowledge that they had won the war, Germany's fighting men were afforded no such comfort. Prior to the outbreak of hostilities, the German nation was one of, if not the, most law-abiding countries in Europe. Its citizens were hard-working, orderly and well mannered. World War I changed all that. Returning from the battlefields, German soldiers had grown accustomed to levels of violence and scenes of carnage never before experienced. On their return home they faced not a heroes' welcome, but a disillusioned and divided populace depressed and struggling to survive in a climate of severe economic instability. By April 1921 the Allies had demanded reparations to be paid by Germany to the tune of 132 million gold marks (approximately £6,600 million). This caused the value of the German mark, which in 1918 had stood at the rate of four to the dollar, to spiral out of all control to seventy-five to the dollar. By the summer of 1922 this had almost quadrupled to four hundred. These were dark times indeed for a country more used to leading the world rather than following meekly behind.

The southern city of Munich, perhaps more than any other principal municipality in Germany – the constitution of the Weimar Republic afforded the old German states such as Bavaria, Prussia and Saxony a certain amount of autonomy by giving them their own state governments and representative assemblies – was worst affected by this mood of dissatisfaction and violence. Even during the war, Munich had stood apart from other cities, with Hitler remarking that 'bad morale and war-weariness were more pronounced in Munich than in the north.'[1]

Faction-riddled and overrun with disillusioned ex-soldiers and impoverished businessmen, Munich was a hotbed of unrest. In 1918 a Jewish journalist by the name of Karl Eisner led a socialist street revolution and established a Bavarian Republic only to be assassinated barely three months later by Count Anton von Arco-Valley. A Social Democratic government was then established only to collapse after two months when a Soviet Republic took over. Barely a month later this, too,

One of the symbols adopted by the Thule Society, dating from 1919 and clearly showing a version of the swastika that would be adopted by the Nazis and become one of the most evocative icons of the twentieth century.

collapsed. Small wonder, then, that against this muddled, divided and divisive background, a group sprang up dedicated to the idea of a strong, single-minded, unassailable Germany. Calling themselves the Thule Society (Thule-Gesellschaft) and meeting in secret, they were to play a significant part in Hitler's rise to power, fomenting support in the beer halls of Munich, the very establishments where Hitler first began practising his charismatic, rabble-rousing speeches. As the author Joanna Kavenna points out in her book, *The Ice Museum*, 'The Thule Society was an early expression of the Nazi fetish for "Aryan" tribes and northern lands, an early elision of an idea of natural purity with a belief in the racial superiority of a people.'[2]

The Thule Society's leader and main activist was a man called Rudolf von Sebottendorff. Sebottendorff's father had been a Silesian railway worker whose last name 'Glauer' young Rudolf seemed to have disowned by explaining how, whilst traveling in Turkey as a young man, he had met and been adopted by a Baron Heinrich von Sebottendorff. In fact, delusions of grandeur were never far from von Sebottendorff's mind, and his adopted persona fitted precisely the type of character his Thule Society aimed to recruit – men of noble lineage, who could trace their families back down through the centuries.

Prior to establishing the Thule Society, having returned from his trip to Turkey, Sebottendorff joined another secret group called the Germanenorden. Formed by a handful of prominent German occultists in 1912 and violently opposed to the Jews, its leader Herman Pohl was obsessed by what he saw as a gradual diffusion of the German race, a slow watering-down of the national blood-lines caused by the introduction of non-Aryan elements. The Germanenorden enjoyed a hierarchical fraternal structure similar to that found in Freemasonry but unlike Freemasonry, the

Germanenorden taught its disciples nationalist ideologies based on racial superiority, and most of the group's literature had an anti-communist, anti-Semitic theme. Sebottendorff fitted in perfectly and soon established his own branch of the group which he named the Thule Society.

Needing an emblem for his new group, Sebottendorff adopted the swastika as the true representation of everything he held dear. Originally the swastika had been an ancient Indian symbol of good luck as well as the traditional symbol of the Norse god of thunder, Thor. In the early twentieth century it had then been taken up by a German neo-pagan movement who named it the Hakenkreutz. Perhaps it was from them that Sebottendorff stole the idea – after all both groups promoted strong anti-Christian ideologies – but it wasn't until a Thule Society member by the name of Friedrick Krohn suggested to Hitler that he adopt the swastika as his new political party's emblem, that this now famous insignia grew to be one of the most feared and hated of all twentieth-century symbols.

Thule was a mythical land (sometimes referred to as an island, sometimes believed to incorporate the lost city of Atlantis) in the most northerly regions of the ancient world, a dark, frozen, mysterious region that existed long before man had mapped the globe with any accuracy. The first mention of Thule appeared in the fourth century BC when a Greek explorer called Pytheas boasted of sailing from the warm regions of southern France to Britain and then onwards north for a period of approximately six days until he reached the land of Thule. Once there he reported that Thule's inhabitants showed him where, on the shortest day of the year, the sun set and how, during the winter everywhere suffered long periods of darkness. But despite Pytheas's account, ancient mapmakers were still baffled about the exact location of Thule, or if indeed it really existed at all. Britain, Iceland and different parts of Scandinavia were all possible locations, although Pliny the Elder seemed to prefer a less concrete interpretation of the place when he wrote that Thule was the 'most remote of all those lands recorded', a country where 'there are no nights at midsummer when the sun is passing through the sign of the Crab, and on the other hand no days at midwinter, indeed some writers think this is the case for periods of six months at a time without a break.'[3]

When the Romans first invaded Britain in 55 BC and traveled to the far north of the country, they sent back word that they had conquered Thule. Many travelers, writers and explorers all wrote reports and sent back messages to the effect that Thule existed, not least a group of early medieval Irish clerics who traveled to Iceland on retreat only to send back word that they had reached Thule. And yet one thing eluded everyone: absolute, unequivocal evidence that such a place existed, for not only could no one agree where precisely Thule lay, they couldn't even settle on how it was spelt. Throughout history Thule's name has changed drifted from one spelling to another as lazily as the changing of the tides: Thule, Thula, Thila, Tila, Thulé being just a small selection. And so it seemed nothing concrete or factual would ever become known about Thule. Instead it grew into an increasingly mysterious, mythical landscape; a place that hovered on the edge of the known world; a symbol of all that was unreachable and remote. Even in Victorian times, when reason might have suggested that Thule was nothing more than an ancient myth, the explorer Richard Burton included it in his notes. Famously, there is also a mention of Thule in Charlotte Brontë's ever-popular novel, *Jane Eyre*. Early in the story the young Jane is seated in her aunt's library trying to escape the reality of her situation by looking at a book on the Arctic when suddenly a reference is made to the rocks of Thule, a reference that sends her off in transports of delight, imagining the icy far north with its 'vast sweep of the Arctic Zone, and those forlorn regions of dreary space, that reservoir of frost and snow, where firm fields of ice, the accumulation of centuries of winters, glazed in Alpine heights above heights, surround the Pole, and concentrate the multiplied rigors of extreme cold.'[4]

In other words, over the centuries Thule had come to represent many things to many people; a mythical landscape; a gothic *terra incognita*; a symbol of remoteness and terror – anyone could interpret the land of Thule in any way they wished and Rudolf von Sebottendorff was no exception. Claiming that his society (only those Germans of pure racial blood over several generations were allowed membership) had been formed so that academics could pursue their interest in the Nordic Sagas, a diary of the group's meetings from 1919 to 1925 shows a series of lectures on such topics as the original homeland of the Teutons, German poetry, megalithic culture and German myths. But these innocent-seeming agendas hid a much darker secret, one that was far more in keeping with the Germanenorden's aims – the search for and reinstatement of the Germanic race's true roots; a search that would eventually call for the expulsion from or, worse still, the annihilation of any 'alien' elements within the country. Little wonder that among the society's members were included prominent industrialists and millionaires, not to mention high-ranking state officials such as Munich's chief of police. At Thule Society meetings, the guests and guest speakers were men such as Adolf Hitler, Rudolf Hess, Alfred Rosenberg (Hitler's chief propaganda minister) and Dietrich Eckhart.

In fact, it was Alfred Rosenberg who, during the 1920s, ran the Thule Society's newspaper, the *Völkischer Beobachter*. Set in the kind of heavy, gothic-style typeface so beloved of Nazi and neo-Nazi groups, the paper spouted a mixture of anti-Semitic and anti-communist rhetoric. When, for instance, Kurt Eisner was in control of the local Bavarian government, the *Völkischer Beobachter* swore that it was a communist-Jewish attempt to 'take over Bavaria'. They were obsessed by 'outsiders' overrunning their country and some journalists even forwarded articles expressing the opinion that Germany had lost the war due to the fact that it was not more firmly rooted to its Teutonic origins. In other words, the Thule Society were mesmerized by the idea of an heroic past, where their forebears lived and died heroic lives. Romantic? Yes. But this is what far right groups of that period tended towards – a sublime vision of mountains and forests that injected into the populace an inner strength; one which could not be defeated.

It was a winning formula. By late 1918 Sebottendorff boasted that the Thule Society had over 200 members. By the autumn of that same year he claimed the number had swelled to over 1,500 in Bavaria alone. Yet it wasn't all plain sailing, for after Kurt Eisner's assassination and the setting up of a Soviet Republic in Bavaria, civil unrest broke out. This was helped along by the Freikorps, private armies of disillusioned veterans organized by the far right, who clashed with the communists and fought them tooth and nail. Naturally, the Thule Society sided with the Freikorps, as a consequence of which their head office was raided and several Thule Society members were taken away and executed. Unperturbed by this bloody turn of events, Sebottendorff hailed his fallen men as martyrs, true Germans who were not afraid to stand up for their beliefs.

As Thule group membership grew and initiates continued to do battle with their communist adversaries, so another organization was also beginning its political life, the German Workers' Party, which would eventually become the National Socialist Workers' Party, or Nazis. Living in Munich during 1919, Adolf Hitler soon aligned himself with this group. 'I went through the badly lighted guest-room,' wrote Hitler in *Mein Kampf,* describing their first encounter, 'where not a single guest was to be seen, and searched for the door which led to the side room; and there I was face to face with the Committee. Under the dim light shed by a grimy gas-lamp I could see four people sitting round a table [. . .].'[5] Satisfied with their credentials, Hitler joined as the seventh member of the group[7] and began his assault on the beer halls of Munich, stirring up his listeners with a stream of racist invective guaranteed to appeal to his lower-middle-class audience. In *Mein Kampf,* Hitler stated that he was in his early twenties before he became aware of the 'Jewish problem', but in light of the fact that he had been raised by an anti-Semitic father, it seems more likely that he had always harbored this deep animosity. The 'Jewish problem' became one of Hitler's life-long obsessions, one which obviously drew him towards the Thule Society whose racist opinions were as virulent as his own. Hitler also expressed an abiding interest in the origins of the Aryan race, a passion he shared with the head of the Gestapo and the Waffen-SS, Heinrich Himmler who, according to the historian Robin Cross, also enjoyed membership of the Thule Society. Both these men knew the powerful appeal of what the Thule Society represented to the average man in the street, particularly in post-war Munich, but also throughout Germany, for Thule doctrine gave support to the idea that Germany could reassume Teutonic supremacy after its shattering defeat in World War I. Both the Thule Society and Hitler, together with his henchmen, were also giving credence to the idea that Nazism wasn't just a political doctrine or a semi-religious manifesto, it was the means by which a whole race could be reborn.

Himmler's romantic dream was to establish a whole country of blue-eyed, blond heroes, the exact image that the Thule Society promoted by emphasizing their ancient Germanic heritage. But whereas Sebottendorff believed that Thule existed in the far regions of the north – Himmler (and to some extent Hitler) now began to be

Hitler with his ministers at a meeting in the Hotel Kaiserhof in Berlin in 1933. To Hitler's left stands Hermann Goering, with Alfred Rosenberg looking over Goering's left shoulder and Heinrich Himmler in uniform on the far right of the picture.

influenced by yet another Thule Society member, Karl Haushofer, who asserted that the true origins of the Aryan race were more likely to lie in, of all places, Tibet.

In 1933 Hitler assumed the role of Chancellor of Germany, realizing both the Thule Society and Himmler's dreams. But while the Nazi Party's sun was in the ascendant, the Thule Society's light began to fade. Membership dropped off with several ex-Thulites setting up splinter groups to cater for their increasingly bizarre beliefs. Even Sebottendorff didn't survive, being ousted by his own members and for several years afterwards he disappeared from view as he took to traveling around the world. But if the bricks and mortar that constituted the Thule Society were disintegrating before Sebottendorff's eyes, Thule Society ideals were by this time flourishing and, more frightening still, being made law.

Given the task of implementing Hitler's ideologies – particularly those involving racial superiority – in 1929 Himmler became leader of the SS or Schutzstaffel (protection squads) who were modeled on the Teutonic knights of old, supposedly representing a fighting force that was superior in strength to any other in the world. By 1939 the SS numbered approximately 500,000 and were the principal enforcers of the Nazis racial doctrine. It was the SS who ran the majority of Hitler's concentration and extermination camps as well as forming the Einsatzgruppen (special forces) who were given the task of cleansing eastern Europe of Jews. In January 1937, Himmler made a speech during which he stated that the sole mission of the German people was 'the struggle for the extermination of any sub-humans, all over the world, who are in league against Germany, which is the nucleus of the Nordic race; against Germany, nucleus of the German nation, against Germany the custodian of human culture; they mean the existence or non-existence of the white man, and we guide his destiny.'[6] These could have been the words of any member of the Thule Society so in tune were they with the group's beliefs, but unlike the Thules, Himmler actually had the power to put his dreams into action. From the outset of his career in office, Himmler pursued his idea of racial selection and introduced special marriage laws which encouraged the coupling of people of 'high value'. In turn this led to the establishment of a human stud farm known as the Lebensborn.

Initially the Lebensborn, which was set up by Himmler in December 1935, worked with one aim in mind, that of permitting racially pure young girls the possibility of giving birth to a child which would afterwards be adopted by an SS family. But with the passing of time Himmler's plans grew ever more sinister and on 28 October 1939 he made a speech which included the now famous edict that, 'it will be the sublime task of German women and girls of good blood acting not frivolously but from a profound moral seriousness to become mothers to children of soldiers setting off to battle.'[7] He subsequently turned the Lebensborn into a place where German women with perfect Nordic traits could 'meet' SS soldiers with the sole intention of producing children who would then be classed racially superior because of their parentage. Himmler also sanctioned the kidnapping of children who matched the Nazis' idea of racially pure stock – blond hair and blue eyes – from the Reich's eastern occupied territories. Thousands of children were transported to the Lebensborn and told that their parents had abandoned them. Afterwards they would be 're-educated' (Germanized) with a few lucky ones being adopted into SS families. The rest, those who refused to co-operate with their kidnappers, were later transported to concentration camps and killed.

But the most extreme example of Himmler's wickedness occurred in 1942 when an SS unit was sent to the Czech village of Lidice after the assassination of the local SS governor Reinhard Tristan Heydrich in Prague. In reprisal for the killing of Heydrich, the SS executed the entire male population of the village. They then selected ninety-one children whom they considered met the Nazis' racial standards and these children were taken away to be resettled at the Lebensborn while those left behind were sent to extermination camps.

To this day no one has been able to calculate just how many children were kidnapped from the eastern occupied territories although, in 1946, the estimate ran at approximately 250,000. After the war a mere 25,000 were tracked down and returned to their proper families but many SS parents refused to let their 'adopted' children go, with some of the children even refusing to be repatriated because they had been so indoctrinated that they believed themselves to be 100 percent Germanic.

As horrific as the Lebensborn project was, it was only one of many criminal schemes perpetrated during the war in the name of racial purity. What the Thule Society had begun blossomed during the Nazi era in ways unimaginable to most of humanity. On 15 September 1935 Hitler implemented the Nuremberg laws which effectively stripped the Jews of their basic human rights by separating them from the rest of the population. The Jews, though extremely disturbed by the situation, had little choice but to comply. In common with most of the rest of the world, they hadn't recognized the full implications of what Hitler had said, for hidden in the same speech the Fuhrer explained that if the plans for these arrangements broke down then it would be necessary to pass further laws, 'handing over the problem to the National Socialist Party for final solution'.[8]

Hitler's Aryanization programme continued apace until, on September 1, 1939, the Final Solution started in earnest. Initially the killings were confined to the mentally or physically disabled in what Hitler termed his euthanasia programme, but soon these murders merged with the extermination of the Jews. Killings were carried out by two methods: in gas chambers within the concentration camps and by mobile killing units. The six biggest death camps were Auschwitz, where over one million people died, Majdanek, Treblinka, Belzec, Chelmno and Sobibor. But the horrors of the gas chambers were not the only atrocities lying in wait for the inmates of these camps. Racially motivated experiments were carried out on a daily basis, for the Party required concrete evidence that proved they were racially superior to all other men. In *Mein Kampf* Hitler states that 'anyone who wants to cure this era, which is inwardly sick and rotten, must first of all summon up the courage to make clear the causes of the diseases.'

The Nazis chose to believe that 'the causes of the diseases' centered around the Jews, the gypsies, the mentally infirm and any other group they chose to victimize. Thousands of men, women and children were photographed and examined by Nazi doctors, who declared that, among the many other outrageous 'results' derived from their experiments, gypsies produced a different blood to the rest of us and were more inclined to criminal behavior.

At Auschwitz a laboratory was set up (known as Block 10) the main aim of which was to discover a means of mass sterilization, while the infamous Joseph Mengele, who was as obsessed as Himmler with the Nazi ideology of racial purity, began to conduct experiments on identical twins. Each twin would be examined, body part by body part with measurements and notes being taken on the length of the nose, the shape of the mouth, skin coloring, eye coloring and any number of other details. The children would be made to stand for hours whilst these examinations took place,

Alfred Rosenberg had become Nazi Minister for the Baltic States by 1940, when this photograph was taken during a Hitler Youth gathering in Kiev.

while some unfortunate victims had dye dropped into their eyes which often caused partial loss of sight. These latter experiments were Mengele's attempts to change the color of Jewish children's eyes from brown to blue. Two victims, Hedvah and Leah Stern, later recalled that, 'Mengele was trying to change the color of our eyes. One day, we were given eye-drops. Afterwards, we could not see for several days. We thought the Nazis had made us blind. We were very frightened of the experiments. They took a lot of blood from us. We fainted several times, and the SS guards were very amused. We were not very developed. The Nazis made us remove our clothes, and then they took photographs of us. The SS guards would point to us and laugh. We stood naked in front of these Nazi thugs, shaking from cold and fear, and they laughed.'[9]

All these experiments were conducted with Himmler's full approval but they were only one of several research areas in which the Nazis became involved.

Certain sections of the Thule Society, including to some extent Sebottendorff himself, harbored a curious mixture of beliefs that included not only Teutonic myth, but also Eastern mysticism and that all-encompassing, late-nineteenth-century obsession, anthropology. Following on from where the Thule Society left off, Heinrich Himmler continued to study all the above disciplines with the sole intention of supporting his (and the Thule Society's) theories on the origins of the Aryan race. In 1935 Himmler created yet another branch of the SS, this time called the Ahnenerbe Forschungs und Lehrgemeinschaft – the Ancestral Heritage Research and Teaching Society.

Much as members of the Thule Society had previously believed, there were those among the Nazi Party who were convinced that the true origins of the Thule lay in the lost but not-so-mythical city of Atlantis located somewhere between Greenland and Iceland. In direct contradiction to this, Karl Haushofer, who was the founder of yet another far-right secret society called the Vril, believed that the origins of the Aryan super-race lay in central Asia or, to be more precise, in Tibet. The Swedish explorer (and practising Nazi), Sven Hedin supported Hausofer in this theory and in 1938 Himmler's Ancestral Heritage Research and Teaching Society mounted an expedition to Tibet led by a German naturalist and big-game hunter, Ernst Schäfer, who was once described by a British diplomat as being, 'volatile, scholarly, vain to the point of childishness, disregardful of social convention or the feelings of others, and first and foremost always a Nazi.'[10] The second principal figure on the expedition was Bruno Beger, an anthropologist and member of the SS who believed that the Aryans might well have originated in central Asia because the physical characteristics of Tibetans in particular, with their high cheekbones and, 'imperious, self-confident behavior'[11] mirrored the prototypical Aryan. Beger and his men took over 60,000 photographs, collected numerous moulds of the Tibetans' faces and shot over 120,000 feet of film after which he concluded that, in anthropological terms, the Tibetans were almost certainly a human type of stepping-stone between the Mongol and European races.

On their return to Germany Himmler declared both men heroes, but although Schäfer remained close to his patron, he never fully understood or agreed with the oncoming Holocaust. In contrast, Bruno Beger continued his studies into the Aryan race by selecting over 100 people from Auschwitz, the majority of whom showed signs of having Asiatic genes, who were studied, photographed, then executed.

Despite the 'success' of Schäfer and Beger's research, however, most people believe that no more Nazi-funded expeditions took place. One exception was the writer Trevor Ravenscroft whose book, *Spear of Destiny,* argues that between 1926 and 1943 other trips were undertaken, all with the aim of studying the origins of the Aryan race. Whatever the truth, Himmler's desire to pin-point where his ancestors originated, led him during World War II to commission a series of archaeological digs in western and southern Russia, afterwards shipping back his 'finds' to the SS headquarters at Wewelsburg. Many people, including Hitler, considered this a step too far, but Himmler remained undeterred and throughout the war continued his researches into what Sebottendorff would no doubt have termed legitimate Germanic studies.

As for Sebottendorff, by the beginning of the 1930s, just as Hitler was starting to realize his dreams of power, the Thule Society's influence was dwindling. After being ousted as leader of the society, Sebottendorff grew increasingly bitter towards Germany's new political movement. Not content simply to fade into the background, he published a book claiming that the origin of the Nazi Party was none other than the Thule Society and that they owed him everything, a theory to which, unsurprisingly, the Nazis took great exception. Sebottendorff's book was confiscated, and every copy the Nazis could find destroyed, while he himself was placed under arrest by the SS who then 'persuaded' him that his best option was to leave Germany for good.

Sebottendorff fled from Germany, a broken, friendless man, taking himself off on a world tour that eventually led him to Istanbul. Shortly after the end of the war, on 9 May 1945, having seen Germany defeated, Sebottendorff died. The circumstances surrouding his demise are somewhat unclear as he drowned whilst swimming in the Bosphorus, but most historians agree that it was probably suicide. Having seen everything he held dear destroyed, there was nothing much left to live for.

An interesting footnote to the Thule Society's history is the present-day plethora of web sites dedicated not only to the preservation of the Society's memory, but also (and more disturbingly) to the promulgation of its vile theories. Tap in the words 'Thule Society' to any search engine and it brings up a multitude of results, although some of the listed sites present 'facts' verging on the ludicrous. The Thule, says one site, were Satanists who practiced Black Magic. Thule Society members also enjoyed a bizarre form of Sexual Magic which 'awakened penetrating visions into the workings of Evil Intelligences and bestowed phenomenal magical powers'. The Thule Society held occult séances. One site spells Sebottendorff's name incorrectly not just once but three times; Sebetondof, Sebettenduff and Sebetendorf while another can't decide when precisely the Thule Society first opened its books, stating that it did so in 1908, and then again in 1910, and then again in 1919. Perhaps realizing that their research isn't quite up to scratch, further sites fantasize that Hitler, far from dying in his Berlin bunker, is still alive, having escaped Allied forces and flown to Thule, which they generally believe lies in a northerly direction. Indeed, if you believe these sites, Hitler has been living happily on an ice floe for the past sixty years.

But perhaps the most curious of all the claims now available comes from a web site called Unexplained Mysteries which claims that Thule Society members believed the Aryan race originated on another planet or star system called Alderbaran whose inhabitants were blond and blue eyed. Their leader was a woman or 'queen' called Isais whilst other eminent Alderbarans included someone called Malok who was 'the commander of their military presence on earth'.[12]

Whatever some may believe, the fact is that the original Thule Society was a secretive, far-right organization whose highly suspect beliefs flavored what was to come in Germany for the next decade and a half.

[1] *Hitler: A Study in Tyranny*, Alan Bullock, Penguin, 1962.

[2] *The Ice Museum: In Search of the Lost Land of Thule*, Joanna Kavenna, Viking, 2005.

[3] Ibid.

[4] *Jane Eyre* (1847), Charlotte Brontë, Penguin, 1994.

[5] *Mein Kampf* (English translation by James Murphy), Hutchinson, 1940.

[6] www.jewishvirtuallibrary.org.

[7] www.thirdreich.net.

[8] *A History of the Jews*, Paul Johnson, Weidenfeld & Nicolson, 1993.

[9] *Children of the Flames: Dr. Josef Mengele and the Untold Story of the Twins of Auschwitz*, Lucete Matalon Lagnado and Sheila Cohn Dekel, William Morrow, 1991.

[9] *Himmler's Crusade: The True Story of the 1938 Nazi Expedition into Tibet*, Christoper Hale, Bantam, 2004.

[10] Ibid.

[11] www.unexplained-mysterious.com.

MUTI – RITUAL SACRIFICE IN LONDON

The victim may be a blood relative or one of their own children, but is never a stranger and definitely never an enemy. The child is not killed because they are angry with it. They are thankful to the child. The child is actually being sacrificed so that these people can have something of an advancement. It is to attain a goal that is unattainable by normal sacrifice [the sacrifice of an animal], whether that goal is prosperity or high political office. To our western minds, the concept of ritual murder is gruesome. But 2,000 years ago Jesus Christ was sacrificed for the good of the community – and the theory is that this is good for the community.

PROFESSOR HENDRIK SCHOLTZ, review of *Goal of Human Sacrifice* by Jeevan Vasagar, the *Guardian*, April 20, 2002

During an average year in London, the Metropolitan Police and the Coroner's Court deal with between forty and forty-five bodies recovered from the River Thames, but on September 21, 2001, officers were shocked to find the badly mutilated corpse of a child floating in the water near Tower Bridge. The body appeared to be that of an Afro-Caribbean boy, aged about five. For want of a real name, the police decided to call him 'Adam.' An autopsy revealed that Adam's legs had been severed above the knees, his arms had been cut off at the shoulders and his head removed. It was concluded that the boy had died from a violent trauma to the neck after which his limbs had been 'skillfully' removed by an experienced butcher.

If this wasn't horrific enough, speculation then grew as to whether Adam had in fact been the victim of a muti-style killing. It was also speculated that this murder might not have been the first of its type in Britain, but was perhaps the latest in a long line of killings by a murderous cult which had established itself within London's African community.

Professor Hendrik Scholtz, an expert in muti murders, was swiftly flown in from South Africa. After examining the body, he concluded that the boy's throat had probably been slit before the head was removed in order to drain blood from the body for use in a ritual. More significant still, it was discovered that Adam's first vertebra (the one located between the neck and the spine) had been removed. In Africa this is known as the Atlas bone, the bone on which Atlas was said to have carried the world.

In muti medicine the Atlas bone is a highly prized piece of the skeleton, for it is said to contain magical powers and give all those who ingest it the property of great strength. Professor Scholtz, together with a London-based forensic team, were also able to establish that the boy had been well-looked after prior to death. He was neither underweight nor malnourished and his stomach contents showed signs of containing Pholcodine, a cough medicine, suggesting Adam was well cared for before he died. In fact, everything pointed to a classic muti killing – the young boy had probably been 'donated' for sacrifice by his own family.

Muti, which in Zulu stands for 'medicine,' is a form of witchcraft prevalent in sub-Saharan Africa. A muti murder is a particular manifestation, therefore, of a traditional type of African healing, but one with an especially black heart, calling as it does for human sacrifices. Some muti witchdoctors (known as Sangoma) make medicine from grinding down the body parts of the dead, and often call for children to be sacrificed because their flesh is said to be 'purer' than that of adults. Less than a decade ago in Africa, almost 300 murders a year were blamed on muti and even as recently as 2003 cases were being reported of muti killings. Six people were arrested by police near to a squatters' camp in Bloemfontein, South Africa, after they had been seen trying to sell the body parts (head, hands, heart, feet, genitals and liver) of a twenty-year-old man. But although this case was gruesome in the extreme, it was only one among numerous other such cases in South Africa during 2002 and 2003.

In 2004 in Cape Town, two men and one woman were charged with killing a baby and afterwards frying her intestines in order to eat them. According to the accused, the intestines were supposed to help all three find a job. In South Africa, the incidents of muti killings have grown to such proportions that theirs is the only police force in the world to have established a special muti task force. The head of the task force, Gerard Labuschagne, admits that, although several hundred muti murders are investigated every year, most killings go unreported.

> They happen in South Africa fairly regularly, at least one a month. But
> for many police officers they are nothing unusual. They are just treated
> as another murder, so there are a lot of muti-related killings out there
> that never come to our attention.[1]

Not all muti medicine or muti practices result in death. The Sangomas' powers are said to be based on their being either directly connected to, or the reincarnation of, an ancestral spirit and more often than not the type of healing they practice is completely harmless. Sangomas are often involved in everyday affairs as mediators to sort out arguments between different parties. They are also called upon to heal souls, mend broken hearts, promote good luck and generally soothe their clients' ruffled feathers. Research has shown that over 80 percent of South Africa's population has, at one time or another, consulted a Sangoma – sometimes up to three times a year.

In this role, the Sangoma can be seen as vital to maintaining order within a community, and most of the 300,000 Sangomas working in Africa openly condemn any type of 'black magic.' Even when most Sangomas practice medicine, the type of products he or she uses will almost always be vegetable-based – roots, bark, herbs and flowers. Muti medicine can, therefore, be seen as another type of herbal healing and the practice of muti is simply the act of balancing ethereal elements with the physical complaint. For the more adventurous muti practitioner, animal products are implemented. Ingredients such as dried puff adders, crocodile fat or any number of potions made up from different parts of the elephant, lion and hyena may feature in the Sangoma's healing repertoire. Visit any African market and there will be stalls piled high with animal bones, skulls and skins as well as fresh herbs. Women sit hollowing out gourds which are then used as medicine bottles. There might even be small huts erected next to the medicine stalls which act as consulting rooms. Yet for all that mainstream muti is innocuous, but when it is extended to include the use of human body parts to heal or bestow special powers on the patient it can surely only be described as evil.

Investigations in several African countries (other than South Africa) have concluded that it is the Sangoma who orders a killing to be undertaken, normally because he has a client who has made a particular request for help. If someone has suffered a stroke, for instance, the muti medicine required to remedy the condition would be a paste made up from the ashes of a severed hand mixed with water. Below is a short list of some other muti medicines made up from human body parts.

  • Male and female genitals are often used to confer virility
  • The eyes of a child would bestow far-sightedness
  • A victim's blood would help restore vitality
  Other body parts can also be used to promote vague concepts, such as good luck.
  • The breasts of a female victim would bestow good fortune
  • The Adam's apple would be used to silence someone
  • The tongue would help smooth the path to a young girl's heart
  • Body fat would ensure a good harvest
  • Brains would improve one's mental abilities

Further to the 'Adam' case in London and the police concerns that his killing was connected to a muti-style cult, officers began investigating allegations that human flesh was now readily on sale in London. Police were already aware that West African gangs were importing large quantities of exotic animal meat such as that from lions, chimpanzees and giraffes, but now they were concerned this illegal trade was hiding darker secrets. Operation Swalcliffe was launched and in one dawn raid by environmental health officers on a shop in north London, two tonnes of unfit meat were confiscated along with the head of a crocodile which was being prepared for use in an upcoming ritualistic ceremony. The *Observer* newspaper, which reported on this raid, also recorded that Clive Lawrence, a meat transport director at Heathrow airport, was convinced that human flesh was finding its way into Britain and that this trade was inextricably linked to gangs who smuggled both illegal immigrants and drugs into the country.

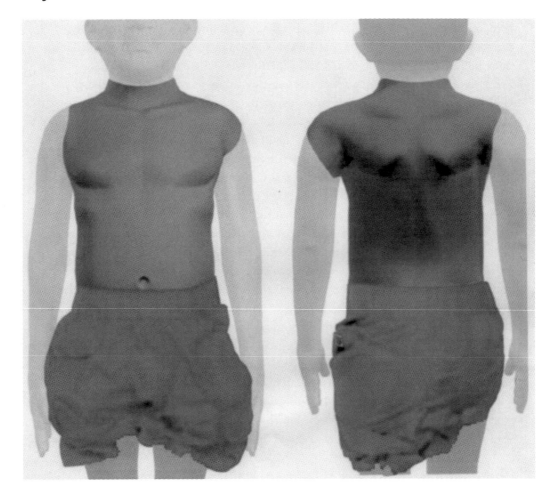

This image was prepared by police investigating the murder of 'Adam' and shows a computer graphic reconstruction of the boy's body, utilizing the red shorts that provided a vital clue to the mystery of 'Adam's' identity.

The intelligence we are receiving suggests human flesh is coming into this country. We are dealing with some very nasty people.[2]

If further illustration were needed of this, a BBC 2 television documentary, *Nobody's Child*, highlighted the problem of muti killings by broadcasting the story of a woman called Helen Madide who came from the Thohoyandou area of South Africa. At eighteen-years-old she was the mother of a small boy, Fulufhuwani, but was separated from the child's father, Naledzani Mabuda, who was a traditional healer or Sangoma. The documentary went on to explain how, while the couple were trying to sort out their marriage, Helen returned to live with her parents while Fulufhuwani frequently went to stay with his father and grandmother. The child's father, as a healer, would most often confine his practice of medicine to traditional herbal remedies; however, as has already been illustrated, a small number of Sangoma prefer more potent medicines with which to practice their craft. Helen explained what ultimately happened to Fulufhuwani:

> He [Mabuda] began to tell me stories. His ancestors said that he must kill me and the child so that he can be rich. He showed me the path and forced me to go along that path. He was pushing me and demanding me to go whether I like it or not. He said he was going to kill the baby first while I see the baby, then secondly he will kill me.[3]

Horrifically, Mabuda carried out his threat, slitting the child's throat while forcing Helen to hold down her son's legs. Once the child was dead, Mabuda began cutting off its hands, legs and sex organs. He then locked Helen away in a room along with her child's remains. Mercifully, Mabuda's family, fearing for their grandson's safety, called the police. Helen was released and her husband arrested. He was sentenced to life in prison but, although justice was seen to be done in this case, there are hundreds of other victims. 'We have children going missing every week from our townships,' said Dr. Anthony Minnar of the Institute for Human Rights and Criminal Justice in South Africa. 'The assumption is that those missing children are being put into prostitution and also that they are being used for muti murder.'[4]

So widely spread is the problem that in 1998 this particular type of killing became one of the main subjects of the bestselling novel by Alexander McCall Smith, *The No. 1 Ladies' Detective Agency*. When a boy goes missing, the horrific conclusion that everyone comes to is that muti was involved.

> We don't like to talk about it do we? It's the thing we Africans are most ashamed of. We know it happens but we pretend it doesn't. We know all right what happens to children who go missing. We know.[5]

As if to underline this, the *Nobody's Child* documentary then went on to record the story of a survivor of one such attack called Jeffery Mkhonto, who told journalists that when he was twelve years old he was abducted by a gang of muti practitioners whose job it was to harvest body parts.

Having been invited over to a neighbor's house, Jeffery found himself being attacked and having his genitals removed with a knife. Nor is Jeffery's the only recorded account of a muti-style attack for in 2002, *Times* reporter Steve Boggan wrote an article outlining the horrific harvesting of body parts practiced on a ten-year-old boy, Sello Chokoe.

Chokoe, who was from a tiny village called Moletjie in Limpopo province approximately 250 kilometers from Johannesburg in South Africa, was searching for a neighbor's donkey on July 30, 2004 when he was snatched by a group of men who subsequently held him down and brutally removed his right hand, right ear and genitals, after which they made a small hole in his skull and sliced away part of his brain. Miraculously, the boy survived the attack, only to be found a few hours later by another youngster, Bernard Ngoepe, who was out collecting some wood. Raising the alarm, an ambulance was called with the medics doing all they were able to save the young boy, but by the time a helicopter had arrived to rush him to hospital, Sello had slipped into a coma and ten days later he died.

Following the boy's murder, all the children in Moletjie were, unsurprisingly, terrified. Steve Boggan reported that Bernard Ngoepe was so traumatized by what he discovered that he could barely speak for months after the incident and needed special counseling.

Meanwhile, back in Britain, police investigating the 'Adam' murder were continuing to draw a blank. Detectives had little to go on. After all, the body had no face, no fingerprints and no dental records which would normally help identify a corpse. No child of Adam's age had been reported missing, nor were there any witnesses to his murder. The only clue police had to go on were a pair of orange (a

A Sangoma sets out his stall in the West African state of Mali. Taken in the late 1950s, the photograph shows animal skulls for sale alongside plants and other items used to make healing or ritual potions.

lucky color in muti) shorts that the boy had been wearing. The label inside them was 'Kids & Co.,' a brand name for a British company, Woolworths, which owned a chain of stores in Germany. Amazingly, officers were able to trace the shorts back to a batch of 820 pairs in the age 5-7 bracket that had been sold throughout 320 German outlets, but after that, they again drew a blank.

Similarly, when police started questioning London's Afro-Caribbean community, little progress was made. A thorough check was made on attendance records at over 3,000 nurseries and primary schools, but seemingly no child of Adam's age had gone missing. The police even requested that the former South African president, Nelson Mandela, make a public broadcast subsequent to which a press conference was held in Johannesburg. Mr. Mandela said:

> It seems likely that the boy might have come from Africa [. . .] I wish to direct my appeal specifically to people in Africa. If anywhere, even in the remotest village of our continent, there is a family missing a son of that age, who might have disappeared around that time, 21 September 2001, please contact the police in London, either directly or through your local police [. . .] Such cruel wastage of the lives of our children and youth cannot be allowed to continue.[6]

Despite such an impassioned plea, however, still no one stepped forward with any substantial information.

Not that all hope was lost, for with advances in technology a thorough examination of the mitochondrial DNA (mtDNA, which is exclusively passed on from mothers to their children) of Adam's remains did throw some light on his origins. Scientists compared Adam's mtDNA to 6,000 sequences that had previously been garnered in other scientific studies, and found that Adam's sequence matched neither those from southern Africa nor from eastern Africa, but only mtDNA from the north-western section of the country. Secondly, in order to narrow further the search for the boy's origins, Ken Pye, a professor of soil geology at the University of London, was asked to join the operation and run a series of tests on Adam's bone composition. The chemical strontium, which is present in soil and water, can work itself through the food chain from plants to animals and finally, when either of these are consumed, into human bones. Depending on where we originate, our bones also contain a strontium signature that should match our environment. Even if we move from one location to another, it takes approximately ten years for our strontium signature to change so that in the case of Adam, who was still only young, his bones would prove a vital clue to his place of birth. Professor Pye, having carried out the necessary tests, concluded that the young boy's bones showed signs of matching a signature of Precambrian rock predominately found in Nigeria, almost certainly Adam's country of birth. Scientists collated all the available data and concluded that the boy had almost certainly lived within a 100-mile 'corridor' located between Ibadan and Benin in south-west Nigeria (a country renowned for its practice of muti-style medicine). Further tests also revealed that in addition to the cough linctus present in Adam's stomach, the child had also been fed a mixture of bone, clay and gold – a typical muti potion. Pollen found in the boy's stomach indicated that he had been alive when he was brought to Britain. Officers thought that his journey probably involved crossing Northern Europe via Germany, which would explain the purchase of the orange shorts, after which the boy had lived in Britain for a few weeks prior to his death.

But for every small step forward with the case, there were several steps back. There was initial hope that a strikingly similar murder in Holland, which had occurred three weeks prior to Adam's death, might throw some light on the case. The naked torso of a white girl, aged between five and seven years, had been discovered in a lake at Nulde, while her head was found many miles away by fisherman in the Hook of Holland. It was the manner in which both of the youngsters' bodies had been mutilated that suggested there might be similarities between the two cases, but, as the investigation dragged on, no substantial link could be made.

Hope also grew when, a few days after the discovery of Adam's body, police found a number of half-burned candles wrapped in a white cloth with a Nigerian name written upon it. The bundle had washed up two miles upstream (in Chelsea) from where Adam's body had been found. Detectives thought they had stumbled across further evidence in Adam's murder; later however it transpired that both the sheet and candles had been used as part of an innocent ceremony held by a Nigerian family who were giving thanks that none of their relatives had been killed in the Twin Towers tragedy in New York on September 11, 2001.

Almost a year passed before police were given any further clues to the killing. An employee within the Social Services department in Glasgow contacted Scotland Yard in London to report that a client of hers, a thirty-one-year-old West African woman by the name of Joyce Osagiede, had been overheard by witnesses saying that she wanted to perform a ritual sacrifice of her two children. This was a lead that seemed to good to be true, but when detectives traveled to Scotland in order to question Joyce Osagiede and discovered, amongst her children's clothes, a pair of orange shorts made by the exact same company that had manufactured Adam's, they believed a breakthrough had occurred. The reality however was that although Mrs Osagiede had lived for a short time in Germany and had purchased the same type of clothing as Adam's, these facts alone were not enough to charge her. Later that month she and her children returned to Nigeria.

But the police's luck hadn't run out completely for, by investigating Mrs. Osagiede, police tracked down her estranged husband, Sam Osagiede, who had recently appeared in court in Dublin due to extradition proceedings against him filed in Germany. In his absence, the German courts had sentenced Sam Osagiede to seven years imprisonment for offences relating to people trafficking. Osagiede was tested to see if his DNA matched that of Adam's but, as with a test that had been run on Mrs. Osagiede, neither party was apparently related to the boy.

Undiscouraged, police continued to question Osagiede; questioning that resulted

Although many Sangomas, or witch doctors, offer cures for ailments using only herbal remedies, some believe that animal and human body parts have special powers to bring good fortune.

in the Metropolitan Police mounting a dawn raid on nine addresses in east and south-east London. They arrested twenty-one people (ten men and eleven women) whom they suspected of being involved in child trafficking.

Disturbingly, UNICEF (the United Nations International Children's Emergency Fund) had only recently published a report estimating that thousands of children from third-world countries were being smuggled into Britain for use as either prostitutes or as a form of slave labor. Where prostitution was concerned, myths such as the belief that having sex with a virgin would cure HIV and AIDS ran rife, especially in African countries. UNICEF also outlined the following facts and figures:

• 1,000 to 1,500 Guatemalan babies and children are trafficked each year for adoption by couples in North America and Europe.

• Girls as young as 13 (mainly from Asia and Eastern Europe) are trafficked as 'mail-order brides.' In most cases these girls and women are powerless and isolated and at great risk of violence.

• Large numbers of children are being trafficked in West and Central Africa, mainly for domestic work but also for sexual exploitation and to work in shops or on farms. Nearly 90 percent of these trafficked domestic workers are girls.

• Children from Togo, Mali, Burkina Faso and Ghana are trafficked to Nigeria, Ivory Coast, Cameroon and Gabon. Children are trafficked both in and out of Benin in Nigeria. Some children are sent as far away as the Middle East and Europe.[7]

The majority of the twenty-one people arrested were also from Benin in Nigeria, the very place outlined in the UNICEF report and the very place detectives had previously indicated Adam was likely to have lived. When police raided the various houses and apartments, they came across damning evidence that some kind of muti medicine had been practiced in at least one location due to the presence of an animal skull with a nail driven through it. Detective Inspector William O'Reilly who was in charge of the raids said:

> We are pretty confident we have a group of individuals who could have
> trafficked Adam into the country. In West Africa there are several reasons
> for human sacrifices – for power, money, or to protect a criminal
> enterprise. We believe the prime motive for the murder was to bring good
> fortune. We suspect Adam was killed to bring traffickers good luck.[9]

Despite O'Reilly's confidence that he had arrested the people responsible for Adam's kidnap and subsequent murder, none of the twenty-one detainees were charged with any crime involving the young boy. Indeed, it appears that no one is going to be brought to justice over this most horrific crime. That said, the idea of dismissing this case as an isolated incident is, for a variety of reasons, no longer possible. Dr. Yunes Teinz, a senior environmental health officer for the Borough of Hackney and health advisor to the London Central Mosque recently stated:

> We know that much of the bush-meat trade is used in potions and
> ointments for black magic treatments and we know that other animals
> are sacrificed for voodoo purposes in the African community. But we
> have a very deep concern over human body parts. We think they could
> be coming in with the bush meat.[10]

As recently as May 2005, the London Metropolitan Police reported that over a two-month period as many as 300 black children aged between four and seven years old have vanished from school registers within the British capital. Many believe this to be a conservative estimate and some experts put the figure much higher with thousands of children disappearing from the school system each year. Most of these are not thought to come to any harm, but if just one child is abused or murdered, it is one child too many. Barbara Hutchinson, the deputy chief executive of the British Association of Adoption and Fostering has stated that she is horrified at the figures.

'Many privately fostered kids,' she said, 'get passed on from household to household. They may be moved around to avoid immigration control; they may be exploited. We know some children are being trafficked to be used as domestic servants or for sexual exploitation.'[11] Similarly, Chris Bedoe, the director of End Child Prostitution, Child Pornography and Trafficking for Sexual Purposes has stated that governments worldwide are failing to take the problem seriously enough. Indeed, she has gone on record as saying their failure could be responsible for the sexual exploitation of large groups of children and numerous deaths. 'We heard recently,' she said, 'of a thirteen-year-old girl who told her teachers her parents had gone home and left her on her own in the UK, and some time later she too disappeared. The teachers don't know what happened to her. We are hearing this type of thing all the time.'[12]

Bearing this and all of the other evidence in mind, it seems that, although Adam's case was probably the first of its kind in London, it will almost certainly not be the last.

[1] 'Magic Medicine Murders Bedevil South Africa,' Michael Dynes, *The Times*, October 4, 2003.

[2] 'Human flesh on sale in London,' Antony Barnett, Paul Harris and Tony Thompson, the *Observer*, November 3, 2002.

[3] *Black Britain: Nobody's Child*, BBC 2, April 2, 2002.

[4] Ibid.

[5] *The No. 1 Ladies Detective Agency*, Alexander McCall Smith, Polygon, 1998.

[6] www.news.bbc.co.uk.

[7] 'Trafficking and sexual exploitation,' www.unicef.org/protection/index_exploitation.html.

[8] 'Where were their eyes as this boy bled?,' Steve Boggan, *The Times*, August 17, 2004.

[9] 'Missing: the mystery of 300 boys who have disappeared from school,' Steven Morris and Rosie Cowan, the *Guardian*, May 14, 2005.

[10] Ibid.

THE TONG –
ROMANCING THE
DRAGON

> I remember in the last of the Tong Wars there was a guy named
> Wong Quong, who was killed on January 6, 1926, in Ross Alley.
> And on April 20, Ju Shuck was killed in the back of the Chinese
> Theater (at 420) Jackson. They were all from different Tongs, and
> we knew they'd been killed because of a war, but we could never
> figure out just who did it. The Chinese were a secretive lot
> anyway, by and large, but none of them could talk about a murder
> like that. They would have been violating the code.
>
> DAN MCKLEM, *Chinatown Tong Wars of the 1920s*,
> Virtual Museum of the City of San Francisco

Long before the Tongs and the Triads became known worldwide for their criminal activities, they operated as resistance organizations in seventeenth-century China, established to fight against the Ching, who had taken over their country. The Ching were not popular with the majority of Chinese as they originated in Manchuria, a country to the north of China. The Manchus invaded China in 1644, overthrowing the ruling Ming emperor to establish the Ching Dynasty.

From the very beginning, Ching rule was marred by difficulties. Apart from the resentment that was caused by having a non-Chinese governing body, its rule was also beset by the ever-increasing presence of foreign colonial powers that were seizing sizeable tracts of Chinese territory and insisting that China allowed the import of large amounts of foreign goods into the country. This was upsetting the finely balanced Chinese economy, making the harsh life of the average Chinese citizen even harder, and creating a breeding ground for dissent and planned insurrection. The resistance was fostered within the folds of the secret societies – the Tongs and the Triads – which, right up to the twenty-first century have struck terror into the hearts of millions of ordinary people all over the world.

The family name of the Ming emperors, for whose return these secret societies were fighting, was 'Hung' and many of these organizations incorporated the Hung name into the name of their own group. Their name, however, was generally all any outsider might know about the group. Secret codes and clandestine rituals were adopted in order that society members could operate without detection. All members were required to learn the martial arts – something that came in very useful when these secret societies aided and abetted several rebellions against the Manchus, notably during the White Lotus Society rebellion in the mid 1790s, the Cudgels uprising between 1847 and 1850, the Taiping uprising between 1850 and 1864, and the Boxer Rebellion which took place between 1896 and 1900. However, unfortunately for those supporters of the former Ming Dynasty, when the Ching were eventually ousted from power in 1911, there were no Mings left to restore to the throne. Consequently, the first president of the newly formed Republic of China was a former military general by the name of Yuan Shikai. He was, unfortunately, no more able to rule the country than the average man in the street and China continued to flounder in an atmosphere of near-total political chaos. With the political leadership in disarray, the people looked elsewhere for guidance and reassurance. They turned to the secret societies which flourished as never before. For the majority of Chinese people, the most significant event of the early twentieth century was the first wave of Chinese emigration to America. Suddenly a whole range of 'Chinatowns' sprang up all the way down both the west and east coasts of the USA. These communities not only gave the new Chinese settlers a sense of 'home' in their otherwise foreign surroundings, but they also had a secondary, far more sinister, role to play. The different Chinatowns served to facilitate the establishment and growth of those Chinese secret societies that had wielded so much influence back in the old country. Two groups in particular were of special importance: the Tongs and the Triads.

Defining precisely what the Tongs represent is a complicated affair because it involves a cursory knowledge of how Chinese society operates. Originally the word was an anglicization of the Mandarin *tang*, meaning a lodge or a hall, although this generally referred to the group operating within such a hall, rather than to the building itself, much as a Masonic Lodge refers to the members of the society rather than the place in which they meet and a 'church' can be the congregation as much as it is the building where the congregation worships.

A Tong group consisted largely of 'unrelated Chinese people united to assist one another by a bond that includes secret ceremonies and oaths.'[1] Traditionally, therefore, whenever the Chinese found themselves transplanted en masse to new surroundings, as they did when the emigrated to Canada or America, the Tong would be one of the first organized groups to set up operations. A prime example of this occurred in British Columbia in 1862 when, on arrival in their new country, the Chinese immediately set about establishing the Chi Kung Tong to aid and abet them in both family and business matters. The Tongs were, and still are, deeply respected within Chinese society, due for the most part to their revolutionary history, in particular those times when they fought against the Manchus and the Ching Dynasty. The Chinese look back with pride on those days, revering the Tongs and bestowing on them an almost legendary status.

Yet, had they relied on their revolutionary credentials alone, it is doubtful the Tongs would have survived. Instead the Tongs have fashioned themselves to serve as a particular type of social unit, looking after all those who belong to their group, ensuring their safety above all others, protecting their interests by any means

Tong and Triad secret societies provided many freedom fighters for the resistance movement against the Manchus, including this flag- and spear-carrying warrior from the Boxer Rebellion of 1896-1900.

available. In this way the Tongs have adopted the manners and values of that other, most Chinese of subcultures, the Triad organizations. Particularly in North America, where Tong groups sprang up in every major city, the society has provided a network of social contacts for its members. Naturally, where criminal activities are concerned these contacts prove incredibly useful, providing funds, manpower and weaponry. Indeed, it is the criminal element, more than any other, that comprises the majority of Tongs, for since their inception they have been renowned for running illegal gambling operations, drugs rings, extortion gangs and prostitution rackets. Where the latter is concerned, the Tong wars, which raged in America in the late nineteenth and early twentieth centuries, were almost entirely based on internecine warfare between different Tong gangs fighting over prostitution rackets.

From the moment the first Chinese settlers set foot on American soil, they began setting up Tongs and other secret societies to help establish themselves in their newly adopted surroundings. But one thing was in short supply: women.

> From 1870 to 1910, the ratio of male to female Chinese immigrants in California (the primary point of entry for Chinese to the United States) was always at least 10 to 1, and a ratio of 20 to 1 was much more common. From 1881 to 1890, as little as 1 percent of the Chinese in America was made up of women.[2]

Inevitably this shortage meant that Chinese prostitution rackets were incredibly lucrative: after all, those Tong gangs who set up Chinese whorehouses had a ready-made customer base, eager to pay over-the-odds for the product. And as for the 'product' itself, in the nineteenth century the bulk of women involved in the trade would have been sold into it by their impoverished families back in China. A smaller percentage of girls would have been kidnapped, with only a very few volunteering to enter into the practice, in order (or so they believed) to earn good money which could then be sent back to relatives. Chinese girls were popular amongst America's white population, but their main source of income would have been amongst their own kind. This meant that a great deal of competition developed between different Tong gangs, all of which vied for the same trade in an attempt to gain bigger and bigger slices of the proverbial pie.

With so much money at stake, violence was never far from the scene. In 1864 the first Tong war erupted in America when a male member of the relatively large Suey Sing Tong gang kidnapped one of his rival's mistresses. Battle was declared, with several men on both sides being killed. The matter was only settled when the Suey Sings eventually caved in and returned the woman to her 'rightful owners.' Disputes such as this broke out frequently between different Tong gangs, exacerbated by the fact that shipping prostitutes from China to America was a costly affair, making the prostitutes – for want of a better phrase – worth their weight in gold.

The preferred weapon of the Tong gangs during this period was a six-inch-long hatchet – a relic from their ancestral past, but one which also earned the Tongs a great deal of notoriety in America. Other weapons included knives and, of course, guns. The writer Herbert Asbury gives a fascinating insight into the type of weaponry and clothing worn by a typical nineteenth-century Tong 'warrior' along San Francisco's Barbary Coast: '[. . .] their queues [pigtails] wrapped around their heads, black slouch caps drawn down over their eyes, and their blouses bulged with hatchets, knives, and clubs.'[3]

When Tong warfare broke out, white journalists liked nothing better than to write up the events for the simple reason that it made great copy. Hatchets meant blood and blood ensured a large readership. Nowhere was this better illustrated than in Los

Angeles in 1871 when two gangs, the Hong Chow Tong and the Nin Yung Tong, began fighting each other in a dispute over a woman. The fighting went on for days, during which time men on both sides were badly injured, whilst others were arrested. Finally one of the city's white sheriffs was shot in the shoulder whilst pursuing one of the Tong leaders. The injured man was rushed to hospital, but the wound was deep and became infected and eventually he died. Enraged by what they saw as a rising level of violence within the immigrant Chinese population, something in the region of 600 people mounted a mass demonstration through Los Angeles's Chinatown district during which further violence broke out. The man said to have been responsible for the sheriff's death was caught by the mob and subsequently lynched. The mob then looted and ransacked every Chinese property they could lay their hands on. In addition to the damage to property, the mob also attacked any Chinese man, woman or child they came across: it is estimated that a further nineteen Chinese were lynched while countless others were shot or hacked to death with their own hatchets. Eight white men were arrested that day and given jail terms, but none served longer than a year in prison.

These were horrendously tough times for the new immigrants and it is little wonder that after such incidents, Tong membership rocketed as more and more Chinese felt the need to stick to their own kind and keep all their dealings secretive. Possibly because of this secrecy, the rites of passage Tong initiates were required to take remained shrouded in mystery. Luckily, the same is not so true of the vows Triad members are said to undertake, which are no doubt similar (if not in content then in tone) to those of the Tong.

Excerpt from Triad Society Initiation Ceremony:

Incense Master: As a vanguard are you versed in civil and military matters?
Vanguard: I am well versed in both.
[. . .]
Incense Master: Name the eighteen kinds of military arts you learned at Shao Lin.
Vanguard: First I learned the use of the rattan shield.
Second the use of metal darts.
Third the use of the trident.
Fourth the use of the metal rod.
Fifth the use of the spear.
Sixth the use of the wooden staff.
Seventh the use of the sword.
Eighth the use of the halberd.
Ninth the use of the fighting chain.
Tenth the use of the iron mace.
Eleventh the use of the walking stick.
Twelfth the use of the caltrops.

Elaborate carvings and ornamentation decorate this centerpiece of the headquarters of the Hop Sing Tong in San Francisco's Chinatown in 1929.

Thirteenth the use of the golden barrier.
Fourteenth the use of the double sword.
Fifteenth the use of the duck-billed spear.
Sixteenth the use of the tsoi yeung sword.
Seventeenth the use of the bow and arrow.
Eighteenth the use of the lance.[4]

Given the nature of the above, it is hardly surprising that both the Tongs' and the Triads' feuding, particularly amongst their own kind, was particularly bloodthirsty. In New York the first Tong wars were said to have broken out around 1900, only a little later than those on the west coast of America. New York, in fact, suffered from prolonged bouts of internecine warfare among various Tong factions, in particular between the Hip Sing Tong and the On Leong Tong.

The On Leong Tong, whose leader at that time was a man by the name of Tom Lee, for the most part controlled the so-called 'property rights' system, which meant that they made their money from the lucrative gambling and opium dens in New York's Chinatown. In contrast, the Hip Sing Tong's power lay in the number of criminal associates that were attached to its ranks and the diversity of their activities. For approximately a decade, the two Tongs operated without significant rivalry between them, but when the Hip Sing Tong (whose leader was called Mock Duck) attempted to usurp its rival and take over some of the On Leong Tong's property rights, fighting broke out. Mock Duck arranged for his men to attack On Leong members in a downtown Chinese theater. The result was a massacre the like of which had rarely been seen in New York before. Several further acts of violence occurred and an increased police presence became required – something neither Tong was happy about. Indeed, so uncomfortable were the Chinese with an 'outside' police presence on their territory that eventually both Tongs sat down at a negotiating table and reached an agreement. Not that this was the end of Tong rivalry in New York. During the 1920s and 30s several more wars broke out – one of which hit the headlines as follows:

> Two shots were fired in the poolroom. About forty billiard cues clashed on the floor, as the young Chinese, who had been gathered around ten tables, dashed in a panic for the doors. In about a second the place was empty of pool-shooters and employees. In another second it was filled up with curiosity-seekers, mostly Americans and Italians, and policemen.
>
> There was a swarm of policemen on the scene before the smoke had cleared away, because about twenty had been posted by Inspector Bolan at former gambling houses in Chinatown which he had closed up in recent weeks.[5]

Naturally, none of the above outbreaks of violence endeared the Chinese to their white Americans cousins for, despite most of the immigrants being hard-working, law-abiding citizens, it was always going to be a case of the minority ruining things for the majority.

Soon white Americans were pressing for radical changes to be made so as to exclude the Chinese from mainstream American life. Under the terms of the 1898 Burlingame Treaty (named after Anson Burlingame who was the US minister to China during the Lincoln and Johnson administrations) both China and America had recognized 'the inherent and inalienable right of man to change his home and allegiance, and also the mutual advantage of the free migration and emigration of their citizens and subjects, respectively for purposes of curiosity, of trade, or as permanent residents [. . .] Chinese subjects visiting or residing in the United States, shall enjoy the same privileges, immunities and exemptions in respect to travel or residence, as may there be enjoyed by the citizens or subjects of the most favored nation.'[6] In other words, the American government had initially been more than willing to provide the Chinese with laws that protected them against exploitation, violence and discrimination. After the Tong wars however, all this changed. The US Government came under increasing pressure to do something about the 'Chinese problem' and the Burlingame Treaty was replaced with the Chinese Exclusion Act of May 6, 1882.

This was the first major restriction on immigration that the United States had ever implemented and illustrates just how high feelings were running in regard to the Chinese in general and the Tongs in particular. The new Act stated:

> Whereas in the opinion of the Government of the United States the coming of Chinese laborers to this country endangers the good order of certain localities within the territory thereof:
> Therefore,
> Be it enacted by the Senate and House of Representatives of the United States of America in Congress assembled, That from and after the expiration of ninety days next after the passage of this act, and until the expiration of ten years next after the passage of this act, the coming of Chinese laborers to the United States be, and the same is hereby, suspended; and during such suspension it shall not be lawful for any Chinese laborer to come, or, having so come after the expiration of said ninety days, to remain within the United States.[7]

After ten years the above law (renamed the Geary Law) was extended for a further decade, at the end of which it was then made permanent. Further to this, the Scott Act of October 1, 1888 also prevented any laborer of Chinese origin who had left the United States on a temporary basis i.e. to visit his family back in China, from returning to America. In this way almost 20,000 Chinese immigrants were refused re-entry into the country. In 1924 Chinese wives were also prevented from joining their husbands in their newly adopted country. It was the first and last time legislation such as this, involving the exclusion of a specifically-named nationality, was ever passed in America and in some ways it stands as testimony to the fear the Tongs had instilled into the heart of white America. The situation didn't really improve until World War II when the United States became allied to China in the fight against Japan.

In 1943 the Chinese Exclusion Act was repealed and 105 persons of Chinese origin were allowed into the United States per year, after which they could become naturalized American citizens. Further to this, after World War II more legislation was passed softening America's anti-Chinese stance – for instance the Displaced Persons Act of 1948 permitted approximately 3,500 persons of Chinese origin who were

Tong feuds cost many lives among the Chinese community in America and great efforts were made to maintain peace between rival factions, as at this conciliation meeting between the Hip Sings and Ping Koongs in San Francisco in 1921.

stranded on America's shores due to the political situation back in China, permanent refugee status. Following on from this, in 1953 the Refugee Relief Act was passed allowing hundreds more Chinese to settle in America and become legal citizens.

From the mid 1940s onwards, therefore, the Chinese population increased rapidly on American shores. Chinatowns were once again in abundance – enclaves where Chinese culture could be both protected and encouraged. Naturally this 'culture' included not only the Chinese language, the study of Chinese history and the arts, the practice of Chinese medicine and the appreciation of Chinese food, but also the return to the old Chinese customs, which included the acceptance of the Tongs as a Chinese way of life.

Stronger than before, with more Chinese communities in which to operate, the Tongs grew and prospered. Extortion rackets proliferated. The Chinese – notoriously reticent at going to legitimate police agencies in order to report crime – made for rich pickings for the Tongs. Businessmen were only too eager to pay protection money, but, for the Tongs, the financial gains weren't the only reason behind their actions. The more shopkeepers and restaurateurs who belonged to a particular Tong, the stronger and more important that Tong became, with an even larger 'turf' area or kingdom over which they could rule. Not all Tongs, however, used out-and-out violence to get what they wanted. One tried and tested method to squeeze money out of a reluctant restaurant owner involved a whole group of Tong members arriving at a restaurant, but sitting down at separate tables. Each person would then order only very little from the menu, but stretch out his or her meal for hours on end therefore blocking the tables so that no other customers could sit down and eat. This type of behavior could stretch on for days or weeks, considerably reducing a restaurant's takings and ruining the business. However, the moment the owner began paying protection money, the problem would melt away. The Tong achieved exactly what it desired without so much as a drop of blood being spilt.

A different method of squeezing extortion money out of a reluctant restaurateur was to post guards at the door of his establishment who would then warn customers away. Only a very rich businessman could afford to allow this type of practice to continue for long, so once again the Tongs won out and raked in the profits.

Kidnapping was also a popular way by which Tong gangs earned an income. Historically Chinese criminals have often fallen back on this practice as a means of achieving monetary gain, kidnapping not only the relatives of the very rich, but also those from middle and working-class backgrounds in the certain knowledge that ransom demands will be met. Where women were concerned, however, the outcome was rarely satisfactory as women have not always enjoyed a particularly high status within Chinese society. Families where a girl had been kidnapped were often unwilling to pay a large sum for her return, particularly when it was supposed that her status as a virgin had been compromised and that her prospects for successfully finding a suitable husband were, therefore, substantially reduced. This meant that young women who were kidnapped were just as likely to be sold into slavery or prostitution as they were to be returned safely to their families. These days kidnapping is still prevalent amongst Tongs as it is often seen as the easiest, most effective way in which to earn money or achieve some other goal. A modern twist on the practice is the kidnapping of large numbers of illegal immigrants who are often employed en masse in Chinese sweatshops or other low-paid industries. The target of the kidnapping is the immigrants' employer whose business will not be able to operate without cheap labor, although, if all else fails, the immigrants' families will be targeted for payment. 'In one such case in Baltimore,' reports Peter Huston, 'sixty-three men, women and children – a mixture of kidnappers and kidnap victims – were taken into custody by the police from one small three-bedroom house. The victims had been transported to the premises at night in rented U-Hauls and had made little attempt to escape.'[8]

Revenge killings are also common among Tong societies, with certain elements of Chinese communities looking upon revenge almost as a tradition that is tightly aligned to the Chinese honor system. But perhaps the most popular illegal activity with which the Tongs are involved, and one which brings in substantial amounts of money, is that of illegal gambling. Often this takes the form of small 'friendly' games between acquaintances, but more frequently the Tongs like to form multi-state, underground gambling rings, which rake in huge revenues while also serving as a means of laundering vast amounts of 'dirty' money. Mah-jong, cards and fan-tan are all popular games pursued during these activities and all relatively harmless when played for small stakes, but gamblers are regularly enticed to bet beyond their means and entire businesses can be put up as collateral, with ownership changing hands overnight. In California, recent State law has tried to address this problem by legalizing most forms of gambling, thereby preventing the Tongs from operating illegally and causing misery amongst the Chinese population.

Another area in which the Tongs frequently operate is the dangerous world of people trafficking. Given the nature of the business there are no accurate statistics available as to how many illegal immigrants are present in the United States at any one time but it has been estimated that approximately 11 percent of Chinese people living in New York's Chinatown are working there illegally. The lure of the rich pickings to be had in America is, no doubt, partly responsible for this – after all, the average farmer in rural China probably makes less in one year than the average American citizen makes in a week.

Tongs can smuggle people into America in many different ways, though two of the most popular routes in the past have either been via Mexico or Canada. The Tongs will supply their 'cargo' with false visas and identity papers which, naturally, come at a very high price. There are undoubtedly more clandestine ways of smuggling people into the country, though once again there is very little information available on the precise way in which this is done. That said, there is evidence to suggest that international smuggling rings often work together in groups, passing illegal immigrants from one country to another across the globe until they reach their desired destination. In this way hundreds of thousands of Chinese citizens make their way into America every year, with a fair number of Tongs using these routes to smuggle in criminal associates who can be of use to them in their illegal activities. The fees for this type of operation are enormous and whole families will save up their money for years in order to send just one member of their group to America – hopefully to earn enough money to then send back home. However, in practice this rarely happens as, more often than not, once the illegal immigrant has reached the United States, the Tongs make certain that they take a percentage of any income he, or in some cases she, makes.

Once successfully smuggled into the country, the illegal immigrants are normally 'housed' by the Tongs, which in effect means that they are almost certainly imprisoned until a job can be found for them, working in a sweatshop or in another

Tong-run business where a constant eye can be kept on them. After all, for the Tongs, these immigrants are an investment on which a return must be made. For the women who have been smuggled in, the situation can be even worse. Frequently they find themselves being sexually abused whilst being transported or sold into prostitution once they reach America.

The Tongs also frequently combine their people smuggling operations with that other, most lucrative pastime, drug smuggling. Marijuana, amphetamines and heroin are the Tong drugs of choice, with the latter being the most lucrative and, therefore, the most popular. Although previously the so-called 'Golden Triangle' of heroin production comprised of Thailand, Burma and Laos, these days China is also part of the equation. For the Tongs and all the other operatives involved, this is big business and the methods they use vary dramatically. While heroin can be smuggled into the country in large consignments hidden in shipments of legal merchandise, this is a high-risk strategy as a consignment intercepted by the authorities represents a major loss in revenue. A more popular way of smuggling drugs is by way of drug couriers and 'foreigners' (non-Chinese people) will often become involved in this process. The most likely candidates for the job are Filipinos and Thais, desperate to make money for their families. There are countless ways in which drugs can be hidden and smuggled; any number of objects, such as children's toys, souvenir ornaments or religious artifacts, can be hollowed out and used to hide small packages. Alternatively, drugs can be stuffed into condoms and swallowed by the drug courier, or 'mule', although, as has been seen on numerous occasions, this can result in the condom splitting and the death of the mule.

Perhaps the strangest fact of all when one considers the criminal nature of the Tongs is just how little their ways have changed over the past hundred years. Illegal gambling, drug smuggling, people trafficking – these were all as much a part and parcel of Tong activity back in the nineteenth century as they are today. More than any other secret society still in existence, the Tongs have remained practically as they were at their inception and will probably go on operating in much the same way for the forseeable future.

---

[1] *Tongs, Gangs and Triads: Chinese Crime Groups in North America*, Peter Huston, Paladin Press, 1995.

[2] Ibid.

[3] *The Barbary Coast*, Herbert Asbury, Old Town Books, 1933.

[4] *Triad Societies in Hong Kong*, W.P. Morgan, Government of Hong Kong, 1960.

[5] '300 Sightseers See Chinatown Murder,' *New York Times*, November 22, 1920.

[6] *The Chinese Experience in America*, Shih-shan Henry Tsai, Indiana University Press, 1986.

[7] The Chinese Exclusion Repeal Act, 1882.

[8] *Tongs, Gangs and Triads: Chinese Crime Groups in North America*, op. cit.

KU KLUX KLAN – THE INVISIBLE EMPIRE

They beat me and they beat me with the long, flat blackjack. I screamed to God in pain. My dress worked itself up. I tried to pull it down. They beat my arms until I had no feeling in them. After a while the first man beating my arm grew numb from tiredness. The other man who was holding me was given the blackjack. Then he began beat me [. . .] All of this on account we want to register.

Part of the testimony given by FANNIE LOU HAMER to the Credentials Committee at the 1964 Democratic Nominating Convention in Atlantic City

O f all the secret societies named in this book it is the Ku Klux Klan which, with its white robes and hoods that supposedly represent the ghostly forms of fallen soldiers returning from the American Civil War, has become (with the exception of the Nazi swastika) the most evil of twentieth-century icons. Far from being mere apparitions or harmless ghouls, over the years the Ku Klux Klan has become one of the most pervasive threats to American civil liberties, numbering amongst its targets not only the African-American community, but also Jews, homosexuals, feminists, anti-Christian liberals and foreign-born citizens.

Established at the end of the American Civil War on December 24, 1865, in the small town of Pulaski, Tennessee, the Ku Klux Klan was formed by six disenfranchised southern men who had all, at one time or another, been officers in the defeated Confederate Army. Disgusted by the idea that the black population was no longer bound in servitude to their white masters, the group's plan was to establish a secret brotherhood comprising Protestant, white-supremacist individuals eager to enjoy the benefits of a secret organization that was hell-bent on redressing what they viewed as a social injustice. Naming their group the Ku Klux Klan after the Greek word for 'circle' (*kyklos*) and then adding an alternative spelling of 'clan' for its alliterative value, the group set about capitalizing on their victims' superstitious natures by choosing a costume of white robes, masks and hoods, leading members of the black community to believe that they were the ghosts of dead Confederate soldiers who lived in hell and rode out at night in search of water. The ruse worked; the KKK's prey were terrified and duly subdued.

The KKK could not have chosen a better time in history to form their society for, as Stanley F. Horn in his book *Invisible Empire* succinctly puts it, the time was 'rotten-ripe' for the establishment of an institution such as the Klan. After all, the black population was not yet accustomed to its new-found freedoms and there were plenty of southerners both willing and able to snub the victorious north. Eyewitness accounts of KKK outrages are plentiful, the black civil-rights leader, Malcolm X having written in his autobiography:

> When my mother was pregnant with me, she told me later, a party of hooded Ku Klux Klan riders galloped up to our home in Omaha, Nebraska, one night. Surrounding the house, brandishing their shotguns and rifles, they shouted for my father to come out. My mother went to the front door and opened it. Standing where they could see her pregnant condition, she told them that she was alone with her three small children, and that my father was away, preaching in Milwaukee. The Klansmen shouted threats and warnings at her that we had better get out of town because 'the good Christian white people' were not going to stand for my father's 'spreading trouble' among the 'good' Negroes of Omaha with the 'back to Africa' preachings of Marcus Garvey.[1]

Soon, the association that had begun as a small group of discontented white men within one town, started to grow in number and spread further afield (in particular to Nashville), until in April 1867 General Nathan Bedford Forrest was elected Grand Wizard. On assuming his new role, Forrest immediately began sectioning off Ku Klux Klan territory and appointing Grand Dragons, Giants, Cyclopses and Night Hawks (names given to denote varying degrees of authority within the Klan), not to mention the Ghouls who were the bedrock of the society. Each had its own dominion, province or den, and each was governed by a set of strict rules, though naturally in a set-up such as this, participants were answerable only to themselves. Indeed these groups believed they were superior to the civilian authorities such as the police, and were not averse to using violence whenever they chose.

They beat, shot, stabbed and hanged their victims without a hint of conscience, forming vigilante groups to target non-white people who were suspected of breaking the law (although their supposed 'crimes' might be as innocuous as appearing not to show enough respect to their white neighbors), who belonged to political organizations or who were audacious enough to purchase their own land or business. The KKK also aimed their focus on any whites who were thought to be aiding and abetting their black neighbors. This could include white teachers who taught in black schools, white businessmen working with black colleagues, or anyone found 'guilty' of giving a black person preferential treatment over a white person.

Nor did state government intervene for, despite the Civil War having abolished slavery, southern states would still not allow their black citizens the ballot, a constitutional injustice that infuriated the majority of northerners. President Andrew Johnson even moved to invalidate every state government in the south with the exception of Tennessee. Far from alleviating the problem, however, this only served to reinforce support for the Ku Klux Klan. Membership soared, violence escalated. In 1871, in Mississippi, a handful of black political activists were put on trial for making inflammatory speeches and causing civil unrest. To show their support,

Grand Dragon of the Ku Klux Klan Samuel Green, seen here flanked by other Klansmen, became responsible for a resurgence in Klan activity after the Second World War, although his reign was short-lived as he died in 1949.

groups of black men and women assembled outside the court, a gathering that attracted the attention of the Klan. Within minutes violence broke out, gunshots were fired and several black citizens were murdered. When the disturbance outside the court had died down, those on trial were taken from the jail and hanged.

Despite the fact that the society was growing in stature as a political force, by 1869 there were signs that the Klan was experiencing serious internal problems and no longer able to control all its various factions. Perhaps this is unsurprising given that each enclave was autonomous, answerable to no greater authority, and that the basis of the Klan's existence was violence and misrule. Nevertheless, this did not make the problem any easier to manage, and in January 1869, General Forrest made the decision to disband the organization and destroy all Klan documents. Most sections of the KKK followed his orders, with the Klan closing its 'offices' in Georgia, Alabama, Mississippi, Arkansas and Tennessee. The KKK was no longer required, or so it seemed, and when, in 1877, President Rutherford B. Hayes withdrew the last of his federal troops from the south, this only seemed to reinforce the point. Local government was firmly back in the hands of local-born white southern Democrats; the black population knew its place and remained there with barely a whisper of insurrection. All were seemingly at peace, but this state of affairs was not to last and nowhere was this more apparent than within the pages of a 1905 book by Thomas Dixon, Jnr., titled *The Clansman: An Historic Romance of the Ku Klux Klan*, which, ten years later, was made into a film by the renowned director D. W. Griffith under the title *Birth of a Nation*. The film was a triumphant success, grossing in the region of US $18 million, but this achievement pales into insignificance when one compares the true effect of the film; an effect which, barely ten years later, led to the re-establishment of the KKK.

In the autumn of 1915, in the Piedmont Hotel, Atlanta, a man by the name of William J. Simmons gathered around him a small group of men (two of whom had been original Klan members), primarily to recreate the original order. Simmons had arranged it so that he and this group of dedicated followers later decamped to Stone Mountain (approximately 16 miles [26 km] outside of the city), at the top of which they built a temporary altar out of stones. Beside this they erected a wooden cross that had been padded with fabric and doused in petrol. Simmons set the cross alight, and the Ku Klux Klan was reborn. Days later, Griffith's *Birth of a Nation* opened in Atlanta. It was an opportunity too good to miss and Simmons immediately placed an advertisement in a local newspaper, next to one for the film, announcing the re-establishment of 'The World's Greatest Secret, Social, Patriotic, Fraternal, Beneficiary Order.'[2]

Membership swelled rapidly, drawing into its fold all manner of disenfranchised white men. Although in the first flush its main aim wasn't to be a 'night-riding' organization, the Klan certainly emphasized 100 percent white supremacy. Then, when America became embroiled in the First World War in 1917, yet another role was assumed by the white brotherhood – that of maintaining law and order.

The nation was gripped by fear; it had to be defended against alien enemies, Roman Catholic subversion, and those who were politically motivated against the government – union leaders, strikers and draft dodgers. The Klan, therefore, felt it had a crucial part to play. Reveling in its role as a pseudo-secret-service organization, the Klan began not only keeping files on political activists, but also spreading its net to include bootlegging, corrupt business dealings, extra-marital affairs, anything, in fact, that it considered to be un-American. The strategy worked. By 1919 membership had reached several thousand but, even so, Simmons knew only too well that they had hardly begun to realize the Klan's full potential. He decided to employ a couple of key disciples to publicize the cause and drum up further membership. Edward Young Clarke and Mrs. Elizabeth Tyler, who formed the Southern Publicity Association, were the chosen two.

By 1921 the Invisible Empire (as it had become known) had grown in support to boast well over 100,000 members. There seemed to be no end to the number of white Protestant males who wanted to belong to this secretive, fraternal organization with its strange rituals and even stranger costumes.

Two years later the Klan managed to win a place in the United States Senate when one of its members, Earl B. Mayfield, was elected. Towards the end of that year a new Imperial Wizard, Hiram Evans, took over the reins of power from William J. Simmons and succeeded in recruiting even more Klan members. But with the swelling of the ranks came a rapid escalation in Klan violence. Even with the publication of a series of articles exposing the Klan's less than spotless record, membership was unaffected and the violent episodes increased. A newspaper exposé only added to the Klan's popularity, appealing in the main to the lower middle-class, religious fundamentalists who felt that mainstream politics had not just passed them by, but had dragged the entire country away from the kind of small-town Protestant values by which they set so much store. In contrast, the Klan allowed its members a vicarious power. Leonard Cline, a reporter for the *Baltimore Sun*, wrote:

> It must have provided a real thrill to go scooting through the shadowy roads in somebody else's flivver, to meet in lonely dingles in the pine woods and flog other men, to bounce down the fifteen-foot declivity where the ridge ends and swoop at twenty-five miles an hour through the flatlands around Mer Rouge, through phantasmal Lafourche swamp with its banshee live oaks, waving their snaky tresses in the moonlight. It was perpetual Halloween. And even if one didn't care much for church, and took one's shot of white lightning when one could get it, and would pay a dollar any day for five minutes in a trollop's arms, it was reassuring to know that religion approved and sanctified one's pranks. It made one bolder.[3]

There are many examples of floggings and lynchings from this period. The state of Texas was notorious for its tar-and-feather parties, and during the spring of 1922 the southern state was credited with having flogged as many as sixty-eight people in what became known as a special Klan 'whipping meadow' by the banks of the Trinity River. But perhaps one of the best-known Klan incidents took place in Louisiana. Two young black men, Watt Daniel and Tom Richards, were targeted for punishment by the Klan's Mer Rouge (in Morehouse Parish) outfit, at that time led by a Dr. B. M. McKoin. Daniel and Richards had been caught spying on Klan meetings and generally badmouthing the organization, so it was decided that the the two boys would be taught a lesson. After being kidnapped in broad daylight, they were taken to some woods and warned that their behavior was unacceptable. Then they were released. Sadly, however, the story did not end there. A few weeks later, on August 24, 1922, after a baseball game and barbecue which most of Mer Rouge had attended, Watt Daniel and Tom Richards, together with their fathers and one other unnamed man, were ambushed in their car, seized by masked figures, blindfolded, hog-tied and bundled into a waiting vehicle. The prisoners were then driven to a clearing in the woods, at which point the two elder men were tied to trees and flogged. Watt Daniel, seeing his father in distress, succeeded in breaking free from his captors, but in so doing tore off the hood of one of his assailants. In this moment it is thought that both he and Tom Richards recognized their tormentor. Their fate was duly sealed, for while their fathers and the unnamed man were later released, Watt

Klan members gather in full regalia at an initiation ceremony not in the 'Deep South', as one might expect, but in Baltimore in 1923.

and Tom were dragged further into the woods never to be seen alive again.

Back in Morehouse Parish there was a public outcry. Pro- and anti-Klan factions were at each other's throats, ready to fight one another to the death over what had occurred. The Democratic governor of the state, John M. Parker, had lost control. So serious was the situation that he had personally requested help from the Justice Department in Washington. After much deliberation, however, President Harding felt his administration did not have the jurisdiction to take the case further. Governor Parker would therefore have to act alone, a prospect he did not relish. Eventually, he ordered the dragging of a lake where it was thought the bodies of the two boys lay and, after several setbacks, the corpses were recovered. A coroner confirmed they had been flogged and later crushed to the point that every bone in their bodies had been broken.

There then followed a protracted period of time while evidence was gathered against Klan members, but as is the way with any secret society, it proved virtually impossible to identify the culprits. In the small number of cases where there was enough evidence to proceed, two successive grand juries refused to indict anyone, not least because sitting on the said juries were several influential Klan members. The most Governor Parker could do was to attempt to convict some of those involved for minor misdemeanors, which he did with varying degrees of success. Some of the culprits were given small fines, while others left the county never to return.

Parker made it known that no district judges would be appointed if they were known to be Klan members, and in state elections during 1924, all of the candidates for the governorship declared themselves anti-Klan. Was this the beginning of the end for the Invisible Empire? The answer is less than clear, for although the organization was on a downward spiral in several key states, including Texas, Arkansas, Louisiana, Oklahoma and California, membership had reached a peak during the mid-twenties, when it numbered approximately three million. By 1928, however, only a few hundred thousand remained.

Several key factors contributed to this decline. With the end of the First World War, Americans felt more secure and the economy appeared to be picking up, signaling greater prosperity for all. The Klan also had to battle the negative publicity caused by events such as the Mer Rouge murders, together with a handful of other notorious cases including the murder of a police constable which took place in Inglewood, California. The state of Texas's flogging parties were also proving a severe embarrassment. Suddenly, law-abiding citizens began to see the Klan as a divisive force, disrupting communal harmony, causing civil unrest. Many of those who had previously belonged to the organization wanted to distance themselves from it. Even with the onset of the Depression, when it might be thought that the Klan would see a swelling of its ranks, membership dwindled even further. Large swathes of the country were out of work and quite literally starving, yet the best the Klan could come up with was to announce that anyone involved in civil unrest such as hunger marches were nothing better than 'Negroes, Hunks, Dagoes, and all the rest of the scum of Europe's slums.'[4]

By the late thirties, it seemed that nothing could revive the Klan's fortunes, and as if mirroring this decline, Imperial Wizard Hiram Evans retired. Taking over from him was a man by the name of Jimmy Colescott. Colescott immediately put into action a major recruiting campaign, which included the usual Klan tactics of violence and intimidation. However, it was doomed to failure from the start for, alongside the onset of the Second World War, which effectively concentrated everyone's minds elsewhere, major incidents such as the 'Shoemaker flogging' brought nothing but adverse publicity.

Consistently against any kind of organized labor or union membership, the Klan was particularly active in the citrus state of Florida where, in 1935, a political group (the Modern Democrats) began trying to create several labor organizations, as well as campaigning for employment reform. Ever alert to such threats, the Klan sent an undercover agent to spy on the Modern Democrats and, after one meeting of members, they detained several men whom they suspected of being key players in the new movement. Among those detained was Joseph Shoemaker. Shoemaker was taken away, flogged, castrated and tarred all over before having one of his legs plunged into a vat of boiling tar. Nine days later he died of his injuries. Though the incident brought national condemnation, and despite the arrest and trial of several of those responsible, ultimately no one was convicted of Shoemaker's murder.

Drawing confidence from this blatant evasion of justice, the Klan then tried to regroup and regain some lost ground over the next decade, particularly where recruitment was concerned, but Imperial Wizard Colescott didn't seem up to the job, and with the Second World War drawing to a close, Grand Dragon Dr. Samuel Green took over Colescott's position. Reintroducing parades, mystic initiation ceremonies atop Stone Mountain, night raids and floggings, he did his best once again to swell the Klan's ranks. But his recruitment drive was beset by problems, mainly caused by bodies such as the FBI and the Bureau of Internal Revenue, which were keeping a close eye on the white-hooded society.

In 1949, Samuel Green died suddenly, plunging the Invisible Empire into even greater turmoil. Splinter groups formed, creating numerous factions that each clung desperately to its own violent agenda. Burning crosses could be spotted across the whole of the south and yet, although united in violence, the Klan could still not rally around one leader to form a cohesive political whole. One result of this was that many Klan leaders ended up in jail. Even with the abolition of public-school segregation, which took place on May 17, 1954, the Klan could not unite properly.

Violence was the only factor that brought the Invisible Empire together, a fact which is illustrated horrifically in the following extract from a report by the combined forces of the Friends' Service Committee, the National Council of Churches of Christ and the Southern Regional Council, which lists over 500 cases of intimidation and violence after the passing of the Supreme Court's school decision.

• 6 Negroes killed;

• 29 individuals, 11 of them white, shot and wounded in racial incidents;

- 44 persons beaten;
- 5 stabbed;
- 30 homes bombed; in one instance (at Clinton, Tenn.), an additional 30 houses were damaged by a single blast; attempted blasting of five other homes;
- 8 homes burned;
- 15 homes struck by gunfire, and 7 homes stoned;
- 4 schools bombed, in Jacksonville, Nashville, Chattanooga, and Clinton, Tenn.;
- 2 bombing attempts in schools in Charlotte and Clinton;
- 7 churches bombed, one of which was for whites; an attempt made to bomb another Negro church.[5]

But if the violence of the 1950s was horrific, during the 1960s, with the ever increasing influence of the civil-rights movement and the fact that the black population was becoming a growing economic competitor to the working-class white male, it only escalated. The Klan finally succeeded in appointing a new Imperial Wizard, a man who, if not accepted by every Klan member, was at least favorable to the majority. Robert Shelton was a Tuscaloosa rubber worker who harbored a violent dislike of black people, whom he saw as little more than savages. With Shelton at the helm, the Invisible Empire slowly began to claw back some degree of coordination, and once again began to make life for its black victims barely tolerable. Nowhere was this more apparent than in Birmingham, Alabama where, during the early part of the 1960s, bombing of black homes and businesses became an almost weekly occurrence until, on September 15, 1963, one of the most infamous crimes in American history was committed when the Klan bombed the Sixteenth Street Bethel Baptist Church, killing four young girls – Cynthia Wesley, Dennise McNair, Carol Robertson and Addie Mae Collins.

Birmingham's law enforcement agencies at first attempted to blame black activists, but soon even they couldn't shy away from the fact that the KKK was involved. Yet, despite clear evidence pointing towards those responsible, at the time no one was charged with the killings. Eventually all four murders went on file, along with several hundred other unsolved crimes of the period. This did nothing to discourage KKK violence. During the summer of 1964 in St. Augustine, Florida, the black population, with the support of Martin Luther King (or 'Martin Lucifer Coon,' as the Klan nicknamed him), embarked on 'integrationist' marches along with their Jewish neighbors. The most militant of the hooded Klan knights were ready and waiting. The marchers refrained from using any sort of violence, but not so the white knights, who stoned and clubbed and threw acid at them. The clashes between the two groups lasted for weeks, the police seemingly powerless to intervene. The violence eventually died down, but other outbreaks of Klan activity sprung up elsewhere. One infamous incident involved Lt. Col. Lemuel Penn who, along with several other soldiers, was returning from a summer training camp at Fort Benning in Georgia. Colonel Penn was black, as were several of his companions. When their car, sporting a Washington number plate, was spotted by a group of Klansmen, they immediately jumped to the conclusion that the occupants were civil-rights supporters, with the result that Penn's vehicle was peppered with gunshots. Tragically, Colonel Penn died in the attack, but what followed was even more outrageous, for although the culprits were eventually arrested and put on trial, the all-white jury was loathe to convict. As the defendants' attorney put it, no '. . . Madison County jury [ever] converted an electric chair into a sacrificial chair on which the pure flesh of a member of the human race was sacrificed to the savage revengeful appetite of a raging mob.'[6] A verdict of 'not guilty' was returned, and much to the federal government's annoyance, if not embarrassment, the defendants went free.

If the Ku Klux Klan thought it was making any inroads into mainstream American life, however, nothing could have been further from the truth for, a little less than a hundred years after the Invisible Empire's birth, when it was formed primarily to stop black people gaining any foothold in mainstream America, the African-American population had begun to claim its rightful place in society. Educated, economically independent and making huge inroads into middle-class America, the country was more truly bi-racial than it had ever been in its entire history. Nonetheless, a great deal of work still had to be done if African Americans were ever to enjoy equality in their own country. Martin Luther King campaigned vigorously to bring down the racist barriers. Rallies were organized, as well as sit-ins and other means of peaceful protest, yet even then the Ku Klux Klan couldn't resist using violence to make its voice heard.

One victim of the Klan, Mrs. Viola Gregg Liuzzo, was shot dead while transporting demonstrators to and from a march in Lowndes County in 1965. The perpetrators were all brought to court; once again no conviction was secured.[7] The only positive outcome of the whole sorry affair was that it did at least prompt the then President, Lyndon B. Johnson, to denounce the Klan publicly and declare a war against all that the Invisible Empire stood for.

Nevertheless, under United States law, it is impossible to forbid the existence of any type of organization, and it fell to individual counties to gauge the political temperature of the country and begin prosecuting Klan crimes. Slowly but surely, the tide began to turn. FBI agents infiltrated many Klan groups and with the evidence they were building up they began securing convictions against Klan members.

In 1965 a voting-rights law was passed, increasing the significance of black citizens and causing politicians to begin taking note of their non-white constituents. Towards the end of the 1960s, it seemed nothing could stem the increasing growth of black power, and several areas with black majorities voted in black mayors, councilors and sheriffs. In such an atmosphere, the decline of the Ku Klux Klan was inevitable.

So determined was the US government to stamp out the KKK that it sanctioned the FBI's 'disrupt and neutralize' programme, otherwise known by the acronym COUNTERINTELPRO, which, by the early 1970s, led the FBI to claim that one in six Klan members were actually FBI informers.

The specter of the four young girls who were killed in the Birmingham bombing several years earlier, also began to catch up with the Klan. In Alabama there is no statute of limitation where murder is concerned, and a certain young lawyer by the name of William Baxley had forgotten neither the crime nor the fact that convictions could be sought at any time so long as there was enough evidence. On leaving law school Baxley set his sights on becoming Attorney General of Alabama, and by the time he was thirty, he had achieved his goal. In a position of authority, Baxley now began hounding the FBI for their files on the case and eventually, with the relevant documents in his possession, realized that the FBI had had, within weeks of the bombing, enough evidence to convict those men responsible. In September 1977, almost thirteen years after the crime was committed, one of the guilty men was brought to justice when an Alabama grand jury (made up of three black and nine white jurors) indicted and afterwards convicted Robert Edward Chambliss on four counts of first-degree murder.

Baxley promised to pursue everyone else who had been involved in the crime and bring them to justice, too. But perhaps the most poignant yet powerful sign that America was moving away from Ku Klux Klan-type politics was that in 1979, Birmingham, Alabama elected its first black mayor.

With Klan ranks thinning daily, and sheriffs and juries increasingly willing to arrest and convict anyone involved in Klan activities, membership of the Invisible Empire waned once again. Small pockets of resistance did still remain, people whose deeply entrenched beliefs were succinctly expressed by the female jockey Mary Bacon, who not only publicly declared her Klan membership but announced that:

> We are not just a bunch of illiterate, southern, nigger killers. We are good
> white Christian people, hard-working people, people working for a
> white America [. . .] When one of your wives or one of your sisters gets
> raped by a nigger maybe you'll get smart and join the Klan.[8]

Even with a brief renaissance (particularly in the Deep South) toward the end of the 1970s, the Klan struggled to achieve the kind of power it wielded in the 1920s. A young, college-educated man by the name of David Duke tried creating a new Klan image by appealing to America's growing middle class. Duke lectured at university campuses up and down the country, and appeared on television and radio shows, but to little avail. Indeed, the Klan seemed only to have become an organization that ultra-right-wing men and women could look back on with nostalgia. The Ku Klux Klan was part of American history, part of a long tradition that represented a yearning amongst some for white supremacy.

But there were some further hideous throwbacks to times gone by. In the town of Greensboro in North Carolina on November 3, 1979, a sizeable anti-Klan rally was gathering in Greensboro's black district when into their midst drove a nine-car cavalcade of Ku Klux Klan and American neo-Nazis. The demonstrators on the street began pounding on the cars, but what happened next was almost beyond belief. In front of TV cameras and numerous witnesses, several of the men inside the cars stepped out of their vehicles, brandished guns and began firing into the crowds. Four white men and one black woman were killed, and many, many more (including children) were badly injured. The incident drew national attention. President Carter ordered the FBI to investigate. Fourteen of the assailants were arrested and charged with the murders, but the Greensboro incident showed that, although America was becoming a more tolerant, interracial society, there were still deep pockets of bigotry and evil at large.

Today, almost twenty-six years later, nothing much has changed. When the Klan was founded back in 1865, its remit was first as a fraternal organization to fight against black emancipation. During its second flush under the authority of William J. Simmons its goal had changed little. The Klan was to be the savior of the downtrodden, working-class, white American. The society saw itself as defending what it believed were traditional American values: the Constitution, the Bible and racial separation. But perhaps what really bound and still binds the Klan together is something even more deep-seated. It is that original idea of fraternity, of a gathering together of like-minded people. Societies like the Klan have existed for many hundreds of years and the appeal of secret rituals, sacred ceremonies and a hierarchical structure clearly answers some unspoken, yet very real need.

The last word, however, must belong to the four teenage girls who died so tragically in the Birmingham Sixteenth Street Baptist Church bombing, where a memorial plaque bearing pictures of the deceased reads, 'May men learn to replace bitterness and violence with love and understanding.'

[1] *Malcolm X: The Autobiography*, Malcolm X (with Alex Hayley), Ballantine, 1965.

[2] *Hooded Americanism: The History of Ku Klux Klan*, David M. Chalmers, Duke University Press (NC), 1987.

[3] 'In Darkest Louisiana,' Leonard L. Cline, *Nation*, 116 (1923).

[4] Extract taken from an article in the Klan's national magazine and used in *Hooded Americanism: The History of Ku Klux Klan*, op. cit.

[5] *Intimidation, Reprisal and Violence in the South's Radical Crisis*, American Friends' Service Committee *et al.*, 1959.

[6] *Hooded Americanism: The History of Ku Klux Klan*, op. cit.

[7] Convictions were gained several years later.

[8] *Hooded Americanism: The History of the Ku Klux Klan*, op. cit.

ORDER OF THE SOLAR TEMPLE – TRIAL BY FIRE

There is nothing so despicable as a secret society that is based
upon religious prejudice and that will attempt to defeat a man
because of his religious beliefs. Such a society is like a cockroach . . .
it thrives in the dark. So do those who combine for such an end.
WILLIAM HOWARD TAFT, 27th US President, 1909-13

On October 4, 1994 in Morin Heights, a small ski resort near Montreal in Canada, the fire brigade was called out to a burning condominium, beside which they discovered the remains of two badly charred bodies. Initially investigators, who had run a quick check on the building's registered owners, thought the two bodies were most likely those of Joseph Di Mambro and Luc Jouret. Di Mambro, it later transpired, was the leader of a secretive sect, known as the Order of the Solar Temple, while Luc Jouret was Di Mambro's right-hand man, a self-styled prophet whose main role was to recruit new members to the cult. But, as an autopsy later confirmed, neither body belonged to these two men; indeed one of the corpses was that of a woman. So perhaps investigators were looking at the bodies of the couple that were renting the condominium? This theory was also quickly dismissed when fire-fighters, having extinguished the flames inside the building, went in to investigate. On close inspection of the rooms, three further corpses were discovered hidden at the back of a wardrobe – those of a man, a woman and a child. But the grisly horror of the scene did not stop there, for all three bodies were found to be covered in blood. The corpses were those of the property's tenants: Tony Dutoit, Nicki Dutoit and their child, a baby boy called Christopher-Emmanuel. It was quickly established that, rather than dying from the fire, all three had been stabbed to death – Tony a total of fifty times in the back, Nicki several times in the back, chest and neck, and finally Christopher-Emmanuel (who was only three months old), six times in the chest with what appeared to have been a wooden stake. Police put their time of death at a minimum of four days prior to the outbreak of the fire, so it would seem that the murderer had stored their bodies before deciding to burn down the building. But what of the other two corpses? Who were they – the people who had murdered the Dutoits, or yet more victims of a multiple killer?

The police were baffled, although early on they did make one crucial discovery: that the Dutoits had been members of the Order of the Solar Temple. Police also learned of a rumor that the leader of the order, Joseph Di Mambro, had sent out assassins to murder the Dutoits' baby boy because he believed Christopher-

Emmanuel to be the anti-Christ. Arrest warrants were issued for both Di Mambro and Luc Jouret but, unsurprisingly, the pair were nowhere to be found.

Meanwhile, across the Atlantic in Switzerland, more fires were breaking out, fires which no one at first had cause to suspect might be connected to the murders in Canada.

At midnight on October 4, 1994, less than a day after the Morin Heights' deaths, Swiss fire-fighters were called to the home of an elderly farmer, Albert Giacobino, who lived near the tiny ski resort of Chiery. On entering the burning building, Giacobino's body was found slumped across the kitchen table with a plastic bag over his head. Investigators initially concluded that he had committed suicide, however, on closer inspection, it was discovered that Giacobino had been shot in the head. Police also discovered that the farmhouse and outlying buildings were peppered with incendiary devices. It all seemed very strange, but the Swiss authorities could not even guess at this point just how sinister these findings really were. One of the outlying buildings appeared to have been turned into a meeting room inside which belongings lay scattered about, although there was no sign of the owners of these items. Then one of the investigators, realizing that the building seemed much larger from the outside than it looked inside, started searching for a hidden door or panel. Suddenly all was revealed: an entire section of wall was found to slide back, on the other side of which lay a secret chamber decorated from floor to ceiling with scarlet furnishings. To the investigator's horror, in the middle of the floor lay eighteen corpses, arranged in a circle with their feet in the middle and their heads towards the outside. Many of the corpses were dressed in what appeared to be red, gold and black ceremonial capes, and some had plastic bags over their heads. A second secret room or chamber was then discovered in which lay another three corpses. There was a great deal of blood in both rooms, indicating that many of the victims had been shot. Forensic specialists estimated the time of death to have been on October 3, at around the same time as the Canadian murders had occurred, allowing for the time difference. Serge Thierren, one of the many investigators who attended the farmhouse massacre, described it thus:

> It was a horrible scene. Some of the bodies were in the chapel, in the basement and some in what looked like a conference room with a round table. There were empty champagne bottles lying on the floor.[1]

Tragically, there were further such deaths to come only two days later. In another Swiss ski resort, Granges-sur-Salvan, located a little over 100 miles away from Chiery, the fire department was called out to deal with a fire in three adjacent chalets. On entering the buildings twenty-five corpses were discovered (including three teenagers and four children), many of whom had been shot in the head several times. The obvious conclusion was that the two tragedies were closely related, but what was the link? The answer to that came when all of the dead from both incidents were identified through dental records and discovered to have belonged to the Order of the Solar Temple. Autopsies also revealed that only fifteen out of the forty-seven had been willing suicides. An international search for the leaders of this now murderous cult was swiftly launched.

Joseph Di Mambro was born on August 19, 1924 in southern France and, though he trained as a clockmaker and jeweler, from an early age he expressed an interest in esoteric religions. In 1956, at the age of thirty-two, he became a member of the Rosicrucian Order, AMORC (Ancient and Mystic Order of the Rosy Cross), and continued his involvement with this group until 1969, by which time he had founded his own brand of religion, one for which he had more than a few disciples.

Moving from southern France to settle near the Swiss border, in 1973 Di Mambro founded the Center for the Preparation of the New Age, a society to which those who joined had to donate vast sums of money in order, Di Mambro said, that he could care for the whole community. This was not the sect's only dubious practice, for Di Mambro also persuaded members that he was the reincarnation of several political and religious leaders ranging from the Egyptian god Osiris to Moses. He also ruled that he alone could decide who was to marry whom and who was allowed to bear children. The idea behind this latter 'law' was that all cult members were, in fact, reincarnations of famous personages and to produce children of a superior quality it was vital that marriages and procreation only took place between suitable candidates. His own son, Elie, was apparently one such gifted child whose destiny was to usher in the New Age, while Di Mambro's daughter, Emmanuelle, was supposedly one of only nine 'cosmic children' and as such was allowed no physical contact with anyone save immediate family members. Extraordinarily, his ideas drew many respected citizens, some extremely wealthy, to the sect. In 1978, Di Mambro founded a core group of followers initially known as the Foundation of the Golden Way and afterwards, around 1984, renamed the Order of the Solar Temple.

Di Mambro had always felt he needed a second-in-command, someone who could dedicate himself to the recruitment of new members. He turned to a man to whom he had been introduced a couple of years before, a Belgian medical doctor by the name of Luc Jouret. Born on October 18, 1947 in the Belgian Congo (present-day Zaire), Jouret was a charismatic, eloquent individual who soon doubled the number of new recruits to the order as well as inspiring existing members by claiming not only to have been (in a former life) a member of the fourteenth-century order known as the Knights Templar, but also to being the third incarnation of Christ.

By 1989, the Order of the Solar Temple appeared to have a worldwide membership of 600, with followers living not only in Canada, Switzerland and France, but also in the USA, Spain and the French Caribbean. Jouret was in his element, traveling between all these countries, giving lectures and seminars and receiving large donations. A report in *Time* Magazine by journalist Michael Seville estimated that Jouret and Di Mambro had accumulated a fortune of approximately $93 million over the years by reigning in their followers' assets. So what could followers expect in return for their generous donations? According to Luc Jouret, after members had died and left their physical bodies, they would rejoin each other via 'death voyages' on another planet named Sirius. Jouret also, during his lectures, advanced the theory that the end of the world ('the time of disasters') would arrive due to human neglect, but that a handful of chosen people ('noble travelers') would transcend this cataclysm before it occurred and ascend to Sirius via a pathway of fire. In fact fire was, disturbingly, a recurrent theme where Luc Jouret was concerned.

Obsessed from an early age by stories of the Order of the Knights Templar, an ancient monastic military order formed in AD 1118 by nine men from the First Crusade who banded together and vowed to protect pilgrims traveling to the Holy Lands, Jouret was particularly absorbed by the manner of their deaths. Over a period of 200 years the Knights Templar grew to be one of the most powerful secret organizations in Europe, not only fighting alongside King Richard I (the Lionheart) of England but also enjoying the support of, amongst others, Pope Innocent II. Feared as warriors, they were also revered for their wealth and essentially invented banking as we now know it today. Their powers seemed limitless, but such wealth and power inevitably caused jealousy and fear among other equally powerful European rulers. Finally, in 1307, King Philip (the Fair) of France, desperately in need of funds to support his war against Edward I of England, decided to move against the Knights Templar on the grounds that they had committed heresy. On October 13 he had all the knights arrested, seizing their lands and assets and forcing them to confess a whole gamut of sins including the worship of the Baphomet, homosexuality and sodomy, trampling and spitting on the holy cross and heresy. In 1310 King Philip had fifty-four of their number burned at the stake, and Pope Clement V subsequently

made membership of the order illegal. The last Grand Master of the Knights Templar, Jacques de Molay, was burned on March 19, 1314, and during his ordeal he is said to have cursed both King Philip and Pope Clement, claiming they would die within the year. Whether the story is apocryphal or not, Clement did pass away one month later and Philip seven months after that.

Jouret was enthralled by the Knights Templar, having fed off the stories surrounding their grisly deaths. He

Swiss-born Luc Jouret was, with Joseph Di Mambro, one of the leaders of the Solar Temple secret society. Both committed suicide along with twenty-one others at a farmhouse near Chiery in the Swiss Alps in 1994.

The sinister chapel of the Order of the Solar Temple which was discovered at the farmhouse in Chiery behind a secret sliding wall panel. On the floor lay eighteen corpses.

traveled extensively giving lectures claiming that elite members of the Solar Temple could absorb the original Knights Templar's spirituality by donating large sums of money. Ludicrous as these claims sound, there were plenty of men and women willing enough to believe Jouret and become members of the group. The academic, Jean François-Mayer, quotes from the statement of one such individual attesting to these beliefs:

> I, a Lightbearer since the most remote times, the time which was given to me on Planet Earth is completed, and I go back freely and willingly to the place from which I came at the beginning of times! Happiness fills me, because I know that I have fulfilled my duty, and that I can bring back in Peace and Happiness my capitalized energy enriched through the experience which I have lived on this Earth – back to the source from which everything comes. It is difficult for the man of the Earth to understand such a choice, such a decision – to leave willingly one's terrestrial vehicle! But such is it for all those who carry with them Light and Cosmic Consciousness and know where they go back.[2]

Given such a mindset, it was only a matter of time before members of the group began talking about 'the end of the world' and how when that time came, members of the Solar Temple would leave this world and go on a death voyage together, back to the planet Sirius.

But why the precise dates that the two leaders finally chose? Sadly, it appears that, far from having any spiritual significance, the truth of the matter was far more worldly. Several members of the cult had become disenchanted with Di Mambro and Jouret and were demanding the return of their investments. Undoubtedly a factor in this rebellion was the demise of another cult. In February 1993, a fifty-four-day siege at Waco in Texas had begun when David Koresh, the leader of the Branch Davidians sect, decided the time was ripe for his cult to commit mass suicide. Eighty-four followers (including many children) died in the ensuing fire, pictures of which were broadcast around the world. This caused a huge drop in the number of new recruits into cults, not to mention a wave of desertions by people desperate to leave the cults they had already joined. Membership of the Solar Temple plummeted.

It was a worrying time for Di Mambro, but his troubles were only just beginning. Later that same year a long-time member of his group became wise to Di Mambro's implementation of laser tricks to make the spiritual 'Grand Masters of the Solar Temple' appear to believers. This man was Tony Dutoit; the same Tony Dutoit whose body was later found stuffed in a cupboard in Canada with fifty knife wounds in his back. Thierry Huguenin, a Swiss dentist, also spoke of the type of tricks Di Mambro liked to play on his disciples.

> Two women began to get undressed as the first notes of Wagnerian music sounded. As they revealed their underwear, a lightbulb detached itself from the spotlight, severed the head of a rose and smashed at the foot of the altar. Jo [Di Mambro] brandished a sword and cried, 'By the powers invested in me, I trace a protective circle around this holy assembly.'[3]

It all sounds exceedingly childish, yet to members of the cult it was obviously a serious display of Di Mambro's powers. Nevertheless, sceptics such as Dutoit were adding to the pressure on Di Mambro, who was also being investigated by several banks for money laundering. As if to add insult to injury, his own children, Elie and Emmanuelle, had begun growing less inclined to believe their father's teachings. Indeed, Elie was more than happy to expose his father's fakery, which he did on a number of occasions, causing at least a dozen members to leave the Solar Temple.

But if Di Mambro had problems, he wasn't alone, for Luc Jouret also had his fair share of concerns. At some point prior to 1994 he was voted out as Grand Master of the Canadian branch of the Solar Temple due to his increasingly eccentric behavior, coupled with his controlling leadership style that many key members had grown to resent. Several testimonies state that prior to the beginning of one of the Solar Temple's many rituals, Jouret would insist on having sexual relations with a female member of the cult in order to give him 'spiritual strength.' But it was Jouret's leadership style that really led him into trouble and finally saw him being demoted. In turn, this led to major disagreements among the European branches of the society and angered Di Mambro, who had always trusted Jouret implicitly. As several investigative journalists later discovered, however, this wasn't the first time Jouret had been ousted from office. Prior to joining the Order of the Solar Temple, Luc Jouret had belonged to a racist, neo-Nazi magical organization, co-founded by a former

Gestapo officer called Julien Origas. After a failed grab for overall control of the group Jouret left, only to join Di Mambro's Solar Temple where he made the same mistake all over again. The police were also interested in Luc Jouret's business dealings as it had come to light that he had begun dealing in illegal arms. Along with two other Solar members he was convicted and fined $1,000.

Di Mambro and Jouret both, therefore, had reason to be concerned about the Solar Temple's future and, more importantly, their own positions as leaders. The straw that appeared to break the camel's back concerned Tony Dutoit. Dutoit's wife, Nicki, had previously been ordered by Di Mambro not to have any children but, desperate to start a family, she ignored Di Mambro's directive and gave birth to her son, Christopher-Emmanuel. On hearing the news, Di Mambro immediately declared the child to be the anti-Christ, sent by negative forces to challenge his daughter's position as the true messiah.

The only way out of this seemingly messy state of affairs, or so it seemed to Di Mambro and Jouret, was to declare that the time had come for both them and their followers to leave this Earth and proceed to a higher level of spirituality. Fire was required for the transition to be successful, so on October 4, 1994, following the murder of Tony Dutoit and his family, their building was set alight. Their murderers (later identified as thirty-five-year-old Gerry Genoud and sixty-year-old Colette Genoud) then committed suicide, believing they were on the path to Sirius. At almost the same moment, on the other side of the world, leaders Di Mambro and Jouret were putting the finishing touches to their own (and several others') suicides in the Swiss farmhouse owned by Albert Giacobino. After the deaths at Chiery and those of October 5 at Granges-sur-Salvan, there was a temporary cessation of activity among the surviving members of the Solar Temple. To what this was due has never been established, but one can surmise that with Di Mambro's and Jouret's deaths, the Solar Temple was finding it difficult to function. Nevertheless, a little over a year after the first three mass suicides, even more blood was to be shed.

In December 1995, in a sparsely wooded area better known as the Well (or Pit) of Hell located just outside Grenoble in France, sixteen people (including three children, six-year-old Tania Verona, nineteen-month-old Curval Lardanchet and four-year-old Aldwin Lardanchet) were found dead. Some of their number had suffered terrible burns while fourteen of them were discovered spread out in the telltale, wheel-like pattern later identified as a star. That day had been the apex of the winter solstice and all the corpses were later identified as having been members of the Solar Temple. Although some of the dead had obviously committed suicide, others showed signs that they had been brutally murdered. One woman's jaw was badly fractured, other people had gunshot wounds and nearly everyone in the circle was shown to have taken a combination of the drugs Myolastan and Digoxine. A few had left suicide notes stating that the purpose of their actions was to leave this life and travel to a higher spiritual plane. Chillingly, the notes also indicated that another mass suicide was going to take place.

A year passed with no further incidents, but police were still keeping a close eye on remaining Solar Temple members, paying particular attention to the winter and summer solstice and equinox dates. Perhaps, because nothing occurred on either occasion, they were lulled into a false sense of security, or perhaps they simply didn't have the resources to keep a constant watch over everyone. Whatever the case, the surveillance was relaxed only for tragedy to strike yet again.

On March 22, 1997 in the small village of St. Casimir in Quebec, yet another mass suicide took place, bringing the total number of Solar Temple deaths to seventy-four. Gathering at the spring equinox on 20 March, five adult members of the group along with three teenagers tried to set off an incendiary device intended to burn both them and the building to the ground. Luckily, the device failed, allowing the teenagers enough time to persuade their parents that they didn't want to die. Once released, the youngsters fled to a nearby house, but the adults continued with their plan, and this time they succeeded. Having taken tranquillizers, they arranged themselves on the floor in the sign of the cross, then set light to themselves. Later a note was discovered explaining that the victims believed this the only way to transport themselves to another planet.

The authorities may have failed to prevent this tragedy but they were much luckier the following year, for in 1998 they discovered that a German psychologist had gathered together twenty-nine members of the Solar Temple in the Canary Islands with the express purpose of staging yet another mass suicide. Meanwhile, back in France, relatives of the Grenoble victims were pressing the authorities to arrest any surviving members of the cult, especially any surviving leader, with a view to prosecuting them.

One such leader was Michel Tabachnik, a world-renowned musician and conductor, who lived in Paris but had worked for both the Canadian Opera Company and the University of Toronto Symphony Orchestra. He was indicted for 'participation in a criminal organization' involving ritual killings, and was brought to trial in Grenoble on April 16, 2001. Although previously not thought to be a main player in the organization, further investigation concluded that he had been a facilitator in the 1994 suicides and all those that followed. In fact, Tabachnik had written a great deal of the group's literature (which was sold to believers for huge sums of money), and therefore had played a vital role in the priming of members to believe self-annihilation was necessary to achieve the Temple's goals.

At the trial, the French magistrate, Luc Fontaine, forwarded the opinion that two of the deceased members of the cult – a police officer named Jean-Pierre Lardanchet (whose two sons also died in the 1995 tragedy) and an architect by the name of Andre Friedli – had been the men who, at the Grenoble mass suicide, shot and murdered several cult members who weren't willing to take their own lives. It was a pattern that had been repeated at all the other incidents – two chosen members of the Temple shooting all those who weren't on a high enough spiritual level to achieve suicide. Afterwards, the crime-scene reconstruction demonstrated how Lardanchet and Friedli then poured gasoline over the bodies before setting them alight and afterwards killing themselves. It was all extremely grisly and unsurprisingly, given that prosecutors were pressing for a jail term of between five and ten years, Tabachnik denied all charges. After all, there was very little concrete evidence, apart from the writings, to link him directly to the deaths. Yet two former Solar Temple members testified that the order to commit suicide came only from the higher echelons of the group, which included Tabachnik. They also testified that it had been Di Mambro and Tabachnik who had set up the Solar Temple, having traveled together to Egypt where they had been inspired by the ancient pharaohs and where Di Mambro had interpreted ancient carvings for his acolyte, informing him that the god Sothis (later known as Sirius) represented knowledge. In addition to this evidence, during the course of the trial, *The Times* newspaper in London printed an interview it had conducted with the son of a former member.

> Edith Vuarnet, the wife of an Olympic ski champion, could not resist the lure of the cult, despite the fact that fifty-three members of the order had already died.
>
> The first that [Alain] Vuarnet or his father knew of the sect's existence and their family's connection with it was in October 1994, when fifty-three of its followers perished in three fires in villas in Switzerland and Canada. The names of Mme Vuarnet and Patrick, her youngest son, were mentioned in a police report.
>
> 'It was as though our world had fallen in,' says the tall, athletic Vuarnet, who now heads the family business. 'But in a sense we were relieved – the two gurus had killed themselves. A few months later, I asked my mother whether she still saw other members of the Order of the Solar Temple. She went pale and replied, "Alain, after all that those people have done, do you really think I could have anything to do with them?"' A year later, in the early hours of December 16, 1995, Edith and Patrick were among sixteen Solar Temple members who climbed through the forests of the Vercors mountains in southwest France to a clearing known locally as the Pit of Hell.[4]

Alain Vuarnet then proceeded to describe how, back in 1990, his mother had been suffering from a mild bout of depression when she met Luc Jouret. She wanted to find something she could believe in, some type of faith, and Jouret's cult obviously fitted the bill.

Meanwhile at the trial, Tabachnik, although admitting he had become involved with the group, stated categorically that he was not one of its leaders, but simply someone who had been duped by Di Mambro. 'My great difficulty, your honor,' he said during one particularly grueling eight-hour court session, 'is to explain my role in what happened, because I was completely naïve.'[5] But the lawyer acting on behalf of the families of some of the Grenoble victims dismissed this defence. 'Tabachnik,' said Francis Vuillemin, 'is trying to pass himself off as an imbecile, when in fact he is trying to treat others as imbeciles. In truth he was the doctrinarian behind the deaths.'[6]

Respected international conductor and composer Michel Tabachnik was suspected of involvement in the deaths of the members of the Solar Temple sect but was acquitted of all charges. He went on to win many accolades for his music and was recently appointed chief conductor of the Noord-Nederlands Orkest.

The prosecution then went on to try to prove, through witness statements, that Tabachnik had been one of the leaders who had announced the end of the cult shortly before the first series of three massacres and that he, therefore, knew precisely the nature of the coming events. Yet no matter how much mud the prosecution flung at Tabachnik, no matter how much they tried to link him to the Solar Temple's leaders, on June 25 he was acquitted of all the charges.

Naturally, Tabachnik's own lawyer, Francis Szpiner, was delighted with the result, declaring that the trial judges had rightfully resisted media pressure to convict his client. However, contrary to this opinion, the Association de defence de la famille et de l'individu – an anti-cult organization – declared the result disappointing and called for the government pass a law banning the existence of cults. 'With this law on the books,' stated the association's lawyer, Francis Buillemin, 'Michel Tabachnik wouldn't have been able to escape punishment.'[7] Tabachnik walked from court a free man and has remained so, despite prosecutors appealing against his aquittal. Today he continues to enjoy a successful career as a highly respected conductor.

Police authorities in France, Switzerland and Canada all decided that there was a very real possibility the millennium might prove the spark to ignite another series of mass suicides. In Quebec, approximately seventy-five investigators focused on sects operating in the province and officer Pierre Robichaud of the Sureté du Quebec was quoted as saying:

> They [the Order of the Solar Temple] say they are inactive, but unfortunately, we cannot say without doubt that, yes, they are inactive. We are not worried but, unfortunately there are things we cannot predict. Tomorrow, another massacre like the one in St. Casimir can blow up in our face. It is a very touchy matter.[8]

In Switzerland, too, moves were afoot to prevent another tragedy, this time by opening a public information center on religious cults so that, while not infringing upon people's beliefs, the public could at least become aware of the danger involved in joining certain groups. François Bellanger, president of the information center said:

> We are not fighting these groups. We live in a country where the freedom of religion is sacred. We want to provide neutral and relevant information. In collecting, analysing and providing this data, we are going to act very carefully.[9]

And this softly, softly approach does seem to have worked for, since the Grenoble suicides and the trial of Michel Tabachnik, there have been no further mass suicides. This does not, of course, necessarily mean that such a thing will not reoccur in the future. Interestingly, in his final report after the Tabachnik trial, Judge Fontaine recorded the following: 'Structured like a multinational, the Order was truly a giant commercial operation with financial interests on three continents.' Whether this statement pointed to the fact that many people believed (and still believe) the cult to be a front for organized crime has, however, never been proved. What is certain is that millions of dollars moved through the Solar Temple's accounts, and that it included amongst its members many highly influential people such as police officers, politicians, civil servants and, allegedly (according to a Channel Four TV documentary), Princess Grace of Monaco. It may also be true that Di Mambro and Jouret were being manipulated by someone even higher up in the organization than themselves – someone whose name, in the true nature of a secret society, has never been revealed.

[1] 'Interpol joins Swiss in Solar Temple murder inquiry,' Edward Luce in Granges-sur-Salvan, Claire Trevena in Toronto, and John Mullin, the *Guardian*, October 6, 1994.

[2] www.religiousmovements.lib.virginia.edu/nrms/solartemp.html.

[3] 'Lured by the cult,' *The Times* (London), April 18, 2001.

[4] Ibid.

[5] 'Conductor tells court how New Age Guru inspired doomsday cult,' AFP, April 26, 2001.

[6] Ibid.

[7] 'Conductor not guilty in doomsday cult deaths, French court finds,' *Globe and Mail* (Canada), June 26, 2001.

[8] 'Solar Temple cult worries rise as millennium nears,' Patrick White, Reuters, April 26, 1999.

[9] 'Geneva seeks to temper influence of cults,' SwissInfo (Switzerland), November 3, 2001.

THE HASHISHIM – THE FIRST TERRORISTS IN HISTORY

> With the jugglery of deceit and the trickery of untruth, with
> guileful preparations and specious obfuscations, he laid the
> foundations of the fida'is, and he said: 'Who of you will rid this
> state of the evil of Nizam al-Mulk Tusi?' A man called Bu Tahir
> Arrani laid the hand of acceptance on his breast, and, following
> the path of error by which he hoped to attain the bliss of the
> world-to-come, on the night of Friday, the 12th of Ramadan of
> the year 485 [. . .] he came in the guise of a Sufi to the litter of
> Nizam al-Mulk, who was being borne from the audience to the
> tent of his women, and struck him with a knife, and by that blow
> he suffered martyrdom.
>
> RASHID AL-DIN

These days, the word 'assassin' is common parlance, used to define any murderer of an important person or anyone hired in the role of professional killer, but originally the word came to the West via the Arabic language just before the time of the Crusades, when it was used to denote a secretive Islamic sect feared throughout that region for the many murders it committed. The Hashishim (also referred to as the Ismailis or the Assassins) were a group who became infamous for using murder as a political weapon. Unpitying, merciless and ruthlessly systematic in both the planning and execution of their crimes, this radical Islamic sect was, justifiably, one of the most feared organizations in the world at that time.

First mention of the group is believed to be in the report of an envoy who was sent to Egypt and Syria in 1175 by the Holy Roman Emperor Frederick I Barbarossa.

> Note, that on the confines of Damascus, Antioch and Aleppo there is a
> certain race of Saracens in the mountains, who in their own vernacular
> are called Heyssessini [. . .] This breed of men live without law; they eat
> swine's flesh against the law of the Saracens, and make use of all women
> without distinction, including their mothers and sisters [. . .] They have
> among them a Master, who strikes the greatest fear into all the Saracen
> princes both far and near, as well as the neighboring Christian lords. For
> he has the habit of killing them in an astonishing way.[1]

This 'Master,' who was best known by the sobriquet 'The Old Man of the

Mountain' (a nickname which was passed down from one Assassin leader to the next), wielded tremendous power over his followers, engendering in them a fanatical devotion that admitted no other master.

The explorer Marco Polo, who traveled through this part of the world in 1273, made some interesting observations relating to the Old Man, observations that go some way towards explaining the hold he had over his followers. Polo described how the Old Man had established a 'certain valley between two mountains to be enclosed, and had turned it into a garden, the largest and most beautiful that was ever seen, filled with every variety of fruit.' Polo then goes on to explain how the Old Man required his followers to believe that this garden was actually Paradise. 'Now,' writes Polo, 'no man was allowed to enter the Garden save those whom he intended to be his ASHISHIN.' Once the Old Man had selected those he wished to enter, they were given a potion to drink after which they would fall asleep, then be carried into the garden. On waking in such beautiful surroundings the Old Man's victims would immediately believe they were in Paradise. And here they would remain until he needed one of them to return to the outside world as an assassin. The chosen one would once again be given the sleeping potion, only this time he would be carried out of the garden and on awakening be given his instructions. 'Go thou and slay So and So,' wrote Marco Polo in imitation of how the Old Man spoke, 'and when thou returnest my Angels shall bear thee into Paradise. And should'st thou die, nevertheless even so I shall send my Angels to carry thee back into Paradise.'[2]

Whether the above account is true or not (and many historians for a variety of reasons believe it is not), what it does illustrate is the extent to which the Hashishim had invaded public consciousness. By the twelfth century several commentators thought they detected the Hashishim's hand behind all kinds of political murder, not just in Syria but also in Europe. In 1158, while Frederick Barbarossa was laying siege to Milan, one historian alleges that an 'Assassin' was caught in Barbarossa's camp. In 1195 while the English King Richard I 'Lionheart' was sojourning at Chinon, it has been documented that at least fifteen Assassins were captured and later confessed to having been sent by the King of France to kill him. Numerous other accounts began to filter through and before long it became commonplace to

Venetian traveler and explorer Marco Polo came across the cult of the Hashishim when traveling through the Middle East in 1273 – and wrote extensively about the 'Old Man of the Mountain.'

accuse your enemy of being in league with the Old Man of the Mountain for the sole purpose of having you assassinated. The truth is that most European leaders of those times would not have needed any outside help to rid themselves of their enemies by murdering them, so the accusation was actually something of a goading insult.

Nevertheless, the Hashishim continued to arouse Western curiosity and in 1697 a man by the name of Bartholomé de Herbelot wrote a book called the *Bibliothèque orientale* (The Oriental Library) which contained almost all the information then available on the history, religion and literature of this region. The Assassins, so de Herbelot concluded, were an offshoot of the Ismailis (who were themselves an offshoot of the Shi'a, whose quarrel with the Sunnis was, and still is when one looks at modern-day Iraq, the main religious schism in Islam).

Another major study – though from a considerably later date – was by the Arabic scholar Silvestre de Sacy, who posed the theory that the Hashishim were so called due to their liberal intake of hashish; however, this theory was later discredited as the Ismailis never make mention of this drug in their texts. It is also believed that *hashishi* – a local Syrian word – was a term of abuse given to the sect to describe their unsociable behavior, rather than a reference to any drug. Indeed, so 'unsociable' was the Hashishim's behavior that it is thought the original Old Man of the Mountain – a man by the name of Hasan-i Sabbah – didn't leave his mountain retreat for well over thirty-five years.

Sabbah was born in the city of Qumm, around the middle of the eleventh century, but while he was still a young boy his father moved the entire family to Rayy (nowadays known as Tehran), where Sabbah began his first serious attempt at religious education.

> From the days of my boyhood, from the age of seven, I felt a love for the
> various branches of learning, and wished to become a religious scholar;
> until the age of seventeen I was a seeker and searcher for knowledge, but
> kept to the Twelver faith of my fathers.[3]

It appears that Sabbah visited Egypt for a period of approximately three years, staying first in Cairo and afterwards in Alexandria. It was during this time, however, that he turned away from his former faith due to a split within the religion. On his deathbed the Caliph of Cairo, al-Mustansir, had appointed his son, Nizar, to succeed him, but after he passed away a decision was made whereby Nizar's brother, a man by the name of al Musta'li, was made Caliph instead. This caused huge disturbances among the population, with many people choosing not to recognize al Musta'li.

> The dissenting group proclaimed their allegiance to the by-passed
> Caliph Nizar, and it is for this reason that members of the sect which
> became known to history as The Assassins were first known as the
> Nizari Isma'ilis.[4]

Hasan-i Sabbah aligned himself with this latter sect, a decision which later saw him deported from Egypt to North Africa. But the ship he was traveling on ran into difficulties, although he was rescued and taken to Syria. From here Sabbah traveled throughout Persia, also visiting Iran and Kurdistan. His main interest, however, lay in northern Persia in the Shi'ite stronghold of Daylam. This was a place that in the words of Bernard Lewis 'jealously [guarded] its independence against the Caliphs of Baghdad and other Sunni rulers.'[5]

As someone who himself shunned the Caliphs, Hasan-i Sabbah fitted in well with his new surroundings and made every effort to put into practice the 'new' preaching of the Nizari Ismailis, traveling extensively throughout the region until, three or four years later, he decided he needed a permanent base for his teachings. He chose a mountain hideaway which would be inaccessible to his enemies, but from where he could continue his fight not only against the Caliphs, but also against his true enemy, the Seljuq Empire.

In the eleventh century, the Islamic world suffered a series of major invasions, the most serious by the Seljuq Turks, who eventually established a new empire that stretched from Central Asia right through to the Mediterranean. It seemed that the Seljuq were invincible. No one attacked them, no one challenged them. Their military power was second to none, and the only form of dissent came from the Ismailis and in particular from Hasan-i Sabbah who, over the years, fashioned himself into the Seljuq's worst nightmare.

When Sabbah first decided to establish a mountain stronghold, the only place he knew of where all the criteria he demanded existed, was the castle of Alamut. Built more than 6,000 feet above sea level on a narrow ridge in the heart of the Elburz Mountains, dominating a sheltered valley that stretched for approximately thirty miles, Alamut was the perfect location. The building is rumored to have been constructed by a former King of Daylam who, while out on a hunting expedition one day, let loose an eagle that alighted on a rock high in the mountains. Seeing how well positioned the location was, the king immediately ordered a castle be built on the site, thereafter naming it Aluh Almut, which in translation means 'Eagle's teaching'. It was rebuilt in 860 by yet another king, but when Sabbah decided the castle was to be his, he overthrew the building's old incumbent and established himself as the new master of Alamut.

Once Sabbah entered the building, he never again returned down the rock on which the castle was built. Instead, he led an abstemious life, studying, preaching and looking after the affairs of his 'kingdom' which, for the main part, meant winning over new converts to his cause and gaining possession of more castles. He also sent out missionaries to help him accomplish both aims. The historian Juvaynie wrote:

> Hasan exerted every effort to capture the places adjacent to Alamut or that vicinity. Where possible he won them over by the tricks of his propaganda while such places as were unaffected by his blandishments he seized with slaughter, ravishment, pillage, bloodshed, and war. He took such castles as he could and wherever he found a suitable rock he built a castle upon it.[6]

So successful was Hasan-i Sabbah, that his operatives even began spreading their religious propaganda in areas loyal to the Sunnis and the Seljuq. It was Sabbah's operatives who first drew blood in a Seljuq-controlled area of Rayy. Eighteen Ismaili

This illustration from the fifteenth-century manuscript Travels of Marco Polo *shows the Old Man of the Mountain issuing his deadly orders to his followers.*

agents, who had gathered together to conduct prayers, were placed under arrest by local guards. They were questioned, after which they were released. The group then went on to try to convert a muezzin, but this man refused to accept their religious teachings and, fearing that he might report them to the authorities, the group killed him. Hearing about the death, the Vizier of the area, Nizam al-Mulk, gave an order that the group's ringleader be arrested and executed – an order that was swiftly carried out. This was the first of many subsequent crack-downs on the Ismailis by the Seljuqs, but rather than shy away from future conflict, the Ismailis, under Sabbah's leadership continued to fight back, and were soon employing the art of assassination to aid them in their task.

Their first chosen victim was said to be the Vizier himself, Nizam al-Mulk, and the man chosen to carry out his murder was Bu Tahir Arrani.

> [. . .] on the night of Friday, the 12th of Ramadan of the year 485 [October 16, 1092], in the district of Nihavand at the stage of Sahna, he came in the guise of a Sufi to the litter of Nizam al-Mulk, who was being borne from the audience-place to the tent of his women, and struck him with a knife, and by that blow he [Arrani] suffered martyrdom.[7]

Nizam al-Mulk's assassination was only the first in a long line of political killings that then erupted. No one was safe: princes, kings, generals, viziers, governors, divines –

anyone who professed to disagree with the Ismailis and their teachings was considered an enemy and became a legitimate target. The Ismailis considered themselves an elite killing force, striking down all those who opposed them. Their victims, on the other hand, regarded the Ismailis as nothing more than 'criminal fanatics,' men who were willing to break the law and commit murder to get their own way.

As a group, the Ismailis (or Hashishim or Assassins) became a very powerful secret society, replete with all the paraphernalia one would expect of such a group. They had their own system of oaths and a highly pronounced hierarchy, organized into rigid sub-groups based upon each member's initiation into the secrets of the society. The organization of the sect as a whole was known as *da'wa*, which in translation means 'mission', with those involved in the *da'wa* referred to as *da'is* or 'missionaries'. These *da'is* were then sub-divided and graded by rank, the highest echelons of which consisted of teachers and preachers. Beneath these came the *mustajibs*, who made up the lowest rank of initiates, but above everyone came the *hujja* or senior *da'i,* whose role was basically that of an elder.

It was murder, however, rather than any form of religious practice, that was the Assassins' foremost claim to fame and it is no exaggeration to say that the Ismailis were probably the first group of people in history truly to transform the act of murder into an ideology – one that was largely focussed against those Muslim rulers who would not tolerate their extreme unorthodoxy. The Ismailis planned their murders in meticulous detail, all the while trying to eliminate the possibility of killing anyone who wasn't a 'legitimate' target. Typically, they would approach their victims while dressed in disguise so as not to alert suspicion. Their weapon of choice was the dagger because this was easily hidden in clothing and, if used correctly, allowed for the swift dispatch of the victim. Indeed, the use of a dagger – as opposed to poison or strangulation, which for certain murders would have been either easier or safer – seems to have been of the utmost importance to the Assassins. They viewed their killings not only as acts of extreme piety, but also as sacramental rituals.

Another fundamental feature of the Assassins' art was that under no circumstances would they commit suicide, preferring instead to be killed by the enemy. Indeed, survival was not generally an option where an Assassin was concerned, for no self-respecting Hashishim would either wish, let alone expect, to carry on living after he had murdered his target.

Hasan-i Sabbah laid down all the above rules and regulations according to his own creed and the Hashishim saw many successes under his rule. By May 1124, however, the Old Man of the Mountain lay seriously ill. Knowing the end was near, he chose an heir from among his loyal followers, a man by the name of Buzurgumid. The appointment came not a moment too soon, for on May 23, 1124, Hasan-i Sabbah died. It was the end of a remarkable era, for Sabbah had been a man of tremendous talent. Writing about him shortly after his death, one biographer described him as being learned not only in arithmetic, astronomy and geometry but also in magic, while another historian points out Sabbah's unique asceticism, which in its most concrete form meant that during his thirty-five-year tenure of Alamut, nobody was permitted to drink or keep drink on the premises.

But since Hasan-i Sabbah was dead, what of his successor Buzurgumid? Had he enough strength to prevent all that his predecessor had built up from being vanquished by the Seljuq? The answer came two years after Sabbah's death when, in 1126, the Seljuq launched a full-scale offensive against the Ismailis. Two major successes were achieved: the conquest of an Ismaili-held village called Tarz where the entire population was executed, and another raid, this time on a village called Turaythith, where, again, many of the civilian population were killed.

Naturally, the Ismailis did not wait long to exact their revenge. In true Hashishim style, Buzurgumid sent two of his most skilled men to seek employment as grooms in the house of the local Seljuq vizier. This task accomplished, on March 16, 1127, when the Vizier summoned the two grooms to help him choose a couple of Arab horses to be sent as a gift to the Sultan, he was deftly assassinated. During Buzurgumid's tenure as leader of the Ismailis, although he did not order as many killings as Hasan-i Sabbah had done, the list of victims was considerable. Bernard Lewis, in his book *The Assassins*, mentions a handful of such cases including '[. . .] a prefect of Isfahan, a governor of Maragha [. . .], a prefect of Tabriz, and a mufti of Qazvin.'[8]

Buzurgumid's reign as leader of the Ismailis continued until his death on February 9, 1138, at which point he was succeeded by his son, Muhammad who swiftly put into practice all he had learnt from his father in the art of killing. His first victim was the ex-Caliph al-Rashid, who was in Isfahan in Persia suffering from a minor illness when Muhammad's men found and assassinated him on June 6, 1138. After his death, it is said that celebrations were held at Alamut to mark the new Ismaili leader's first so-called 'victory'.

Fourteen assassinations then followed al-Rashid's, with one of the most notable victims being the Seljuq Sultan Da'ud, who was murdered by four Syrian assassins in Tabriz (north-western Persia) in 1143. But if a tally of fourteen seems large, in comparison with the number of assassinations committed during Hasan-i Sabbah's reign it was paltry. A shift had occurred or, to be more precise, over the years the Ismailis appear to have lost some of their religious fervour. Instead, they began to concentrate on more mundane matters such as cattle rustling and border disputes. Yet there were still some among them who longed for a return to the 'good old days', the days when Hasan-i Sabbah had ruled and when religious matters had inspired them to commit bold deeds. This group began to congregate around a new leader, Muhammad's son, Hasan, but it wasn't until Muhammad's death in 1162 that Hasan eventually took over and began to reinvigorate his followers.

Two years after he was crowned leader, in the middle of the fasting month that is Ramadan, Hasan announced the dawning of a new Millennium. There are several accounts of this momentous occasion – first and foremost within texts belonging to the sect themselves, which describe the event in detail down to the color (white, red, yellow and green) of the banners that were erected around the pulpit from which

Hasan spoke. The positioning of the pulpit itself (facing west) was also of great significance, meaning that Hasan's entire congregation had to stand with their backs towards Mecca. Hasan then entered the scene dressed in white robes, with a white turban on his head. Standing in the pulpit, he spoke to the crowd and declared that from this moment forward they were free from the rules of Holy Law. He declared himself their spiritual leader or 'Living Proof' who must be obeyed in all religious and worldly matters. Hasan's message was that of the Imam – 'His word is our word'.[9] Directly after this address, Hasan then declared that everyone should join him in a banquet, thus breaking Ramadan. This, together with the congregation standing with their backs to Mecca, symbolized, for them, nothing less than, for them, an end to Shari'a law.

Most Ismailis celebrated and embraced the new era; however, there were still a few who refused to break with tradition and dispense with the old ways. Hasan dealt with them severely.

> Hasan maintained, both by implication and by clear declaration, that just as in the time of the Law if a man did not obey and worship but followed the rule of the Resurrection that obedience and worship are spiritual, he was punished and stoned and put to death, so now in the time of the Resurrection if a man complied with the letter of the Law and persisted in physical worship and rites, it was obligatory that he be chastised and stoned and put to death.[10]

Yet, although Hasan's proposals were radical, ironically, given that he had just declared himself the closest thing there was to the hidden Imam, shortly after his declaration at Alamut he was killed by his brother-in-law, who had refused to relinquish the old ways.

If at this point the Ismailis were undergoing turbulent times, it was in the last years of the eleventh century that they succeeded in setting a firm hold in Syria where they converted a Seljuq prince of Aleppo called Ridwan ibn-Tutush. By the mid-twelfth century they had also succeeded in capturing the hill fortress of Masyad as well as several other citadels in northern Syria, including al-Qadmus and al-Kahf. But it was at Masyad that one of the most famous Assassin leaders resided – Rashid-al-Din Sinan.

As a young boy, Sinan had been educated at Alamut alongside Hasan who, on taking over from his father Muhammad, ordered Sinan to go into Syria and spread the word throughout that region. This Sinan did to great effect, although perhaps his most notorious action during the period was the assassination of the Marquis Conrad of Montferrat, King of the Latin Kingdom of Jerusalem in Tyre, who was taking part in the Third Crusade. The two assassins whom Sinan chose for the job are said to have disguised themselves as Christian monks and inveigled their way into the confidence of the Marquis before stabbing him to death. Sinan appears to have instilled in his followers an extraordinary degree of devotion. This account by the German chronicler Arnold of Lübeck illustrates the power he wielded over his acolytes:

> This Old Man has by his witchcraft so bemused the men of his country,
> that they neither worship nor believe in any God but himself. Likewise he

entices them in a strange manner with such hopes and with promises of such pleasures with eternal enjoyment, that they prefer rather to die than to live. Many of them even, when standing on a high wall, will jump off at his nod or command, and, shattering their skulls, die a miserable death. The most blessed, so he affirms, are those who shed the blood of men and in revenge for such deeds themselves suffer death. When, therefore, any of them have chosen to die in this way, murdering someone by craft and then themselves dying so blessedly in revenge for him, he himself hands them knives which are, so to speak, consecrated to this affair, and then intoxicates them with such a potion that they are plunged into ecstasy and oblivion, displays to them by his magic certain fantastic dreams, full of pleasures and delights, or rather of trumpery, and promises them eternal possession of these things in reward for such deeds.[11]

As well as killing those whom he saw as politically opposed to his point of view, Sinan (and those who followed in his footsteps) also discovered a means of turning their evil reputation as ruthless killers to another advantage, that of exacting large pay-outs from their adversaries. One contemporary source has it that the Emperor Frederick II (the Holy Roman Emperor and German King as well as the King of Jerusalem from 1229–50), who had traveled to Palestine on a Crusade, brought with him a whole bevy of servants carrying gifts worth over 80,000 dinars to give to the Assassins. Ironically, this new-found method of financing their organization also spelt the beginning of the end of their cult, for as the Crusades continued over a long period of time, it was only natural that more and more information about the Assassins gradually became available. A small handful of Europeans even began to meet up with a few of their number, to discuss their religion and their politics, to the point that the Templars and the Knights Hospitaller (an order first founded in the eleventh century and originally dedicated to providing sick-bays for Christian pilgrims in Jerusalem, but later to become a military order as well) even managed to establish some sort of influence over them. Eventually these orders were to demand an annual tribute from the Assassins, rather than the other way round.

In 1228 the English historian, Matthew of Paris, reported that a delegation of Muslims had arrived in Europe seeking advice and help from both the English and French, because of the imminent threat of a Mongol invasion of Syria from the east. This really was the end for the Syrian Assassins, who were not only facing this Mongol invasion, but were also being squeezed hard by the Mamluk Sultan of Egypt, Baybars. Baybars was himself under threat from the Mongols as well as the Christian Franks, and was not prepared to tolerate the presence of a highly dangerous clique of heretics within Syria's midst. Assigning all the Assassins' lands and property to one of his generals, he further diminished their power by collecting taxes from them and confiscating all the gifts of money they received from the various princes in the region. All of this weakened the Assassins considerably, and it is said that in March 1271 Baybars arrested two Assassins who had been sent to murder him. After being questioned the two suspects were released, but only after two Ismaili leaders had relinquished hold of their castles. Humiliated, broken, vanquished, by the thirteenth century all mention of the Assassins disappears and any small pockets of Ismailism that survived probably did so for only a very short time, never again to achieve the kind of political importance they had once so enjoyed.

Before the Ismailis, many other sects whose main purpose was dissent from mainstream thinking existed, but according to several commentators on the period, none were as effective or as systematic in the use of terror as the Assassins. In fact, it is safe to say that this group of fanatics were the world's first terrorists. Hasan-i Sabbah knew this instinctively. Without stating it openly, he realized that preaching alone could not combat Sunni Islam or the armies of the Seljuq. Only by forming small, self-disciplined units of trained killers could he hope to have any effect on those forces whose manpower and weaponry far outstripped his own. And, with a handful of notable exceptions, including the murder of the Marquis Conrad of Montferrat, the Assassins' victims were almost entirely made up of Sunni Muslims – the ruling elite. It was their strong hold over the region – political, military and religious – that so incensed and angered the Ismailis, for they rarely targeted the Shi'ites and they barely posed any threat to the native Christians, Jews or, contrary to what is commonly assumed, to the Crusaders either.

But perhaps the most significant point to be made about these, the earliest of terrorists, is that they failed utterly in their dream of overthrowing the existing order. For decades they caused ripples of fear throughout the regions they targeted, but

Lacking the manpower and weaponry to wage all-out war, the Hashishim were not, as is often assumed, any real threat to the Crusaders, unlike the Saracen warriors depicted in this illustration from the thirteenth-century French manuscript Chroniques de Saint-Denis.

ultimately they did not succeed in gaining control of even one major city. They possessed several significant castles and the land thereabouts, but in reality these were no more than 'petty principalities'.

Although the Ismailis eventually faded away, the same cannot be said for the manner in which they operated. History has proved only too well that their revolutionary tactics have trickled down through the centuries, finding countless converts along the way. One only has to look towards the Middle East and the suicide bombings that occur there, or to the Twin Towers attack in New York on September 11, 2001, to notice the striking resemblance between those terrorist activities committed in medieval times and those committed today. The absolute secrecy of the terrorist cell, the complete dedication of the assassin to his cause in return for guaranteed entry into Paradise, the calculated implementation of terror – the parallels are numerous. The medieval Assassins and terrorists operating today do, however, show one marked difference. Whereas Hasan-i Sabbah and his successors targeted the leaders of the existing order – that is to say Sunni generals, ministers, monarchs and religious functionaries – they went to great lengths not to involve or harm any civilians. Their counterparts today appear not to care whom they kill, be they men, women or children, Christian, Muslim or Jew, black or white.

There is one last parallel that might still be drawn between the two groups. It could be argued that Osama bin Laden, the world's most wanted terrorist is, in a very real way, our present-day Old Man of the Mountain. After all, who can forget the video footage of bin Laden addressing (and threatening) the world from his mountain hideaway somewhere in Afghanistan? Let us hope that, like Hasan-i Sabbah, he fails to realize his dreams.

---

[1] Extract from the report of Gerhard, *vice dominus* of Strasbourg, quoted in *Chronicon Slavorum* (1172-1209) by Arnold of Lübeck, ed. W. Wattenbach, Deutschlands Geschictsquellen, 1907.

[2] *The Book of Marco Polo*, translated and edited Sir Henry Yule, 1903.

[3] Autobiographical fragment preserved by historians and here taken from *The Assassins: A Radical Sect in Islam*, Bernard Lewis, Weidenfeld & Nicolson, 1967.

[4] *The Assassins: Holy Killers of Islam*, Edward Burman, Aquarian Press, 1987.

[5] *The Assassins: A Radical Sect in Islam*, op. cit.

[6] Ibid.

[7] Ibid.

[8] Ibid.

[9] Ibid.

[10] Ibid.

[11] *Chronicon Slavorum*, op. cit.

THE MAU MAU –
AFRICAN
INSURRECTION

The settler knew a lot about how to use African labor. But he
could not see what the use of that labor and the production of
money was beginning to bring about. He could not see the
political change.

WILLOUGHBY SMITH,
District Officer in the Colonial Service, 1948-55

To understand the nature of the Mau Mau and of the Mau Mau uprising, it
is first necessary to understand a little of the history of Kenya and in
particular of the British Colonial administration from approximately the
mid-nineteenth century until 1963.

The first Europeans to penetrate East Africa are thought to have been British and
German missionaries who, as well as bringing the word of God and so-called
Western civilization to the natives, also brought an attitude of acute moral outrage,
particularly over the type of heathen practices in which, in their opinion, the natives
were prone to indulge. For instance, a large number of the indigenous population did
not wear clothes and their nakedness shocked and offended the Europeans, as did the
custom of placing their dead in animal traps so as to entice prey to eat. For all their
efforts, however, the missionaries made little headway in Kenya. It wasn't until
around 1880 that the British Imperial East Africa Company began to prospect in the
region, looking for suitable land that could either be farmed or mined, or better still,
both. At this point the Germans had an established protectorate over the Sultan of
Zanzibar's coastal regions, but in the 1890s Germany handed these holdings over to
the British who subsequently, in 1895, established the area as a British settlement
under the name of the East African Protectorate. Slowly but surely, the British
brought the southern half of Kenya under their control too, although the northern
half didn't truly come under British rule until well after World War I (1914-18),
during which time both British and South African settlers moved in to the highland
regions of the country (soon to be nicknamed the White Highlands). This area
contained rich farming land together with a climate perfectly suited to the business
of growing coffee. The only drawback was that most of the territory belonged to
Kenya's Kikuyu tribe – a fact the British neither appreciated nor cared to
acknowledge. The Kikuya were driven out of their homes and effectively excluded
from owning their own land. As if this were not humiliation enough, the Kikuya also
suffered when the European settlers decided they required ever increasing amounts

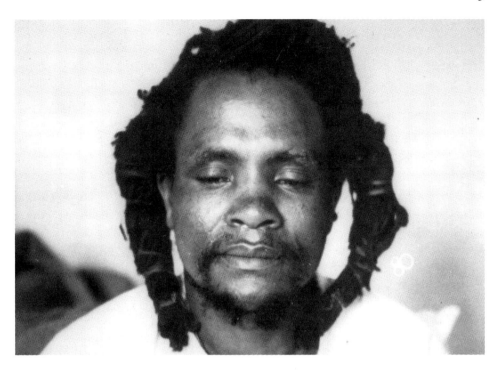

Dedan Kimathi was the last of the Mau Mau leaders to be brought to justice. Shot and captured by a Kenyan police officer in October 1956, he was tried and executed for his crimes.

of cheap labor in order to run their businesses efficiently. They persuaded the administration to raise taxes on their African neighbors so that increasing numbers of black Kenyans would either be forced to seek work on the farms in order to pay off their tax debts, or to find employment in urban areas such as Nairobi.

In 1920, Kenya was named a British Crown colony and Sir Charles Eliot was appointed Governor, with an elected Legislative Council to provide him with both advice and support. Naturally, given Britain's dismal colonial record, native Kenyans were not allowed on this committee; it would not be until the 1940s that a small number would, begrudgingly, be given seats. Eliot, who was first and foremost a scholar of languages (he had published several books, including one on Finnish grammar and another on the Ottoman Empire), was an inflexible man of the old school who believed that Kenya was a 'white man's country in which the interests of the European must always be paramount.'[1] This attitude was commonplace during the period – based as it was upon the earlier Victorian conviction that it was the white man's duty to civilize his African cousins. This was the proverbial 'white man's burden': to civilize the Africans and teach them to know their place and accept it.

Given the extent to which the native Kenyans were subjugated and brow-beaten by the British, it is hardly surprising that resentment grew not only at their gross mistreatment but also due to the lack of proper representation in government. Not long after World War I, a political party, made up solely of Kenyan Africans, mobilized themselves into an opposition movement protesting against the government's crippling tax system, as well as the general lack of opportunities for black Kenyans, the colonial labor-control policies and, most important of all, the illegal appropriation of land, which by 1948 saw approximately 1.25 million Kikuyu restricted to 5,200 square kilometers of scrubland. This was in sharp contrast to the 30,000 European and South African settlers, who enjoyed 31,000 square kilometers of the most desirable farmland.

One of the first of these opposition groups was called the East African Association, but the British swiftly outlawed this organization in 1922. In 1924 a second group was formed called the Kikuyu Central Association (KCA), which demanded not only that the British return all farmlands previously stolen from the Kikuyu to their rightful owners, but that they respect the Kikuyu culture and Kikuyu society. This group, however, much like its predecessor, failed to make any significant headway. Then, in 1945, following the end of World War II , opposition to British rule became increasingly nationalistic and far more noticeably vociferous. This was undoubtedly partly due to the fact that many Africans had been conscripted to help fight alongside the British during the war, and as a result their political consciousness had been raised to the extent that when they returned to civilian life they were no longer prepared to live as second-class citizens in their own country. In 1944 a new political organization had been formed – the Kenyan African Union (KAU). The main leader of this party was a Kikuyu by the name of Jomo Kenyatta who had previously belonged to the KCA. Kenyatta was determined to address the problems of his native Africans and improve their lot but, much as with the KCA, when it came to challenging British colonial rule, the KAU had made little progress.

It was at this point, during these turbulent post-war years that a secret Kikuyu guerrilla organization called the Mau Mau first came into being.

Mau mau is, experts on African languages assert, a term of uncertain provenance. Some people claim it is the Kikuyu word for a group of hills bordering the Rift Valley and Lake Naivasha in northern Kenya, while others maintain the word is a rough alliteration of the Kikuyu war cry. A third interpretation has it that Mau Mau is a British invention meant not only to denigrate the insurgents, but to demonize them. In a British television Channel 4 documentary, *How Britain Crushed the Mau Mau Rebellion*, the historian Professor Lonsdale remarked how the Mau Mau were first portrayed by the British government as 'the welling up of the old unreconstructed Africa, which had not yet received sufficient colonial enlightenment and discipline, which proved that colonialism still had a job to do.' In other words, the Mau Mau were little more than savages bent on misrule and destruction.

Whatever the provenance of the word Mau Mau – be it a form of demonization or the Kikuyu war cry – it is believed that the group was first established some time between 1947 and 1952 with one aim in mind: to free Kenya from colonialism at any cost. In practice, this involved the Mau Mau in a campaign of anti-colonial terrorist violence in which large numbers of both Europeans and Africans were killed.

There had always been a minority of native Kenyans who had cooperated with, and therefore benefited from, colonial rule. Targeting these groups (who mainly lived and worked in the Nyeri District of the Central Province) was relatively easy, and many black 'collaborators' subsequently died. Yet the Mau Mau's violence was, at least initially, directed against the white settlers – a violence that was reflected in the group's wild initiation ceremonies. These ceremonies made extensive use of ancient symbols and black magic together with the number seven which, for the Kikuya, has huge significance as it is directly linked to their most sacred initiation rites.

Writing extensively about such initiation ceremonies in his book on the Mau Mau, and basing much of his work on the writer L.S.B. Leakey's original research, Fred Majdalany describes one such ritual:

> It is quite dark and he [the initiate] is ordered to remove his clothes. In the darkness he is pushed forward and receives his first Shock when his naked body is brushed by the outline of an arch. This is totally unexpected, but he knows it is the arch of sugar cane and banana leaves through which he has to pass during his initiation into manhood [...] Now they would go to work on him quickly. He would be ordered to eat a piece of sacrificial flesh thrust against his lips. This would be done seven times and after each he would have to repeat the oath. Then the lips would be touched with blood seven times, the oath being repeated after each. Next a gourd of blood would be passed round his head seven times; he would be ordered to stick seven thorns into a sodom apple and pierce the eye of the sheep.[2]

This blend of both the sacred and the profane had a lasting effect on the initiates, who would usually be totally overcome by the ceremony. 'We used to drink the oath,' one ex-Mau Mau insurgent, Jacob Njangi, admitted. 'We swore we would not let white men rule us for ever. We would fight them even down to our last man, so that man could live in freedom.'[3]

Majdalany also listed the set of oaths he believed Mau Mau initiates were required to take:

(a) If I ever reveal the secrets of this organization, may
     this oath kill me.
(b) If I ever sell or dispose of any Kikuyu land to a
     foreigner, may this oath kill me.
(c) If I ever fail to follow our great leader, Kenyatta,
     may this oath kill me.
(d) If I ever inform against any member of this
     organization or against any member who steals from the European,
     may this oath kill me.
(e) If I ever fail to pay the fees of this organization,
     may this oath kill me.[4]

The deaths that ensued from failure to adhere to such oaths were savage in the extreme. Many of the corpses of former Mau Mau that were discovered had wounds that were characteristic of the ritual mutilation favored by the Kikuyu. Despite the bloodshed, however, or perhaps because of it, more and more people joined the Mau Mau until, in 1950, having enjoyed unimpeded growth, the organization was declared illegal. In August of that year Kenya's Internal Security Working Committee had been tasked with evaluating the insurgency question. Its report was a corrosive denunciation of the Mau Mau, which was defined as follows:

> This is a Kikuyu secret society which is probably another manifestation of the suppressed Kikuyu Central Association. Its objects are anti-European and its intention is to dispossess Europeans of the White Highlands. Its members take an oath not to give information to the police, and may also swear not to obey certain orders of the Government. It is suspected that some members employed on European farms indulge in a 'go slow' policy and that they may also have committed minor acts of sabotage on farms. Successful prosecutions against the society are believed to have checked its growth; or at least to have curbed the forceful recruitment of adherents. The potency of the organization depends on the extent to which it possesses the power latent in all secret societies, of being more feared than the forces of law and order.[5]

Despite the above recognition of the problem, and despite the Mau Mau having been declared illegal, during January 1952 reports continued to trickle through about 'oathing ceremonies' not only in Kenya's northern territory, but also in the Nairobi district. It was a desperate state of affairs, yet the colonial Governor at that time, Sir Philip Mitchell, who was an acknowledged expert on African matters, didn't appear too concerned. Following the Internal Security Working Committee's report he glibly stated that Africans were nothing but a primitive people and, therefore, what could one expect them to do but dabble in black magic and oath-taking ceremonies? By February 1952, events had become even more grave, with several reports of crops being set alight on land belonging to the white settlers. But the attacks were not only restricted to the white-owned coffee plantations – there were additional reports of Mau Mau violence in Nairobi's white suburbs. In May 1952 intelligence reports suggested that the content of the Mau Mau's oaths had begun to change character – moving away from a general promise to commit violence against European settlers in favor of more specific threats of murder against named individuals. The practice of oath-taking was also being seen on a larger and larger scale, with massive initiation ceremonies taking place involving up to 800 people. Those Kikuyu who would not take the oath, or informed on those that did, were summarily killed and mutilated.

On September 25, 1952, five white-owned farms were attacked. Outbuildings were burnt to the ground and over 400 sheep and cattle were either maimed or killed. With all this going on, it might be expected that Governor Mitchell would change tactics, instead of which he continued to dismiss claims that any major problem existed in Kenya. It wasn't until his departure from the country (on authorized terminal leave) that any serious effort was made to combat the Mau Mau.

The new Governor was a man by the name of Sir Evelyn Baring who, on arriving in Kenya, immediately conducted a week-long tour of the colony. He was made aware that the Mau Mau had murdered in the region of forty people in the past month alone, and were also beginning to acquire large quantities of firearms. Baring swiftly concluded that the only remedy to the situation would be to declare a full-scale State of Emergency accompanied by an increase in the number of British Army personnel in Kenya.

In a letter addressed to the Secretary of State for the Colonies Baring wrote:

> I have just returned from a tour [of Kenya] and the position is now abundantly clear that we are facing a planned revolutionary movement.
> If the movement cannot be stopped, there will be an administrative breakdown followed by bloodshed amounting to civil war.[6]

On October 21, a State of Emergency was finally declared and troops began pouring into the country. Anyone suspected of being a political agitator was rounded up, including Jomo Kenyatta, president of the KAU, who was now accused of belonging to the Mau Mau. It is a generally accepted view among modern researchers and historians that the militant branch of the KAU was linked to the Mau Mau, and it is also agreed that the Nairobi criminal underworld comprised of a high percentage of Mau Mau operatives as well. What has never been proved satisfactorily, however, is Kenyatta's link to this secretive and extremely violent organization. After all, his modus operandi was always to present himself as a rational African leader through whom the British could reach a satisfactory resolution with the Kenyan people.

Following the declaration of the State of Emergency, events moved swiftly with the Kenyan government making every effort to suppress the Mau Mau and protect its white citizens. Kenyatta was flown to Kapenquria, where he was placed under heavy armed guard to await trial (in 1953 he was sentenced to seven years' imprisonment with hard labor), while approximately 112 others were also arrested on suspicion of Mau Mau involvement. On the morning of October 22, Nairobi's citizens were alarmed to find the Lancashire Fusiliers patrolling their streets, and the next day the Royal Navy cruiser *Kenya* arrived in Mombassa carrying a detachment of Royal Marines, who were deployed to suppress any Mau Mau activity in that city as well.

Yet, despite the mass arrests in Nairobi and the surrounding areas, it soon became apparent that the Mau Mau were still growing in strength. A Kikuyu chief who was sympathetic towards the British administration's goals attempted to break up a Mau Mau oathing ceremony, only to be hacked to pieces with machetes by the crowd. Shortly afterwards the Mau Mau claimed their first white victim, a farmer by the name of Eric Bowyer. Bowyer lived with two African servants on an isolated holding. While he was taking a bath, Mau Mau rebels broke into the house and slaughtered all three

Guards escort Mau Mau suspects to cells in Nairobi in November 1952. The month before, the Mau Mau problem had become so acute that a State of Emergency was declared and British troops were deployed in Kenya.

occupants. Acts such as this continued apace, leaving the colonial administration feeling frustrated and impotent. Their problems appeared to be threefold. Firstly, there was an acute lack of reliable intelligence to indicate the Mau Mau's organizational structure, how well it was armed and what its intentions were. This meant that government forces were unable to plan an appropriate strategy to overcome the rebels. Secondly, the armed forces operating in Kenya were of very mixed abilities. There was the British military, the colonial military, a critically understaffed civilian police force and an unarmed tribal police unit. Finally, all of the above units operated independently from each other, with very little organized coordination.

To resolve some of these problems it was decided that Kenya's only intelligence agency (a Special Branch unit of the Kenyan police) would be upgraded and trained specifically to combat the Mau Mau. The Lancashire Fusiliers were deployed up-country to the Rift Valley province around Thomson's Falls, Naivasha and Nakuru, which had all been designated Mau Mau trouble spots, while the King's African Rifles were deployed mainly in the native reserves of the Central province as well as around Nairobi. The colonial administration also saw to it that those Kikuyu who were loyal to the British were allowed to form a self-defence unit known as the Home Guard. Slow headway was being made by the British administration, but it was always set against a background of continuing Mau Mau activity.

Charles Hamilton Ferguson lived on a remote farm in the Thomson's Falls area of Kenya when, on January 1, 1953, while enjoying a late dinner with a friend, Richard Bingley, a gang of Mau Mau insurgents swept into the house and murdered the two men where they sat. The next evening, the Mau Mau attacked another farmhouse, this time located near Nyeri. This house was owned by a Mrs. Kitty Hesselberger and her companion Mrs. Raynes Simpson. Mrs. Simpson, according to a later police report on the incident, was seated in the living room of the house with her face to the door, and on the arm of the chair she was sitting in she had placed a gun. When the houseboy entered, Mrs. Simpson, noticing something odd about his appearance, swiftly picked up her weapon and was immediately confronted by a gang of Mau Mau thugs piling into the room. Her first shot mortally wounded the gang's leader while it is believed her second shot distracted another Mau Mau member who was about to kill Mrs. Hesselberger. Mrs. Simpson then continued to fire her weapon, giving Mrs. Hesselberger the opportunity to pick up a shotgun, at the sight of which the remaining Mau Mau fled.

Other victims of Mau Mau attacks were not so fortunate. Over the following two weeks, it is believed that thirty-four Africans were murdered by the Mau Mau, yet it wasn't until the events of January 24, 1953 that the world became fully aware of the type of atrocities the Mau Mau were prepared to commit in the name of freedom. On that night, at a remote farm owned by a Mr. Ruck, a gang of Mau Mau were smuggled onto the premises by Mr. Ruck's African employees. At 9.00 p.m., while Mr. Ruck was having dinner with his wife, he was asked by one of his servants to step outside as they had caught an intruder on the premises. Mr. Ruck did as he was requested, only to be struck down as he exited the house. On hearing his cries for help, his wife grabbed a gun, but was quickly overcome by the insurgents before she could fire a shot. Both bodies were later found outside in the scrubland, where they had been badly mutilated. But as if that wasn't sickening enough, the Mau Mau conducted a thorough search of the house, during which they came across the Ruck's six-year-old son, Michael, asleep in bed. What was done to this little boy does not bear description.

However horrific these single incidents were, two months later on March 26, the Mau Mau stepped up their programme of terror and instigated two large-scale operations. The first targetted Naivasha police station – a change from previous operations, which normally concentrated on isolated farms. Just after midnight on March 24, approximately eighty-five Mau Mau, having shot the watchtower sentry, broke through the station's outer perimeter of barbed wire. They then split into two groups. The first group headed for the police station's main office, where they killed the duty clerk, while the second group headed straight for the station armory where they stole as many weapons and as much ammunition as they could carry. Having driven a truck into the compound, the armory raiders loaded it with their newly acquired arsenal while the other group breached the walls of a nearby detention center, releasing 173 prisoners. Naturally, during all this mayhem several gunshots were fired, awakening all those off-duty officers who were asleep in their barracks. Luckily for them, on realizing the nature of the attack they fled to safety rather than face up to the Mau Mau, who by this time were making away with their arms haul.

While the Naivasha raid was in full swing, another Mau Mau unit was gathering around the settlement of Lari, located approximately thirty miles south-southeast of Naivasha. Lari was home to many hundreds of Kikuyu men, women and children, most of whom were opposed to the Mau Mau or, worse still, were members of the Kikuyu Home Guard. Lari was also a base for the King's African Rifles, but on the night of the 26th most of the soldiers had been sent to the Athi River Prison, where it was feared a mass break-out was planned.

With its defences down, Lari made an easy target for the Mau Mau. An estimated 1,000 insurgents, split into a number of groups, spread themselves throughout the village so that they could attack the homesteads simultaneously. Each unit had a specific task, with one group ensuring that all the huts were bound with cable around the outside to prevent the doors from opening. Another unit then soaked the huts with petrol while a third squad was tasked with attacking all those trying to escape the ensuing fires. Over 200 huts were burned to the ground during the attack at Lari. Thirty-one people are believed to have survived, but nearly all of these suffered horrendous injuries. Because a large percentage of Lari's male population was out on patrol on the night in question, most of the dead were women and children. It has also been estimated that over 1,000 cattle were slaughtered during the raid.

Worldwide reactions of horror over both the Naivasha and Lari attacks bolstered the British administration's resolve to wipe out the Mau Mau. More reinforcements were required so that the military could get on with the job. In addition, the police, the army and all the various civilian loyalist groups also began working more closely together and began conducting large-scale raids through areas that were thought to be Mau Mau strongholds.

> 6000 Africans in the shanty village of Kariobangi (near Nairobi) were rounded up for questioning April 24 and their village was ordered destroyed by bulldozers. 7000 natives in two villages northeast of Nairobi were evicted April 17 and their homes were leveled similarly April 19. The area was called Nairobi's Mau Mau headquarters.[7]

The administration also instigated what became known as the Kikuyu Registration Ordnance Act, which in effect meant that any Kikuyu living outside a designated reserve had to carry identification papers. But nothing was as easy as it seemed, for when the Mau Mau heard of this new initiative they 'persuaded' most of the Kikuyu to resist this order by returning to the reserves. The majority of white farmers, now more than ever before fearing Mau Mau attacks, dismissed their black servants and land workers who, having nowhere else to live, also returned to the reserves. Suddenly, tens of thousands of people were converging on land meant to house a fraction of that number, a situation which in turn led to overcrowding and bitter resentment among the largely Kikuyu population. The Mau Mau took full advantage of this disaffection, recruiting new members by the dozen. Yet, despite this sudden eagerness of Kikuyu to join the Mau Mau, there were still a fair number unwilling to sign up to such an organization – particularly given that the massacre at Lari, far from targeting white landowners, instead involved the murder of their fellow countrymen. Indeed, by mid-

1953 the biggest question on the minds of most Kikuyu tribesmen was whether to join an organization which actively promoted the brutal and often irrational murder of their own kind, or to take a stand against them. Many chose the latter option, joining the British administration's Home Guard. 'Whatever use the Government made in publicizing the Lari Massacre to the world,' wrote A. Marshall McPhee in his account of this time, 'the fact remains that it was the turning point against the Mau Mau; many more rallied to the Kikuyu Guard and from this time on Mau Mau would meet increasing resistance from the people they sought to liberate.'[8]

This resistance was further strengthened by the British who, on the advice of a senior member of the army, now decided to provide the Home Guard with firearms – a move they had previously dismissed, fearing the Mau Mau would try to appropriate the weapons.

But the British had a long way to go before any of their military operations bore fruit, for despite an increase in the number of soldiers being deployed to Kenya, and despite the rapid growth within the ranks of the Home Guard, tracking the Mau Mau down was an almost impossible task. The British administration's biggest break didn't come until early in 1954 when Waruhiu Itote (better known by the nickname 'General China'), one of the Mau Mau's most powerful leaders, was wounded during a minor skirmish with government troops and subsequently captured. While he was in custody, the police's Special Branch unit questioned Itote for days, trying to elicit from him not only information, but also an agreement that in return for his freedom he would attempt to negotiate a mass surrender of those men directly under his command. Before long, General Kaleba and General Tanganyika, both Mau Mau leaders like Itote, were also captured and 'persuaded' to participate in a negotiated surrender of their men. On March 30, 1954 members of the police, the army and the government sat down with a selection of Mau Mau representatives to thrash out a deal. The government guaranteed that all those who gave up their arms would not be executed, although inevitably their leaders would face long jail sentences. Furthermore, all those Mau Mau who weren't thought to have been actively involved in terrorist activities would be gradually rehabilitated into the community. It was a good deal, one which the British administration gave the Mau Mau ten days to consider. In the interim, however, another Mau Mau general called Gatamuki, who was adamantly against surrender of any description, kidnapped several of those who had attended the government negotiations. Government forces now had to move very swiftly to address what was rapidly turning into a major crisis. Manoeuvring their troops into position they mounted a full-scale attack on Gatamuki and his men, killing twenty-five Mau Mau and capturing nine others, including Gatamuki himself.

Placed under arrest, Gatamuki announced that, having spoken at length with the Mau Mau he had kidnapped, these men had persuaded him that surrender was the best option considering how low morale was within the Mau Mau's ranks. Conditions in the forests, where most of them were hiding out, had become intolerable. Food supplies were low, as were ammunition supplies, while the increasing strength of the government forces had left the Mau Mau's communications system in disarray.

Meanwhile, back in Nairobi, operations were under way to settle the Mau Mau question once and for all. Knowing that large pockets of insurgents were both living and operating within the city itself, Operation Anvil swung into action. On April 24, 1954, British troops sealed all exits to the entire city, thus preventing anyone from entering or leaving Nairobi. Then police began a methodical house-to-house search of the city. All identification papers had to be produced, with anyone who was suspected of belonging to the Mau Mau was arrested and sent to a detention center at Langata, five miles from Nairobi where they underwent further investigation. Similar screening operations were also carried out in the reserves, as were large-scale military sweeps through the Aberdare Mountain Range, where it was known that large numbers of Mau Mau operatives were still hiding out. Naturally, given that the enemy was well-practiced in guerrilla warfare, there were as many steps back as there were forward, but slow progress was made until finally, with the deployment of small tactical units made up entirely of Home Guard officers who knew the terrain better than anyone, arrests started to mount up.

By the autumn of 1956, it was believed that there were only around 500 Mau Mau

Former Mau Mau leader Jomo Kenyatta became Kenya's first black Prime Minister in May 1963 and is pictured here (right) with Ugandan Prime Minister Milton Obote at a meeting in Nairobi the following month.

members still at large. The administration's main concern now was to track down and capture the last major player in the Mau Mau organization, a commander by the name of Dedan Kimathi, who was thought still to be hiding out in the Aberdare Mountains.

On October 17, 1956, Kimathi was wounded by Henderson's [Superintendent Ian Henderson, who conducted operations against the Mau Mau] men, but succeeded in escaping through the forest, but after traveling non-stop for just under twenty-eight hours and covering nearly eighty miles, he collapsed near the forest fringe. There he remained for three days, hiding in the day time, foraging for food at night. Early on the 21st he was found and challenged by a tribal policeman who fired three times at him, hitting him with the third shot. He was then captured, in his leopardskin coat, and in due course brought to trial and sentenced to death.[9]

Indeed, it seemed only fitting that it was an African who brought down one of the last of the Mau Mau, for despite being a group who were ostensibly fighting for African rights, during their operations it was their fellow Africans who bore the brunt of the violence. The statistics agree; for it has been calculated that during the whole State of Emergency while 32 Europeans were killed and 26 wounded, a total of 1,817 African civilians died, with 910 wounded.

The general State of Emergency was finally lifted in December 1960 and shortly thereafter Jomo Kenyatta was released from prison. While he had been in jail, the newly-formed Kenyan African National Union (KANU) party had voted him their president, and on his release he was also admitted onto Kenya's Legislative Council.

In May 1963 Kenyatta became Kenya's first black prime minister, and led the country to full independence on 13 December of the same year.

[1] *State of Emergency: The Full Story of Mau Mau*, Fred Majdalany, Houghton Mifflin, 1963.

[2] Ibid.

[3] From an interview broadcast in Channel 4's 'Secret History' series, *How Britain Crushed the Mau Mau Rebellion.*

[4] *State of Emergency: The Full Story of Mau Mau*, op. cit.

[5] *Kenya*, A. Marshall MacPhee, Praeger, 1968.

[6] *State of Emergency: The Full Story of Mau Mau*, op. cit.

[7] *Facts on File: World News Digest with Index*, reports for 1953, Facts on File.

[8] *Kenya*, op. cit.

[9] *State of Emergency: The Full Story of Mau Mau*, op. cit.

AUM SHINRIKYO – THE 'SUPREME TRUTH' SECT

Some strange malaise, some bitter aftertaste lingers on. We
crane our necks and look around, as if to ask: where did all that
come from? . . . We will get nowhere as long as [we] continue to
disown the Aum phenomenon as something completely other, an
alien presence viewed through binoculars on the far shore.

HARUKI MURAKAMI, from an article in the *Guardian*
by Richard Lloyd Parry, March 18, 2005

The morning of March 20, 1995 began much like any other morning of any
other day in Tokyo, Japan. People all over the city were rising, having
breakfast, then heading off to the subway to get to work. But, unlike any
other day, packages had been placed on five different trains; packages which
contained plastic bags filled with a lethal chemical agent. Once laid on the floor each
parcel was punctured by an umbrella tip, which allowed the chemical inside – a lethal
nerve gas called sarin – to be released. It then spread throughout the carriages. What
Tokyo was experiencing was a co-ordinated terrorist attack, one that was carried out
by a sinister, secretive cult named Aum Shinrikyo. In fact, this was a double tragedy
for Japan, for only nine weeks earlier the city of Kobe had suffered a massive
earthquake in which 6,000 people died. The Japanese novelist Haruki Murakami
described the two events like, 'the back and front of one massive explosion . . . these
twin catastrophes will remain embedded in our psyche as two milestones in our life
as a people.'[1]

The sarin-gas attack not only brought about a serious inquiry into the very heart
of the Japanese state, it also spelt the beginning of the type of global terrorism best
illustrated by the events of September 11, 2001, when two aeroplanes were
deliberately flown into the Twin Towers in New York. But who was behind the events
in Japan, in which thousands of people were injured and twelve people died? And
what was the motive for causing havoc on such a large scale?

The self-proclaimed leader of Aum Shinrikyo was a man who called himself
Shoko Asahara, although this wasn't his real name. His actual name was Chizuo
Matsumoto, and he was born in the provincial city of Kumamoto on March 2, 1955
to impoverished parents, his father earning a living as a tatami-mat maker.
Matsumoto was partially blind from birth, a disability which meant he was sent to a
special government-run boarding school for the blind. Unlike the other children,
however, he could see out of one eye, and it is said Matsumoto took advantage of this

situation to bully and manipulate the other children into doing his bidding. Money was his main motivation; he rarely, if ever, helped out his blind schoolmates without first extracting payment from them. Not everything went his way though, for several times he tried to become president of the student body, but was unsuccessful on each occasion due to his lack of popularity.

Upon graduating, the young Matsumoto spent several years trying to gain entrance to Tokyo University. To attend this establishment was almost a pre-requisite for anyone wishing to enter Japan's governing elite, an ambition that Matsumoto had harbored since he was a child. Whether through bad luck or lack of application, Matsumoto failed to realize his dream – a setback that played bitterly on the young man's mind. Returning to his home town of Kumamoto, he took up a job in a massage parlor. It was hardly an auspicious beginning for an ambitious youngster, but at the age of twenty-three, determined to better himself, he returned to Tokyo. Here he set up the Matsumoto acupuncture clinic and married a nineteen-year-old college student called Tomoko, with whom he was to have six children. Shortly after setting up business in Tokyo, however, Matsumoto was arrested for the first time, for attempting to sell fake remedies to an unsuspecting public. He had apparently concocted a potion out of orange peel soaked in alcohol, that he called 'Almighty Medicine' and which he claimed was a traditional Chinese remedy for treating all types of illness. Together with a three-month course of acupuncture and yoga, Almighty Medicine was sold for $7,000 a pop.

After his arrest and a fine of $1,000, Matsumoto decided, during the 1980s, to travel to India, where he was inspired to take further yoga classes. He became fascinated by the idea of spiritual enlightenment, which certain types of yoga and meditation are said to promote. Suddenly Matsumoto knew what he wanted to do; he would return to Japan, set up his own yoga center, and encourage members not only to study a new type of faith, but also to regard him as this new faith's spiritual leader.

By 1987, Matsumoto's ambitions were realized; he named his group Aum Shinrikyo Matsumoto and it was at this time that he adopted the name Shoku Asahara. Initiates to the cult claimed that their leader had taught them not only spiritual enlightenment based on an eclectic mix of Buddhism, Hinduism, Shamanism, the writings of Nostradamus, apocalyptic Christianity and New Age beliefs, but also supernatural powers such as how to levitate and the art of telepathy. To most people these claims might seem ludicrous, but, disturbingly, within two years of its conception in 1989, Aum Shinrikyo had so many converts that the Japanese government was forced to grant it legal status as a religion (a move which also granted Asahara huge tax concessions). Indeed, at the height of Aum Shinrikyo's powers, in the mid-1990s, membership in Japan swelled to well over 10,000, with over 30,000 admirers and followers around the world, including a large group in Russia.

As the cult grew, so Asahara became increasingly confident. Anything he said was taken as truth. His followers didn't balk even when it came to some of the more bizarre rituals, such as the drinking of Asahara's blood, which they were informed

Shoko Asahara, a partially sighted academic failure and con artist, established a legal religion with himself as its head. He sold his beard clippings and bath water to followers, telling them they had curative or magic powers.

had magical properties. At other times followers were encouraged to buy Asahara's bath water – which was also said to have miraculous powers. Clippings from Asahara's beard were sold with instructions to boil them in water and afterwards ingest the solution. Anything Asahara said was believed. There appeared to be no stopping either the cult or its leader – and naturally with such great power, also came great wealth. In March, 1995, one of Aum Shinrikyo's leading members estimated the cult's net worth as being in the region of $1.5 billion.

Initially, when Shoku Asahara first began teaching yoga, he had shied away from charging his pupils any money or, if they did pay, it was simply by way of a token donation. But, with the legalization of Aum Shinrikyo as a religion, all this was to change. Suddenly donations weren't just welcomed, they were expected. The cult also set up a huge merchandising operation (much as a large corporation might) for the sale of videos, books, magazines and other paraphernalia. Asahara wrote several books himself, a few of the most popular being *Secrets of Developing Your Spiritual Powers* (which promised, among other things, to teach trainees how to see into the future and how to read minds), *Beyond Life and Death* and *Mahayana Sutra and Initiation*. Seminars and training courses were also popular and easy ways to rake in money, with tens of thousands of dollars being charged for each session. Aum Shinrikyo also diversified into running several 'outside' businesses, such as a computer manufacturing company, which imported parts from Taiwan to be assembled in a cult-run factory back in Japan, with the end products sold in Aum Shinrikyo shops in the capital. It has also been suggested by Kyle B. Olson, in an article entitled 'Aum Shinrikyo: Once and Future Threat?', that another method by which the cult raked in money was via the practice of 'green mail' which in effect meant that Asahara would threaten to set up a cult operation in any number of cities – unless the local government paid him not to do so. The ruse worked over and over again, earning Aum Shinrikyo hundreds of thousands of dollars.

With such great wealth at his disposal, it was only a matter of time before Asahara decided to plough some of the money into property. In 1988 he decided that what his cult needed was a temple and compound, within which his followers could live.

Mount Fuji is without doubt one of Japan's most easily recognizable landmarks. An inspiration to artists over the centuries, it has come to symbolize both the beauty and mystery of the country as a whole. Sadly, in 1988, it received a far less noble addition to its grandeur. At the foot of the mountain Aum Shinrikyo, having bought a plot of land, erected a series of bunker-like buildings, which were to serve as its headquarters. Huge dormitories were built, in which the faithful could sleep upon the bare wooden floors. A giant refectory was also erected – here followers (if they were lucky) were served one meal a day consisting of steamed vegetables and rice. With such basic living conditions, and given that they were required to donate huge amounts of money to the cult, it might seem surprising that so many men and women were willing to join this organization. But the numbers kept on growing, with many young professionals among the new recruits. Hideo Murai was one such individual. An exceptionally talented young man who had trained as an astrophysicist, after meeting Asahara he turned his back on his former life and instead joined Aum Shinrikyo. Another member was Seiichi Endo, a genetic engineer with a Ph.D in molecular biology. Many others followed. But, although on the surface the cult appeared to be fulfilling all these people's expectations, underneath cracks were beginning to appear, and several disillusioned followers were now starting to look for a way out.

The disillusionment (or even fear) felt by some newcomers to the sect stemmed in part from the weird, masochistic initiation ceremonies that a large number of them endured, the most famous of which involved boiling water. Candidates would be made to submerse themselves in a tub of boiling water until their skin peeled away, after which they would be forced to meditate night and day, while all the time listening to a tape of Shoku Asahara chanting mantras. Food and sleep were also used as weapons, with initiates receiving very little of either, a well-known cult technique used to lower people's resistance, making it easier to brainwash them. Candidates were also forced to take hallucinogenic drugs, either to subdue them or to help incite them to commit criminal acts. Refusal to do any of the above would result in punishments that included several weeks of hard labor.

Shuji Taguchi had joined Aum Shinrikyo with every intention of making a lifelong commitment to the cult. He was a model member of the group, with a deep-rooted conviction that Asahara was little less than a god. His faith was unshakable – until, that is, one of his closest friends asked permission to leave the cult. Asahara informed everyone that this man must be mentally unstable and needed specialist treatment. The type of assistance he received was closer to torture than counseling – for the man was hung upside-down and then dropped repeatedly into a container of ice-cold water. Eventually, having been submersed so many times that his heart could no longer bear the strain, the man died.

Taguchi was shocked by his friend's death and, understandably, began talking to other Aum Shinrikyo members about his concerns. It was the last they would ever see of him. Angered by what he saw as one of his disciples' insubordination, Asahara had Taguchi executed. His body was then burned. A few weeks later, concerned about their son, his parents tried to contact the compound, only to be told he was unavailable. Further attempts to get in touch with Taguchi also failed to yield results, after which the police were contacted, but, even though they had received several requests from other worried parents concerning their 'lost' children, the police, too, drew a blank. It wasn't until a young lawyer, Tsutsumi Sakamoto, heard about the cult and the anguish of those parents whose children had joined, that questions began to be asked and alarm bells were sounded.

Initially, Sakamoto, who was married with one small child, was employed by one family to demand the release of their under-age daughter from the cult's clutches. Word quickly spread, however, and soon Sakamoto was working on behalf of twenty-three families, all seeking to help their children escape. Firstly the young lawyer organized the individual complainants into one single group, named the Society of Aum Supreme Truth Victims. Only then did he approach the cult with a request to allow the parents proper access to their offspring. This offensive brought him into contact with one of the cult's lawyers, Yoshinobu Aoyama, who had joined the cult in 1988 after being credited as one of the youngest students ever to pass the bar exams at the renowned Kyoto Law School. Aoyama at first tried to placate Sakamoto by allowing one set of parents access to their child, but Sakamoto was having none of this and demanded the release of all the named youngsters. In addition, Sakamoto surprised Aoyama by informing him that he was also acting on behalf of a cult member who had purchased some of Asahara's 'miracle drug' but who had received none of the benefits that the cult claimed would occur upon ingestion of the liquid.

Very soon, given the nature of Sakamoto's enquiries and his persistent hectoring of Aum Shinrikyo, the media became involved, interviewing the lawyer who once

Aum Shinrikyo's chief scientist Hideo Murai (left) and spokesman Fumihiro Joyu leave a press conference at the Foreign Correspondents Club of Japan in Tokyo, after having claimed that chemical stockpiles found by police on the cult's premises were to ensure Aum's survival when the world ended.

again accused the cult of holding members against their will. Asahara was furious and immediately mounted an assault – initially handing out leaflets in Sakamoto's home district, which discredited the lawyer and accused him of all manner of indecencies. When that failed to have an effect, Sakamoto began receiving threatening calls at home and at work until, on November 3, 1989, Asahara upped the stakes and sent three of his henchmen (Hideo Murai, by then the cult's chief scientist, Satoro Hashimoto, a martial arts expert, and Dr. Nakagawa) to Sakamoto's home. The plan was for the three men to wait outside Sakamoto's house until his return from work, then kidnap and kill him. But the plan didn't work because November 3 was a public holiday, and Sakamoto was already at home with his wife and child. In the middle of the night, the three men broke in to Sakamoto's house and, with chilling efficiency, killed not only Sakamoto but also his wife (Satoko) and their baby son (Tatsuhiko). They wrapped the bodies up in old sheets to take them back to Aum Shinrikyo headquarters. Later, each body was loaded into a tin drum and driven out into the countryside. All three corpses were then dumped in separate locations.

The disappearance of an entire family immediately aroused concern and suspicion. Sakamoto's mother, on discovering her son's home empty, called the police, but although they found an Aum Shinrikyo badge on the premises, they seemed unable or unwilling to investigate further. Even when the media took up the cause and stated a link between the family's disappearance and the cult, the police did nothing and soon not even the media were interested in the case.

Safe in the knowledge that he had ordered the execution of an entire family without being discovered, Shoku Asahara now decided to attempt to have a handful of his disciples elected to parliament. It was a bold step, but one that Asahara felt was necessary to achieve his dreams of ultimate power. Of course, as with almost everything Asahara was involved in, his approach to canvassing votes involved a certain level of violence. Opposition party workers were intimidated, they had their phones tapped and threats were made against their families. Asahara fielded twenty-five candidates and threw millions of dollars into his campaign . . . but not one of the twenty-five succeeded in being elected. It was a terrible blow to Asahara, whose thoughts immediately turned to retaliation against the country. He now began speaking of a coming Armageddon. Suddenly, Shoku Asahara's rhetoric included plans to raise an army to fight against all those opposed to his plans. More terrifying still, Asahara charged his chief scientist, Hideo Murai, with the task of creating a means of countrywide devastation. Murai spent months developing different types of chemical weapons, including one toxin best known as Clostridium Botulinum.

As Murai slaved away trying to concoct these poisons, Asahara decided to expand his empire even further. In 1992, the sect set its sights on Russia. Arriving in Moscow in March, Aum Shinrikyo was a huge success, attracting thousands of Russians to its cause within only few months. Even government officials joined the cult's ranks, and soon Asahara had made important contacts not only within the Russian security council, but also within the Soviet scientific community. Aum Shinrikyo now began purchasing ex-Soviet military weapons, enough to form its own army. Indeed, Asahara's plans for Armageddon were growing ever closer to fruition, with biological warfare the preferred weapon of choice. The conventional firearms, supplied by the Russians, were also to be used. By this time Hideo Murai had made huge inroads into developing chemical weaponry, by introducing a nerve gas into Aum Shinrikyo's arsenal – one that was first invented by the Nazis: sarin.

Shoku Asahara's goal was the complete militarization of Aum Shinrikyo. Every member had to receive rigorous training, after which an elite few were chosen to lead separate commando units. Asahara also built a huge factory at his compound, known to cult members as 'The Supreme Science Institute', to manufacture conventional weaponry so that every man and woman could enter battle fully armed. It was only a matter of time before Asahara decided to test out his strength, and the upcoming marriage of Japan's Prince Naruhito appeared to be the ideal opportunity – a date on which the country's leading dignitaries would all be gathered in one spot. Asahara ordered his men to organize the spraying of the botulism toxin throughout Tokyo, with the intention of causing a major epidemic. Although the operation went ahead, the toxin failed to take effect, and not one person was struck down or died. Aum Shinrikyo needed another, more effective weapon of mass destruction – and in late 1993 the deadly anthrax virus was deployed. The results of this second assault were as disappointing as those of the first. Releasing the toxin from the roof of one of his many buildings, Asahara stood back and waited for citizens to start dropping like flies. Instead, local residents complained of stomach pains and headaches, but no one died. So, why hadn't the deadly anthrax spray worked? According to the magazine, the *New Scientist*, the cult had produced the toxin in liquid form as opposed to powder which is by far the more effective killer. Furthermore, the cults's scientists had sourced their anthrax from a veterinary strain of the bacteria, which was far less capable of causing disease. It was at this point that Aum Shinrikyo focused all its attention on one chemical weapon – sarin gas. The substance had first been discovered by the Germans in 1936 while investigating organophosphates, and it was afterwards manufactured by the Nazis, though ultimately it was never used by them as a battlefield weapon. Asahara ordered that an entire building within the Mount Fuji complex be given over to the production of this new gas, stating that he required a minimum seventy tons of the poison – enough to kill not only every man, woman and child on the planet, but also every living creature.

The toxin worked in a particularly vicious way. First the victim's nasal passages would begin to run, after which they would experience an acute tightening of the chest, violent body spasms (accompanied by vomiting), loss of bowel control and afterwards death. It was not a pleasant way to die; but sarin was the perfect weapon for a cult intending to inflict a doomsday scenario on the world.

Despite sarin gas's potentially devastating effects, the initial tests were conducted. At one point, in poor safety conditions the sects's head of security was splashed with the toxin, and only just escaped death after a quick-thinking scientist injected him with an antidote. Nevertheless, the cult was not discouraged from using its latest weapon, and in yet another attempt to test its effectiveness, Shoku Asahara, chose as his first victims three district court judges, who were all engaged in a lawsuit against Aum Shinrikyo.

On June 27,1994, two trucks set out from the cult's compound loaded with sarin gas – but in an episode demonstrating an almost comic ineptitude, a combination of bad timekeeping and hideous traffic jams meant that by the time the vehicles arrived at the courthouse, the judges had gone home. Determined that all their efforts would not go to waste, Asahara ordered that the gas be released in a nearby residential area. His commands were swiftly executed and, although a change in wind direction caused the gas to be blown in the opposite direction to that intended, seven people lost their lives and more than 150 were admitted to hospital suffering from acute stomach pains and shortness of breath.

The incident was reported widely on TV and the police were called in to mount a thorough inquiry. Despite all the official efforts, however, Aum Shinrikyo miraculously escaped even a mention in connection with the attack.

Shoku Asahara must have thought himself invincible. After all, he had not only created his own fully-equipped army, but he had also produced his own chemical weapons and tested them successfully. It was, by the standards of any deranged criminal despot, a major achievement.

There was now, however, mounting pressure from several cult members' families to launch an inquiry into the goings-on within Aum Shinrikyo. For an ordinary cult member to leave the compound was well-nigh impossible, but one elderly woman (who had donated her life savings to Aum Shinrikyo, only to become increasingly suspicious of the group's agenda), did just this, escaping the compound and going into hiding. Asahara ordered her return and sent several squads to hunt her down, all of whom failed in their task. Instead, they kidnapped her sixty-eight-year-old brother, Kiyoshi Kariya, who for weeks after her disappearance had been plagued by phone calls demanding her return. Fearing for his life, Kiyoshi left a note saying that if anything happened to him then those responsible would be Aum Shinrikyo.

Kiyoshi was taken back to the cult's headquarters where he was bound and beaten. He was given drugs in the hope that, under their influence, his tongue would loosen and he would reveal his sister's location. Eventually, Kiyoshi fell into a coma and died. His body was quickly burned and his remains dumped outside the compound in a nearby lake. But Kiyhoshi was now about to avenge his own murder from beyond the grave. The note that he had left behind, identifying Aum Shinrikyo as his abductors, fell into the hands of the police. At last they had the evidence they needed to take action against the group and began to make preparations to mount a surprise raid on the cult's headquarters. Asahara knew nothing about the planned police attack. Instead of bolstering his defences, he was concentrating on his own plans to unleash sarin gas on the Tokyo subway system during the early morning rush, hoping to cause the death of hundreds, if not thousands of citizens.

On March 20, 1995 at 8.00 a.m., a group of carefully hand-picked Aum Shinrikyo members (Kenichi Hirose, Yasuo Hayashi, Masato Yokoyama, Dr. Ikuo Hayashi and Toru Toyoda) stepped on to a variety of trains, all of which were timetabled to converge at Kasumigaseki station. Each member was carrying a small, toxic-resistant plastic bag filled to the brim with deadly sarin, along with specially adapted umbrellas with spiked ends. As each train neared its final destination, all five cult members placed their packages on the floor of their respective carriages and cut them open with their umbrella tips. Immediately sarin fumes began spreading through the trains. Those nearest the packages were coughing and wheezing within seconds of the gas being released. By the time the different trains pulled into Kasumigaseki, those passengers who were still able to were running for the exits, while the less fortunate lay dead and dying all over the platforms. Subway staff and police did all they could to help, but it was an impossible task. Twelve people died almost immediately and over 5,500 others were also affected by the attack, some of whom suffered horrific injuries. In the meantime, the perpetrators escaped and returned to the Aum Shinrikyo compound, where Asahara congratulated them and told them to go into hiding. The attack had been a huge success, but now it was time to lay low.

Asahara also went into hiding. His Rolls Royce was seen leaving the compound shortly after the subway attack. In the early hours of March 22, 1995, the police finally mounted a 1,000-man raid on the cult's headquarters.

There were few, if any, surprises inside. Officers soon located bags of chemicals, all of which were taken away for forensic analysis, as well as countless pieces of equipment used for the chemicals' manufacture. Hundreds of weapons were discovered as well as torture chambers and cells – several of which still contained prisoners. Yet, despite all the evidence that police confiscated from the compound, including the numerous chemicals, they didn't make one single arrest in connection with the sarin-gas attack on the Tokyo subway. Asahara was in his element. He immediately released a video, stating that not only was Aum Shinrikyo not responsible for the carnage, but that the attack had been staged by the US military in an attempt to slur the cult. No one was convinced by his claims and within hours of the video's release, Asahara, together with his most trusted lieutenants, was put on Japan's 'Most Wanted' list. There now ensued further violence, this time directed straight at the authorities. Takaji Kunimatsu, the chief of the national police federation, was attacked by four gunmen and shot four times. Miraculously, he survived, but only hours after the hit, a message arrived at a Japanese television station stating that if the police didn't back off from their investigation into the cult, then many more officers would die. The threat failed to impress anyone.

By April the police had begun arresting some of Aum Shinrikyo's major players including Dr. Ikuo Hayashi and one of its hitmen, Tomomitsu Niimi. Both were charged with imprisoning people against their will. But the police's main target, Shoku Asahara, was still at large, and still producing press releases. One of them threatened that, on April 15, 1995, a disaster would befall Japan on an even larger scale than the Kobe earthquake. The police, together with the army and the city's hospitals, were all put on high alert, but when the fateful day arrived, nothing happened. It seemed as if Asahara was now making idle threats – but four days later a report came through that Yokohama station was the site of another gas attack. Approximately 550 people were rushed to hospital suffering from a combination of sore eyes and throats. Naturally, Aum Shinrikyo was the main suspect but a short while after the attack, a confession was made by a small-time gangster with a grudge against the police.

Still Shoku Asahara was a free man, although the police had made several significant arrests, as yet they hadn't managed to charge anyone with the sarin-gas attack. Men such as Hideo Murai were still operating as if nothing had happened, but all this was about to change.

On April 23, Murai, together with the sect's lawyer, Yoshinobu Aoyama, were on the point of entering their office building when a man rushed up and repeatedly stabbed Murai in the stomach. The assailant, Hiroyuki Jo, later confessed that he had committed the crime because of increasing anger at what Aum Shinrikyo had done on March 20. He later changed his story and said that he had been employed by the Yakuza – Japan's mafia – to kill Murai in order to prevent him confessing to the police and implicating the Yakuza in Aum Shinrikyo's attack. Hideo Murai died shortly after the stabbing, subsequent to which the police mounted further raids on more Aum Shinrikyo buildings, this time finding a basement that had hitherto lain undiscovered. In this room, cowering in a corner, officers were surprised to find two of the sect's main players: Masami Tsuchiya and Seiichi Endo.

Despite their capture, on May 5, at Shinjuku station, staff discovered a burning package in one of the public toilets. Immediately they tried to put out the flames by pouring water over the parcel, but noxious fumes immediately began to rise from it. The police were called in and on later examination the package was found to contain condoms stuffed with sodium cyanide and sulphuric acid. When mixed, these chemicals combine to form hydrogen cyanide – the lethal gas used in the Nazi concentration camps to exterminate Jews. Once again, it seemed as if Shoku Asahara was baiting the police, showing them just how capable he was of wreaking havoc while still eluding arrest. Thankfully, however, his luck was about to run out.

Aum Shinrikyo followers sit on the ground to perform a ritual paying tribute to the sect's chief scientist, Hideo Murai, who had been stabbed to death on that very spot twenty-four hours earlier.

On May 16, 1995, just over two months after the sarin subway attack, police stormed one of Aum Shinrikyo's main buildings (a structure they had searched several times previously), where they eventually arrested Asahara. This was a major coup, but the attacks continued on the Tokyo subway where several cyanide bombs were planted, although none of them actually detonated.

The trials of the different Aum Shinrikyo detainees began in 1996. Asahara was charged with twenty-three counts of murder. Charges against the other Aum Shinrikyo members ranged from murder, attempted murder, detaining people against their will, the manufacture of lethal drugs and a whole catalogue of less serious misdemeanors. A few of those in the dock gave full confessions in the hope that their sentences would be reduced. Other members, including Shoku Asahara, steadfastly pleaded not guilty. On October 8, 1998, the court sentenced Kazuaki Okazaki to death for the murder of the lawyer, Tsutsumi Sakamoto, his wife and child, as well as the murder of another cult member who had wanted to leave the sect in 1989.

Incredibly, it took a further eight years before Shoku Asahara was also handed a death sentence, after being found guilty of the murder of twenty-seven cult members. The sentence was handed down on February 27, 2004, with the presiding judge, Shoji Ogawa, stating that:

> The crimes were cruel and inhuman, and his [Asahara's] responsibility as the mastermind behind all the cases is extremely grave. He deserves the maximum punishment. He had dreams of being delivered from earth's bonds and attempted to rule Japan as a king under the pretext of salvaging people. He had a selfish dogma of killing those who he thought were obstructing his bid, and armed his cult. He threw people in Japan and overseas into terror. It was an unprecedentedly brutal and serious crime.[2]

Asahara showed little emotion as the death sentence was passed, perhaps feeling safe in the knowledge that his legal team would launch an immediate appeal. Many have been reticent about expressing any opinion on the Aum Shinrikyo atrocities, even those directly affected by the organization's activities. There is still grave concern about the kind of repercussions that members of the group could inflict. On hearing of Asahara's sentence, Shizue Takahashi, the widow of a railway worker killed in the sarin subway attack, made the simple comment; 'It was good to hear the death sentence that I had been hoping for.'[3]

On going to press, Asahara's death sentence has still to be carried out.

[1] 'A Lingering Nightmare,' Richard Lloyd Parry, *The Times*, March 18, 2005.

[2] www.crimelibrary.com.

[3] www.guardianunlimited.com.

ODESSA – A NAZI ESCAPE ROUTE

In Nuremberg at that time something was taking place that I
personally considered a disgrace and an unfortunate lesson for
the future of humanity. I became certain that the Argentine
people also considered the Nuremberg process a disgrace,
unworthy of the victors, who behaved as if they hadn't been
victorious. Now we realize that they [the Allies] deserved to lose
the war. During my government I often delivered speeches
against Nuremberg, which is an outrage history will not forgive.

From the private tapes of JUAN DOMINGO PERÓN,
President of Argentina, 1946–55

At the end of World War II and for decades afterwards, historians and
researchers debated the existence of a secret society formed primarily for the
rescue of Nazi war criminals. Stories abounded of crates packed with Nazi
gold either being smuggled out of Germany and deposited in numbered Swiss bank
accounts, or arriving on the shores of Patagonia where they were driven off to secret
locations. Other stories revolved around Hitler living out his last days in southern
Argentina surrounded by loyal followers. Films were made (notably *The Night Porter*
in 1973, starring Dirk Bogarde), documentaries shown, articles written together with
many books (including Frederick Forsyth's hugely popular novel, *The Odessa File* and
Ira Levin's *The Boys from Brazil*), all pointing to the fact that such an organization did
indeed exist. The name Odessa (which stands for *Organisation der ehemaligen SS-
Angehörigen* – Organization of Former Members of the SS) consequently passed into
popular consciousness. But was such a society ever formed and if so by whom and
with what aims?

The famous Nazi hunter Simon Wiesenthal stated that he only heard about
Odessa during the Nuremberg trials, yet ever after was convinced of its reality, while
other scholars have remained more sceptical. Few have done more to raise public
awareness of the Odessa legend than the aforementioned novelist, Frederick Forsyth.
His book, which was first published in 1972, tells the story of a group of former SS
officers banding together to form an escape route out of Germany for high-ranking
Nazis, with the aim of rebuilding their organization and thereafter establishing a
Fourth Reich in order to fulfill Hitler's unrealized dreams. But for all that Forsyth's
book is an engrossing read, and that the plot involves some genuine historical facts,
ultimately the novel is only fiction. The truth, on the other hand, now that so many
top-secret documents have been declassified and so many scholars have pored over
the details, is probably stranger even than Forsyth's fiction. The real story involves an

intimate collaboration of organizations as varied as the Catholic Church, the Argentine government (under president Juan Domingo Perón) and the Allied intelligence services.

As World War II began to draw to a close, it swiftly became apparent that large numbers of Nazi SS (who, due to the nature and magnitude of their war crimes, knew that surrender was not an option), together with those who were sympathetic to their cause, were fleeing Germany for sanctuary abroad in Spain, Portugal, Switzerland and Italy. The SS was the army within an army, devised by Adolf Hitler and commanded by Heinrich Himmler, which was charged with 'special tasks' during the Nazi rule in Germany between 1933 to 1945. These 'tasks' supposedly revolved around the promotion and protection of the Third Reich, but in reality were far more concerned with achieving Hitler's ultimate ambition, to rid first Germany and afterwards the rest of Europe of elements he considered undesirable. As a result, the SS executed in the region of fourteen million people – among them approximately six million Jews, five million Russians, two million Poles and a mix of gypsies, the mentally unstable, infirm and physically handicapped.

No wonder, then, that as the war drew to a close and Germany anticipated defeat, the men who had perpetrated or supported such inhuman acts knew that the civilized world would want retribution for their evil acts. They had no choice but to flee their homeland if they wanted to escape with their lives. For this they needed not only a support network made up of men and women sympathetic to their plight, but substantial amounts of money. To this end it is believed that on August 10, 1944 a secret meeting of top German industrialists (including steel magnate Fritz Thyssen, who bankrolled Hitler's rise to power in the 1930s) convened at the Maison Rouge hotel in Strasbourg. What they discussed has always remained secret, but the main outcome of the meeting was the establishment of a support network to aid and abet the escape of as many high-ranking Nazi officials as possible. Eminent figures such as Adolf Eichmann (head of the Jewish Office of the Gestapo), who was responsible for the murder of hundreds of thousands of Jewish men, women and children, felt the Allied net tightening and the need for escape paramount. Nor were his fears unfounded for, in the Soviet Union, war-crimes trials involving German officers responsible for the deaths of Jewish citizens had already begun. Taking the Russians' lead, the Western Allied forces also announced their intention of punishing all those involved in war crimes.

By April 1945, with the Red Army advancing on Berlin, many SS officers began creating the sort of fake documents they would need to flee the country under assumed identities. Neutral Spain was the initial destination of choice. French, Belgian and German Nazis or Nazi sympathizers turned up there in their droves, including Charles Lesca who would later become a key figure in the secretive Odessa organization.

Lesca had been born in Argentina, but had lived the greater part of his life in Europe, mixing with various key Nazis including the German Ambassador to Paris, Otto Abetz, as well as high-ranking Vichy officials. When he eventually fled Berlin for

This Argentine immigration document from 1949, bears the name 'Helmut Greger,' the alias adopted by the 'Angel of Death' Dr. Joseph Mengele when Odessa helped him to flee from war-crimes trials in Europe.

Madrid he settled at 4 Victor Hugo Street from where, after the electoral victory of Perón in 1946, it is believed Lesca began the systematic transportation of 'all possible German intelligence officers to Argentina.'[1] But the first person to use Lesca's escape route was not a high-ranking Nazi official; instead, Carlos Reuter was a middle-aged banker who had recruited agents for the German intelligence service in occupied Paris. His journey began in late January 1946, taking him from Bilbao to Buenos Aires. The escape route was deemed a success and opened the gateway for many more fugitives, yet none of these 'escapes' could have been possible without Argentina's backing or the full approval of President Juan Domingo Perón.

Perón, as an ultra right-wing politician, had long been a supporter of Hitler and of the Nazi regime. With the aid of his military chiefs he had sought and established a secret alliance with Hitler in 1943, one that guaranteed mutual benefits. On Perón's side, Hitler allowed the Argentine military full access to the Nazi intelligence service's powerful communications network, thus enabling Argentina to spy on her neighbors. This was no small gift, but Perón also gave generously in return. He guaranteed Hitler indefinite freedom from arrest for all Nazi officials in Argentina. The deal was struck and a lifelong bond sealed, despite the fact that in January 1944 the Allies persuaded Argentina to break off all diplomatic ties with Germany. All was not, however, as it seemed, for even though Argentina went as far as to declare war on Germany one month before Hitler's suicide in Berlin in April 1945, the reality of the situation was that Perón only struck this pose to distract the Allies from the fact that he had begun setting up escape routes for Nazi fugitives. As he himself said:

> [. . .] if Argentina becomes a belligerent country, it has the right to
> enter Germany when the end arrives; this means that our planes and
> ships would be in a position to render a great service. At that point we
> had the commercial planes of the FAMA line [Argentine Merchant Air
> Fleet] and the ships we had bought from Italy during the war. This is
> how a great number of people were able to come to Argentina.[2]

Another route by which 'a great number of people were able' to escape to Argentina was via Perón's newly established DAIE (Delegation for Argentine Immigration in Europe) which he set up in Italy, with its main offices split between Rome and Genoa. Ostensibly, the organization was there to facilitate the emigration of Italians and other Europeans to Argentina, but covertly it was processing all the false documentation that was required by fleeing Nazis before they left Europe for South America. Although the DAIE was extremely efficient, prior to approaching it any prospective émigré also had to obtain a landing permit from the Argentine Immigration Office as well as a travel permit from the Red Cross. Acquiring a Red Cross permit using a false name was not as difficult as it might at first seem because the Red Cross documents were intended for refugees who had lost all other forms of identification. Armed with all of the above it was relatively straightforward for the unscrupulous Nazi fugitive to gain entry into his newly-adopted country. Without the offices of, among others, the Catholic Church both in Europe and in Argentina, however, Perón's plans would never have reached fruition.

One church official, Bishop Alois Hudal, wrote to President Perón on August 31, 1948 expressing the wish to obtain 5,000 visas for German and Austrian men, who were not refugees as such, but fighters who had made great sacrifices to save their country. Hudal was named by the Vatican as its special envoy to visit the German internees at the numerous 'civilian' camps dotted all over Italy, camps in which hundreds, if not thousands of Nazi officers were hiding among real refugees. Indeed, Hudal was later praised by several leading Nazi officers for his help during these years, including the Luftwaffe hero Hans-Ulrich Rudel, who wrote:

> Rome became a sanctuary and salvation for many victims of persecution
> after the 'liberation'. More than a few of our comrades found the path
> to freedom through Rome, because Rome is full of men of good will.

Nor was Hudal reticent about documenting his post-war efforts, for in his book *Roman Diary* he noted:

I felt duty bound after 1945 to devote my whole charitable work mainly to former National Socialists and Fascists, especially the so called 'war criminals'.

Joining him in these efforts were numerous other dignitaries of the Catholic Church, including Archbishop Giuseppe Siri of Genoa (one of the main points of departure from Italy to Argentina), who founded the National Committee for Emigration to Argentina. But perhaps the most shocking of all the Catholic Church's officials to help the Nazis was the Pope himself – Pius XII. For many years the Catholic Church denied any involvement of Pius in supporting Germany's war criminals, let alone his sanctioning of the Church's efforts to help them escape Italy. What cannot be ignored, however, is that between 1946 and 1952 Pius sent several pleas to those presiding over the Nuremberg war trials to commute the death sentences hanging over key Nazi officials.

Among the death sentences the Pope wished to see commuted were those of Arthur Greiser, convicted for the murder of 100,000 Jews in Poland; Otto Ohlendorf, who had murdered some 90,000 people as commander of the mobile killing squad Einsatzgruppe D; and Oswald Pohl, head of WHVA, the vast SS agency that ran the Nazi concentration camps, overseeing a slave force of 500,000 prisoners and supervising the conversion of victims' jewelry, hair and clothes to hard currency.[3]

Sadly, the Pope and the Catholic Church weren't the only ones aiding and abetting the escape of Nazi officers. In his book on the subject, Uki Goni explains how the Swiss Federal Archives still hold records revealing that several prominent Swiss officials permitted 300 Nazi Germans to travel through Switzerland, no questions asked, on their way to Argentina.

Naturally, Perón also had his own agents in place, both in Europe and in Argentina. Two such were former SS Captain Carlos Fuldner and Rodolfo Freude, chief of the Perón government's secret service. Fuldner was born in Argentina in 1910 to German immigrant parents who, when Fuldner was eleven years old, returned to Germany with their children and set up home in Kassel. By the age of twenty-one, Fuldner had been admitted into Hitler's SS, where he was quickly promoted to the rank of captain. All was not as it seemed, however, for Fuldner had a penchant for high living, generally paid for with other people's money. According to several accounts from that period, he swindled not only a shipping company out of a sizable sum of money, but also the SS, as a consequence of which he decided to flee Germany and return to his homeland. His escape was not successful and having been captured, he was expelled from the SS and spent some months in jail. Despite this, Fuldner's career was not yet at an end, for at some point between being released from jail and the end of World War II, Fuldner's star rose once more when Heinrich Himmler employed him on a 'special mission' to help set up a German/Argentine rat-line to smuggle people such as Adolf Eichmann and the 'Angel of Death', Josef

Although the existence of the Odessa network has been disputed, Nazi hunter Simon
Wiesenthal (above) was convinced the secret organization had helped senior Nazis to
escape justice from the moment he first heard mention of it at the Nuremberg Trials.

Mengele, out of Germany. In this new role, Fuldner traveled extensively throughout
Europe, often skipping between Spain, Italy and Germany within the space of a few
days. Fuldner also played a key role running Perón's DAIE office in Genoa.

The second key member of Perón's team, Rodolfo Freude, was also of mixed
German/Argentine origin although his father, Ludwig, far outranked Fuldner's
father, being a close personal friend of Perón's as well as having proven Nazi
credentials. With this background it is not surprising that Rodolfo Freude, as soon as
he was of age, went to work for Perón. Nor is it surprising that when Perón was first

elected president, Rudi (as he was known) became his spy chief.

Everything was now in place for one of the greatest multiple-escape stories of all time to unfold. Fuldner, along with many other Nazi agents, had established his network in Europe and Freude, along with his boss Perón, was ready and willing to accept all Nazi fugitives into Argentina. Among these was SS officer Erich Priebke.

Priebke joined the SS in 1936, but due to his flair for languages (in particular Italian and English) he was transferred to the Gestapo, where he was set to work liaising with international police departments, as well as forming part of Mussolini's personal guard when the Italian dictator visited Germany during 1937. Lieutenant Priebke also traveled with Hitler as his personal translator when the Führer visited Rome and worked alongside Reinhard Heydrich, who is best known as one of the perpetrators of Hitler's Final Solution. Perhaps Priebke's most important role during the war, however, was as the main go-between between the Vatican and the Nazi Party. This made him an extremely important cog in a very large machine, but when Mussolini was finally ousted from office by the Italian Fascist Council in 1943, Priebke's position immediately became most perilous.

Furious at what he saw as Italy's ungratefulness towards Germany, Hitler sent his troops into Rome and swiftly captured the city, after which Priebke's official duties changed to include the arrest, torture and, more often than not, execution of Italian Communists and partisans. More gruesome even than this, Priebke is also believed not only to have overseen the deportation of over 2,000 Roman Jews to their deaths in the concentration camps, but also to have taken a leading role in the Ardeatine Caves massacre, one of the most notorious of all Nazi war crimes in Italy.

On March 23, 1944, Communist partisans attacked a company of German soldiers marching through Rome, killing thirty-three men. Outraged by the slaughter, Hitler immediately ordered that for every German soldier that had died, ten Italians were to be executed. Priebke immediately set about searching his files for 330 convicted prisoners to fulfil Hitler's order but, according to his later testimony, there weren't enough victims to make up the number. Finally, he ordered that seventy-three Jews and fifty ordinary prisoners be taken from the city's jails. On the following day, all the detainees were driven out to the mouth of the Ardeatine Caves where they were shot. Priebke later recalled:

> All were tied with rope with their hands behind their backs, and when their names were called they walked into the cave in groups of five. I went in with the second or third party and killed a man with an Italian machine pistol. The executions finished when it was getting dark in the evening. During the evening some German officers came to the cave and after the shooting the caves were blown in.[4]

Not long after this massacre, on June 4, 1944, the Allies entered Rome and Priebke, fearing for his life, fled to Verona. From there he returned to Berlin but afterwards traveled back to Italy where, on May 13, 1945, he was eventually arrested. Despite being formally named as one of the participants in the Ardeatine massacre,

Priebke was not held in a high-security facility. Instead, he was detained in a British-run camp in Rimini from where he managed to escape by cutting through some barbed wire while his guards were drunkenly celebrating the New Year.

> Five of us managed to escape: three non-commissioned officers, another officer and myself. We went to the bishop's palace and that's where our flight really began.[5]

For two years Priebke, along with his wife and children, who had traveled from Germany, lived a peaceful life in the Alto Adige, until he decided it was no longer safe to stay in Europe – war tribunals were still taking place and Nazi officers were still being sentenced to death. Priebke applied for and was granted an application under the assumed name Otto Pape (probably through Fuldner at the DAIE office in Genoa) to emigrate to Argentina. Bishop Alois Hudal also gave Priebke a blank passport bearing the Red Cross insignia, thus granting him the smoothest of passages to his new home. On October 23, 1948, Otto Pape and his family boarded the *San Giorgio* in Genoa and three weeks later disembarked in Buenos Aires.

In 1954 Priebke moved with his family to the Andean retreat of Bariloche in southern Patagonia, where he lived a peaceful, prosperous existence, frequently traveling back to Italy and Germany. But in 1994 Priebke's luck ran out when an ABC television crew door-stepped him at home and asked him straight out whether he had participated in the Ardeatine Caves murders. Without a hint of shame, Priebke replied that he had indeed taken part. His answer sealed his fate. In May 1995 an Italian extradition order arrived in Argentina and by November of the same year Priebke was behind bars back in Italy where he was later sentenced to life imprisonment. But if Erich Priebke's escape with the aid of the Odessa organization was finally foiled, sadly the same cannot be said for another, far more notorious Nazi war criminal, the 'Angel of Death,' Doctor Josef Mengele.

Mengele had been in charge of the women's camp at Birkenau (part of the Auschwitz complex) from 1943 and became known as 'the chief provider for the gas and chamber ovens' because, when it came to choosing women disembarking from the trains, he more than any other SS officer would select the largest number without a flicker of conscience. Even worse, Mengele, who was a trained doctor, was said to move-up and down the lines of Jewish men, women and children searching for twins upon whom he could carry out brutal experiments. Some of these included injecting dye into the eyes of brown-eyed children to see if he could turn them Aryan blue. After the experiments the children would be sent to the gas chambers. But all this was to change in January 1945, when Mengele could see that his days were numbered. On January 17, he packed his bags, collected his medical data and, adopting the disguise of a regular army doctor, joined a retreating military unit.

When the concentration camps were liberated and statements taken, Mengele's name was mentioned on many occasions in relation to the terrible acts he had committed, and in May 1945 the United Nations War Crimes Commission issued a warrant for his arrest on the grounds of 'mass murder and other crimes.' Yet despite the warrant, when he was finally captured by American troops in June of the same year, they failed to identify him correctly and he was later released. Now traveling under the name Fritz Hollmann, Mengele escaped to Bavaria where he worked on a small farm for three years. Although his name was frequently mentioned at the Nuremberg trials, no trace was found of the man himself. Mengele bided his time and it wasn't until the spring of 1948 that he made the first move towards escaping to Argentina.

With Carlos Fuldner's help, Mengele obtained new identity papers under the name of Helmut Gregor and applied for an Argentine landing permit. Most historians believe the applications were routed through Fuldner's DAIE office in Genoa to the Buenos Aires Immigration Office. In fact, the author Uki Goñi points out that at the time of Mengele's application a whole flurry of similar applications were being made by key members of the SS, including Erich Priebke, Josef Schwammberger, Erich Müller, and last but not least Adolf Eichmann. This made mid-1948 one of the busiest periods for Odessa.

On September 7, 1948, news arrived (if it was ever in any doubt) that Helmut Gregor's landing permit had been approved by Argentina after which, save for a brief few months while Mengele tried to persuade his wife to join him in South America, he left Germany for ever, traveling first to Austria and then to Italy. Naturally, his flight involved several border crossings, all of which called for the bribery of officials and the need for yet more forged documents. Once in Italy, Mengele initially stayed in Vipiteno, but after about a month moved to the town of Bolzano where he made contact with a secret agent known only as 'Kurt', who arranged for him to travel to Argentina on a ship called the *North King*.

On May 25, 1949, Mengele set sail for South America. The crossing lasted four weeks before the ship docked in Buenos Aires. At first Mengele stayed in a downtown hotel, but after a brief period he was invited to stay at the home of Gerard Malbranc, a high-profile Nazi sympathizer who soon introduced his new guest to the cream of Argentine/Nazi society. From then on Mengele's life in Argentina became more comfortable and prosperous. He became a successful businessman, enjoying all the benefits that this brought, but when President Perón was finally ousted from power in 1959, Mengele realized that the support he had formerly received from Perón's government could no longer be relied upon. He moved swiftly to Paraguay and then later to Brazil. The move did not come a moment too soon because shortly afterwards, not only did Germany request his extradition from Argentina to face trial back in Europe, but in 1960 Mengele's one-time colleague Adolf Eichmann was abducted from Argentina by an Israeli commando kidnap squad and spirited away.

Adolf Eichmann was one of the last major war criminals to receive assistance from Perón's Odessa group, escaping from Germany to Argentina in the early 1950s. As the organizer of the deportation of Jews from their homes to Reich concentration camps such as Auschwitz and Treblinka, Eichmann was one of the Allies' main targets in their hunt for war criminals. Despite this and his arrest by an American patrol, Eichmann's luck held good. Imprisoned at Oberdachstetten camp along with thousands of other Germans, Eichmann still managed to use his fake documents (under the name Otto Eckmann) to escape detection. Eichmann's plan was to lie low until the Allies had finished their 'witch hunt' for ex-Nazi officers, but on January 3, 1946, a former colleague of Eichmann's by the name of Dieter Wisliceny testified against him at Nuremberg, saying that his old friend had insisted he would commit suicide if Germany failed to win the war.

> He said he would leap laughing into the grave because the feeling that
> he had five million people on his conscience would be, for him, a source
> of extraordinary satisfaction.[6]

Wisliceny's testimony (along with those of defendants such as Herman Goering and Auschwitz commandant Rudolf Hoess) was subsequently printed worldwide, blackening Eichmann's name to the extent that when word filtered back to him he knew he would never be safe in Europe again. Two days after Wisliceny's testimony Eichmann escaped from the American-run camp and fled first to Prien in southern Germany and later to Eversen in the British-occupied northern sector, where he worked in various rural jobs, felling trees and rearing chickens. But if Eichmann thought that with the passing of time his crimes would be forgotten, he couldn't have been more wrong. The Nazi-hunter Simon Wiesenthal never let up in his search for the former SS officer, hunting down Eichmann's parents, wife and even his ex-mistresses in pursuit of his prey, while the press constantly made reference to Eichmann's crimes and supposed 'disappearance'. It was during this period that Adolf Eichmann first made contact with Perón's Odessa organization.

> I heard of the existence of some organizations which had helped others
> leave Germany. In early 1950 I established contact with one of these
> organizations.'[7]

Soon Eichmann was making his way, with Odessa's help, across the Alps into Italy, where he was handed a passport by a Franciscan monk, Father Edoardo Dömöter, made out in the name of Riccardo Klement, together with an Argentine visa. Indeed, by rooming in various Catholic monasteries and convents with the full cooperation of the Catholic clergy, Eichmann easily escaped detection. According to Simon Wiesenthal, one Franciscan monastery in particular, the Via Sicilia in Rome, was a virtual transit station for Nazis hoping to flee Europe and establish a new life abroad.

On July 14, 1950, the ship carrying Adolf Eichmann, the *Giovanna C* docked in Buenos Aires and for the next few years the fugitive lived a relatively quiet life in the northern province of Tucumán (approximately 600 miles from Buenos Aires), working for the water company CAPRI, whose payroll included numerous ex-Nazi officers and technicians. Eichmann also had his wife and children follow him out to Argentina, and later the whole family moved back to Buenos Aires. But, unlike so many other Nazis who had found lucrative employment in Argentina, once Eichmann returned to the capital he struggled to make ends meet, working

Adolf Eichmann, the Nazi official who organized the transportation of Jews and other so-called untermenschen *to the death camps, sits in a protective glass cage during his trial in Jerusalem. Although he escaped to Argentina via the Odessa network, he was later kidnapped by Israeli commandos to stand trial in Israel.*

(somewhat ironically, given his involvement at Auschwitz) for the Orbis gas-appliances company as well as for the Mercedes-Benz factory.

Although his new home afforded him relative safety, Eichmann was aware at all times that the Israelis were still seeeking him out and would not relent until he was caught. Finally, in 1957, the head of Mossad (the Israeli secret intelligence agency), Isser Harel, received the information for which he had been waiting; Eichmann was alive and living in Argentina. Harel wrote in his book recording how Mossad eventually captured Eichmann:

I didn't know what sort of man Eichmann was. I didn't know with what morbid zeal he pursued his murderous work or how he went into the fray to destroy one miserable Jew with the same ardor he devoted to the annihilation of an entire community. I didn't know that he was capable of ordering the slaughter of babies – and depicting himself as a disciplined soldier; of directing outrages on women – and priding himself on his loyalty to an oath [. . .] I knew that he was a past master in police methods, and that on the strength of his professional skill and in the light of his total lack of conscience, he would be an exceedingly dangerous quarry. I knew that when the war was over he had succeeded in blotting out all trace of himself with supreme expertise.[8]

In fact, Eichmann's whereabouts had initially been located, not by any intelligence agencies, but by an aging, blind refugee from Nazi persecution by the name of Lothar Hermann. Hermann, who had been imprisoned in Dachau concentration camp for his socialist politics, was now living with his wife and daughter in the Olivos area of Buenos Aires. There his daughter, Sylvia, had made friends with Eichmann's eldest son, Klaus. The young boy often made anti-Semitic remarks and stated that his father had been proud to serve in the war, but it wasn't until Sylvia's father heard the name Adolf Eichmann in reference to a Nazi trial back in Germany, that he put two and two together and realized the true nature of Eichmann's identity. From that moment on, Lothar Hermann made it his mission to alert the Israeli and German authorities and see to it that Eichmann did not escape justice for a second time. Mossad operatives flew into Argentina and, on May 11, 1960, kidnapped Eichmann as he returned from work, spiriting him away to a secret hiding place outside Buenos Aires.

For the following ten days Eichmann was kept prisoner, blindfolded and handcuffed to a bed, until Mossad was able to arrange to smuggle their captive out of the country without alerting the authorities. Argentina would not, after all, take kindly to Israeli forces operating within its borders, and would certainly block any attempts to extradite Eichmann through official channels. Meanwhile, back at the Eichmann house, pandemonium reigned as his sons contacted their father's former SS friends in an attempt to find out what might have happened. In addition, a 'Perónist youth group' also approached the Eichmanns with an offer to help search for the missing man. They also offered to launch a campaign of terror against the Israelis by kidnapping the Israeli Ambassador to Argentina and torturing him until Eichmann was released, or even by blowing up the Israeli Embassy.

Finally, on May 21, 1960, Mossad managed to move Eichmann out of the country. He was heavily drugged and dressed in the uniform of an El Al flight attendant, his captors explaining that Eichmann was suffering some form of food poisoning, but that he would be taken care of by the rest of the flight staff until they reached Tel Aviv. The plan worked and on May 23 Israeli Prime Minister David Ben Gurion announced: 'Eichmann is already in this country under arrest and will shortly be brought to trial.'

Naturally, the Argentine government was incensed at the kidnapping of one of its 'citizens' and demanded that Israel return Eichmann to Buenos Aires. Argentina's Ambassador to the United Nations, Mario Amadeo, even made a formal protest before the Security Council in New York, but to no avail. Other prominent figures also joined the fray, notably the Argentine Cardinal Antonio Caggiano, who had also been involved in Odessa's escape network. Speaking to the press Caggiano said:

> He [Eichmann] came to our fatherland seeking forgiveness and oblivion.
> It doesn't matter what his name is, Riccardo Klement or Adolf Eichmann,
> our obligation as Christians is to forgive him for what he's done.[9]

But all their outrage and pleading came to nothing. Eichmann was put on trial in Jerusalem where, in court, he was kept in a bullet-proof glass box to prevent him being assassinated by the surviving victims of his crimes, and having been found guilty of all the charges against him was put to death on May 31, 1962. His last words were, 'Long live Germany, long live Argentina, long live Austria. I shall not forget them.'

Sadly, Eichmann's fellow Odessa escapee, Josef Mengele, was not to face the hangman's noose, for although he never enjoyed a peaceful existence in Paraguay, nor later in Brazil, always fearing arrest, no Mossad team spirited him back to Israel to face trial for his terrible crimes. Instead, Mengele died by drowning while swimming off the beach at Betrioga, near Sao Paulo, Brazil on February 7, 1979.

Priebke, Mengele and Eichmann were Odessa's most famous 'members', but it is thought thousands of Nazis escaped Europe using this secret network, engineered and aided by all the various groups and nations previously mentioned. Whether Odessa was a coordinated organization, conceived by the Nazis and made operational by Perón, is not quite so clear. Rather than being established as part of a grand plan to further the cause of the Nazis, it is far more likely that the whole Odessa escape network grew together piecemeal, according to necessity, as the last option for a group of frightened and desperate fugitives running for their lives.

[1] *The Real Odessa: How Perón Brought the Nazi War Criminals to Argentina*, Uki Goñi, Granta, 2002.

[2] *Así Hablaba Juan Perón*, Eugenio P. Rom, Peña Lillo Editor (Buenos Aires), 1980.

[3] *The Real Odessa: How Perón Brought the Nazi War Criminals to Argentina*, op. cit.

[4] Priebke's statement at 209 POW Camp, Afragola, August 28, 1946, *Primetime*, ABC Television; 1994. *El Ultimo Nazi*, Elena Llorente and Martino Rigacci, Sudamericana, 1998; Priebke interview, *La Nación* (Argentina), April 12, 1998.

[5] Priebke interview in *Odessa al Sur*, Jorge Camarasa, Planeta (Argentina), 1995.

[6] Dieter Wisliceny's testimony at Nuremberg, January 3, 1946.

[7] *The House on Garibaldi Street*, Isser Harel, Viking, 1975.

[8] *The House on Garibaldi Street*, op. cit.

[9] *La Razón* (Argentina), December 23, 1960.

THE SOCIALIST PATIENTS COLLECTIVE – LUNATICS IN CHARGE OF THE ASYLUM

> Protest is when I say this or that doesn't suit me. Resistance is
> when I ensure that what doesn't suit me no longer occurs.
>
> ULRIKE MEINHOF, *Vom Protest zum Widerstand*
> *(From Protest to Resistance)*

During the 1960s, perhaps more than any other decade in history, the world was party to some of the most violent, politically radical underground movements it had ever experienced. Governments were attacked were as the military – in fact, all mainstream institutions and ideologies came under fire, with 1968, in particular, coming to symbolize the whole of that decade. Left-wing rebellions broke out in all corners of the world: Paris was affected, as were Tokyo, Berlin, Saigon, New York, Prague and Mexico City. Militant direct action became commonplace, with predominantly middle-class students espousing the teachings not only of Karl Marx, but also, Mao Tse-Tung and Ho Chi Minh, in the hope of combating fascism, imperialism and capitalist exploitation. This was a revolution both an exciting, thought-provoking time, and yet a dangerous, heavily bloodstained one.

In Germany a group known as the Rote Armee Fraktion (the Red Army Faction) or RAF began their campaign of terror hoping to overthrow the government, only to be joined by other, smaller organizations such as the West Berlin Anarchists or 'June 2 Movement', as well as a group which called itself the Socialist Patients Collective (Sozialistisches Patientenkollektiv, or SPK), a gathering of psychiatric patients who had formed their own armed terrorist cell. But what was it that first drove seemingly privileged, middle-class men and women to such extreme lengths? Who were they attacking, and with what aim in mind?

In the 1960s, Germany's fascist past was still a matter of deep concern, particularly to the New Left, whose younger members condemned their forebears' involvement with Nazism and accused them of not facing up to the reality of what they had done. Students could see for themselves that there was a direct personal link between the old Nazi regime and the new German state.

As of 1965, fully 60 percent of West German military officers had fought for the Nazis, and at least two-thirds of judges had served the Third Reich. Students clamored to know the past of their professors and conducted research revealing that many of them had been affiliated with the Nazis.'[1]

The New Left generation felt disenfranchised and angry – an anger that rapidly translated itself into political activism. The Vietnam War was one of the first causes taken up by young Germans, determined to demonstrate their disillusion. Siding with the Viet Cong, they saw it as their duty to oppose the war and America's imperialist stance. They also claimed that their government's support for the conflict ably illustrated just how little Germany's values had changed since the Nazi period.

The student protests escalated, particularly in West Berlin where the Cold War was at its zenith, with right-wing newspapers such as *Bild* and the *Berliner Morgenpost* stirring up anti-student hysteria, a campaign that eventually, on June 2, 1967, resulted in the death of a twenty-six-year-old protestor at the hands of an undercover policeman, Karl Heinz Kurras.

Benno Ohnesorg had been attending his first big, mass rally (organized to protest against the Shah of Iran's imminent arrival in Germany) when he was shot and killed. Later that same night, Gudrun Ensslin – the future founder of the RAF – was quoted as saying:

> This fascist state means to kill us all [. . .] Violence is the only way to answer violence. This is the Auschwitz generation, and there's no arguing with them.[2]

It was against this backdrop of brutality and fighting that the Socialist Patients Collective first came into being. The year was 1969 and the place was the Psychiatric Neurological Clinic at Heidelberg University where Doctor Wolfgang Huber had begun encouraging patients to see capitalist society as the root cause of their illness.

Doctor Huber, who had been appointed to his teaching position (as a scientific assistant) at the age of twenty-nine in August 1964, had already been warned several times by the Director of the university, Doctor von Baeyers, for refusing to collaborate with colleagues. Now he was taking his disdain of authority even further. In group-therapy sessions, Doctor Huber was outspoken in his opinion that the capitalist agenda of the Federal Republic was sick to its very core and was, as a result, responsible for producing physically and mentally sick people – a situation which could only be reversed through violent opposition to the government. His teachings left the university with no choice and, on February 21, 1970, he was dismissed without notice. Huber's lawyer immediately lodged a complaint against the dismissal and on February 28 Huber rallied those of his patients who were psychiatrically fit enough to stage a sit-in in the offices of the university's administration block. Doctor Huber also stated that some of his more fragile patients might well commit suicide if he wasn't reinstated to his post. The university ultimately backed down and agreed to continue paying Huber until September 30, 1970, as well as giving him four rooms out of which to work. Relieved to have his old job back, Doctor Huber began formally to organize his patients into the Socialist Patients Collective. Margrit Schiller, Klaus Jünschke, Siegfried Hausner and Carmen Roll were just a few of the patients from this group who were more than willing to 'cure' their personal mental disturbances through violent action. In her book, *Hitler's Children*, Jillian Becker also points out that although Huber's university contract ran out in September 1970, meaning his work would no longer receive finance, he continued to be funded by the institution:

> [. . . the] university continued to support the organization well beyond this deadline, not out of its normal funds, as hitherto, but out of its special "charity funds". In all DM 31,875 was made available by the "sick system" to those who planned to cure themselves by destroying it, from its inception to its dissolution, at which point the balance of the money was "distributed" to the private accounts of leading members.[3]

But Doctor Huber's group was not the only organization taking up arms at this time. In 1968, another collective comprising Andreas Baader, Gudrun Ensslin, Horst Söhnlein and Thorward Proll – all of whom had previously been convicted and imprisoned on charges of arson – were given temporary parole while their case was sent to appeal. On their release Baader, Proll and Ensslin took up jobs working with troubled teenagers but in 1969, when their appeal was rejected, instead of returning to prison, all three decided to take flight. With the help of Proll's sister, Astrid, they escaped to Paris, but Baader and Astrid Proll returned to Germany shortly afterwards, settling in West Berlin. It was at this point that Ulrike Meinhof (who already knew Baader through his work with the teenagers) helped house both fugitives while they in turn began trying to source weapons for use in forthcoming terrorist activities.

In many ways, Ulrike Meinhof was typical of the kind of white, middle-class, well-educated woman who was signing up to Dr. Huber's terrorist cause. Born in 1934, the year after Hitler came to power, her father, Werner, was the assistant director of a museum, while her mother, Ingeborg, stayed at home looking after the children. It was a comfortable, pleasant life in the type of leafy neighborhood so many films and novels represent as being the perfect place for a family to live in. Sadly, Werner died when she was only six years old – and with his death Ulrike's mother was forced to take a job. Ingeborg coped well with the situation and financially the family wasn't much worse off than before the death of her husband. Even during the war (which her mother survived as a silent critic of the Nazis) Meinhof continued to receive a good education and didn't lack love and attention. Shortly after the war ended in 1945, however, Ingeborg was diagnosed with cancer and died soon afterwards. A close family friend, Renate Riemeck, now took over as Meinhof's substitute mother. Well educated, with a strong maternal streak, she was the perfect candidate for the job. Riemeck ensured Meinhof received everything she required, and also introduced her to a wide range of subjects including philosophy, literature and politics – all of which interested the young girl, who had begun to show a real talent for writing. Soon Meinhof was enjoying the company of young left-wing intellectuals who shared her ideas and goals. In 1960 she joined a Hamburg-based magazine called *Konkret*, which heightened her interest in left-wing politics.

Admittedly, Meinhof had experienced more than her fair share of trauma in her life up until this point, but there can be no argument that her parents, while they were alive, provided their child with a safe, happy home in which to grow up, and that she was given a good education. In this respect she was no different from many of the SPK members whose future reputation, though overshadowed by Meinhof's, was

Andreas Baader was the leader of the Baader-Meinhof Red Army Faction terror group with which the SPK aligned itself. He committed suicide in prison in 1977.

equally violent. In *Hitler's Children* Jillian Becker goes so far as to pose the theory that this post-war generation was indeed united in an unconscious desire to prove to themselves that they would have fought tooth and nail to defeat Nazism had they lived in that era. In effect, they were fighting Hitler 'a generation too late.'

But perhaps Meinhof would never have become involved in such extreme activities if she hadn't come in to contact with the charismatic, incorrigibly rebellious Andreas Baader and his girlfriend, Gudrun Ensslin. The latter, like Ulrike Meinhof, had enjoyed a comfortable middle-class upbringing. Born on August 15, 1940, she was the fourth of seven children. Ensslin's father, Helmut, was a pastor of the Evangelical Church of Germany (EKD), a group that was set up in 1945, the year Hitler was defeated. The EKD's beliefs ran counter to those of the Nazis. More than this, the EKD actively encouraged its members to question authority rather than simply going along with the majority view and to oppose the Federal Republic's plans to rearm. Helmut Ensslin, along with his wife, Ilse, also liked to encourage their children to discuss politics and social issues round the kitchen table and Ensslin was instilled with a good appreciation of world affairs. When she was eighteen years old, Ensslin was given the opportunity to study in America, in Pennsylvania, on a student exchange programme, a time she enjoyed even while harboring a certain disdain for the country's obvious inequalities. Jillian Becker observed that:

> She found much fault with America, its social injustice, its material inequality. But she had not arrived innocent of all prejudgment of the country, so this was not a case of any eye-opener or an education in social realities. She found what she was looking for, and what was certainly there to find.[4]

On her return, Ensslin enrolled in the University of Tübingen and afterwards in the University of West Berlin, there to study a combination of Philosophy and Germanics. The author Günter Grass, who knew her while she was studying at the latter institution later recalled, 'she was idealistic, with an inborn loathing of any compromise. She had a yearning for the Absolute, the perfect solution.'[5]

Again it is easy to draw parallels between Gudrun Ensslin's background and that of her SPK comrades and it is also easy to see why, when Ulrike Meinhof gave shelter to Baader and Ensslin, how the three of them immediately gelled and formed a strong bond. However, the two fugitives' sojourn at Meinhof's apartment was to be short-lived for, on April 3, 1970, Baader was rearrested by the police, after which Meinhof's fate was sealed.

No sooner had the courts despatched Andreas back to prison then his comrades began plotting ways to get him out. For Meinhof, this was to be her first foray into terrorist activity.

On May 14, Andreas Baader – who had been given leave to attend a state library (inside the German Central Institute for Social Issues) for the day – was set free by his friends, but only after two security guards were shot at and one elderly library staff member, George Linke, was so badly injured that he almost died from his wounds. Fleeing from the scene Baader, Ensslin, Meinhof and friends immediately went underground. Triumphant at what they regarded as a major coup (but regardless of the fact that they had nearly killed an innocent civilian) the group subsequently issued a statement which was printed in the May 22 edition of the far-left magazine, *833*, under the logo of a black panther – a direct reference to the American terrorist organization of the same name.

> Did the pigs really believe that we would let comrade Baader sit in jail for two to three years? Did the pigs really believe that we would forever fight with paintballs against bullets. . . ? Did any pig really believe we would talk about the development of class struggle. . .without arming ourselves at the same time? Did the pigs who shot first believe that we would allow ourselves to be gunned down like slaughter-cattle? Gandhi and Martin Luther King are dead. The bullets that killed them, the bullets that hit Rudi [Dutschke][5]...have ended the dream of non-violence. Whoever does not defend himself will die. Whoever does not die will be buried alive: in prisons, in reformatories, in the hovels of Kreuzberg, Wedding, Neuköln, in the stony wastelands of the new housing developments, in the overcrowded kindergartens and schools, in the perfectly furnished, newly built kitchens, in the mortgaged bedroom palaces. . . START THE ARMED STRUGGLE! BUILD UP THE RED ARMY![6]

Although this was the first mention of the Red Army Faction or, as it quickly became known, the 'Baader-Meinhof Gang,' it was to be another full year before they issued their full manifesto, 'Concept of the Urban Guerrilla' (*Das Konzept Stadtguerilla*) by which time RAF members had taken themselves off to Jordan where they trained at a PLO (Palestine Liberation Organization) camp. Here they learned the tactics of terrorism, how to use firearms, throw hand grenades and build bombs, after which they returned to Germany to begin stockpiling arms.

At this point the SPK were just beginning to commit their own acts of random violence. In mid-February 1971, Siegfried Hausner and Carmen Roll attempted to bomb a train on which the Federal Republic's president was traveling. Their plans went completely awry, however, when Carmen Roll turned up late at the station, thus missing the opportunity of placing the bomb (a small, homemade device) on the train.

In June 1971, Doctor Huber, who had moved his offices to his home in Wiesenbach, became aware that the police had begun monitoring the comings and goings of his patients. Two of these, Ralf Reinders and Alfred Mahrländer, were of particular interest to the authorities, so when they were stopped by officers on their way to Huber's home, it wasn't surprising that one of them, Reinders, pulled out a pistol and shot one of the policemen in the shoulder. Reinders and Mahrländer both escaped, but were arrested shortly afterwards.

Following this incident, seven members of the SPK, including Doctor Huber and his wife, were placed under arrest on suspicion of forming an illegal organization as well as for buying weapons and explosives. Although present at the time of the police raid, Carmen Roll and Klaus Jünschke both managed to evade capture.

It was at this point that Jünschke, along with several other SPK members, staged a bank robbery during which a policeman was shot and killed. Then, on September 25, 1971, two police officers, Helmut Ruf and Friedrich Ruf (not related), approached an improperly parked car on the Freiburg-Basel autobahn. Inside sat Holger Meins and Margrit Schiller, both SPK members and both in possession of firearms. Knowing they would be arrested if the police searched them, both terrorists took the decision to fight and opened fire on the policemen. Friedrich Ruf was wounded in the hand, while Helmut Ruf was far more seriously injured. Schiller and Meins then made their escape, leaving the authorities to search their abandoned car – a search that uncovered two underground publications of some significance. The first was entitled, 'Concept of the Urban Guerrilla,' while the second had the seemingly innocuous title of 'Road Traffic Ordinances,' although its undercover title was, 'Concerning the Armed Struggle in Western Europe.' The former, of course, had been written by Ulrike Meinhof, a fact which led officers to believe that SPK members were now beginning to affiliate themselves to the RAF.

Shortly after the Freiburg-Basel autobahn shooting, on October 22,1971, Margrit Schiller was captured by the police in Hamburg, but not before she had spent some time in an RAF safe house which she described as being more than a little exciting. Here, all the higher echelons of the Baader-Meinhof group met up, talked politics, argued, laughed and rested amongst a general mayhem of guerrilla-style equipment, such as a radio that could monitor police frequencies as well as bomb-making equipment and guns.

Schiller's arrest was itself by no means uneventful. She had been staying in Hamburg for a few days, trying to lie low but, on exiting a subway station one night, she noticed a police patrol car was following her. Schiller ducked into the basement garage of a nearby shopping complex, waited a while, then came out from an exit on the far side of the building, only to realize she was being followed once again by the police. Trying to avoid them she took shelter in an abandoned house, but later had to come out in order to meet up with two other SPK members, Irmgard Möller and Gerhard Müller. Naturally, the police were waiting and no sooner had Schiller begun to walk away from the house than two officers – Schmid and Lemke – drove their car onto the pavement in front of her. Schiller, who by this time had been joined by Möller and Müller, fled to a nearby park with the officers in pursuit. Schmid then grabbed Schiller by the arm at which point she pulled out a gun. Möller and Müller, seeing their comrade in distress, opened fire, hitting Schmid who fell unconscious to the ground. Lemke meanwhile had been wounded in the foot, but limped back to the patrol car to alert his colleagues, only to find that someone had stolen it. The delay cost Schmid his life, for by the time the two officers were taken to hospital, he was already dead.

Hamburg's entire police force was put on full alert, a move that paid dividends for not long after two plainclothes officers soon spotted a woman in a phone box whom they suspected to be one of the fugitives. The officers waited outside the box for the woman to exit, at which point she was placed under arrest. Her name, according to her identity papers, was Dörte Gerlach, but what really gave the game away was the discovery of a fully loaded gun in her handbag. Gerlach/Schiller was taken to a police station, where she was formally identified and charged with murder.

Less than a week later, police raided an apartment in the same residential district as the phone box. What they found inside was a fully operational terrorist cell with approximately 2,600 rounds of ammunition, detonators, explosives, wiring, walkie-talkies and even police uniforms. Yet despite the confiscation of all this equipment, the violence continued.

On December 22, 1971, SPK members (many of whom were now working for the RAF) were involved in one of the bloodiest actions taken by their organization when they robbed the Bavarian Mortgage and Exchange Bank, seizing DM 133,987. On that morning, a man entered the bank, placed a tape recorder on a desk and switched it on so that loud pop music blared out. Seconds later, three people dressed in anoraks with balaclavas covering their faces burst in. Two of them carried sub-machine guns, while the third carried a pistol. The three terrorists threatened bank staff and customers alike while ordering them to remain calm. Directly outside the building, a red Volkswagen minibus had parked illegally, something which drew the attention of a police officer called Herbert Schoner. Schoner approached the vehicle to talk to the driver, only to be met by a hail of gunfire. He was shot several times, one bullet blasting into his back, yet he still managed to crawl towards what he thought would be a safe haven, the Bavarian Mortgage and Exchange Bank. On entering the building, instead of finding sanctuary, Schoner was met by one of the robbers who shot him in the chest. He died at the scene.

The robbers, realizing they had just killed a police officer, took off in the red minibus along with their spoils. They had succeeded in pulling off a major bank robbery and, even though one of their number, Klaus Jünschke, had been identified by a witness to the robbery, all of the terrorists appeared to have got away with, quite literally, murder.

At this point, though it was abundantly clear that the SPK were still operative, it was also apparent that many of their number had begun aligning themselves with the RAF, which was a much larger, more high-profile outfit. In 1972, the RAF decided to mount a 'May Offensive', which included the staging of not one but a string of major terrorist events over a two-week period. Two US military bases were attacked, as were police stations in two of Germany's biggest cities and the offices of Axel Springer, who owned most of Germany's conservative tabloids. The first bombing (carried out by, among others, Andreas Baader and Gudrun Ensslin) took place at the Headquarters of the US Fifth Army in Frankfurt and killed one soldier while injuring thirteen other American servicemen. The next day, a second bomb exploded,

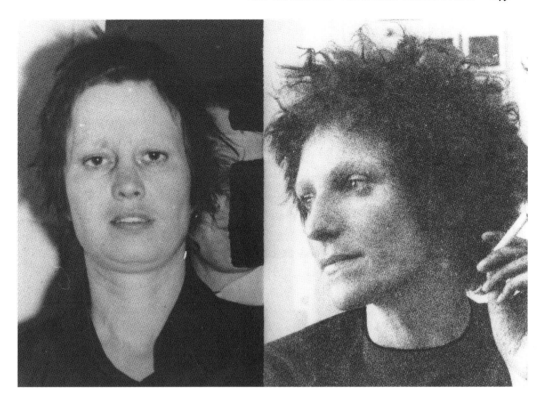

Ulrike Meinhof (left) and Gudrun Ensslin (right) had both enjoyed comfortable, middle-class upbringings, although Meinhof had suffered the trauma of losing both her parents at a very young age. Their privileged lives, however, were something that they certainly had in common with most of their SPK terrorist comrades.

this time outside the Augsburg police station. Fortunately, no one was killed, but the bombing spree was not finished. Later that day yet another bomb exploded next to the Bavarian Federal Police Headquarters in Munich, demolishing at least twenty-five vehicles. Shortly afterwards, the RAF placed a bomb under the car of Wolfgang Buddenberg, a judge who had signed numerous arrest warrants against members of the group. Buddenberg did not get into the car on that day, but his unfortunate wife did, suffering extremely serious injuries in the blast. On May 19 the RAF bombed the Springer corporation offices, an attack that left seventeen workers injured. Finally, on May 24, a car loaded with 400 pounds of TNT was driven into the Headquarters of the US Army Supreme European Command site in Heidelberg, killing three American soldiers and injuring five others.

The RAF presented various 'justifications' for these attacks, but the main cause, so they said, was retaliation for the increased bombing of Vietnam by the United States. They maintained that West Germany should no longer be a safe place from which the American military could operate; indeed, the only way the violence would stop would be if the US withdrew from Vietnam altogether. Ultimately, however, the only people who found themselves unable to operate within Germany were the terrorists, for after the 'May Offensive' the police mounted a massive hunt for all RAF and SPK members. Over 130,000 officers were involved, patrolling the streets, checking border crossings and sifting through the mass of evidence that was coming in from the general public. The pay-off was enormous. In late May in Frankfurt, a resident alerted police, having grown suspicious of three of his neighbors whom he saw mixing an unidentified substance at the back of their house. On June 1, 1972 all three suspects were arrested; Andreas Baader, Holger Meins and Jan-Carl Raspe. The substance they had been mixing was an explosive. On June 7, a shop assistant in Hamburg noticed a young female customer acting suspiciously with what appeared to be a heavy object secreted in her handbag. Again, the police were alerted and the woman, Gudrun Ensslin, was placed under arrest. The object in her bag turned out to be a gun. Finally, on June 15, the authorities captured yet another major Red Army Faction player. The previous evening, a left-wing teacher had received a visit from a friend asking if he could accommodate two acquaintances for a short period. The teacher, though suspicious, agreed, and let the two stay, but later decided to call the police who immediately placed the apartment under surveillance. The next day one of the two guests, Gerhard Müller, left the apartment to use a telephone booth outside on the street, only to be pounced on by several officers, who then also placed the second fugitive, Ulrike Meinhof, under arrest. At first the police were unaware of the identity of either of their captives, and although they soon worked out who Müller was, it took a little longer to establish Meinhof's identity.

There were no previous fingerprints from Meinhof to match up with those of their new captive but the police found an old copy of *Stern* magazine in which an article on Meinhof had appeared, accompanied by a photograph. The photograph was of an X-ray of her skull taken after an operation she had undergone back in 1962, when a metal clip was placed over an engorged blood vessel. The police now took an X-ray of their captive's skull and, on comparing the two, found they were identical. The authorities were ecstatic. They had captured one of Germany's most wanted terrorists. To cap it all, three weeks later they arrested Irmgard Möller and Klaus Jünschke.

It was at this time that a subtle change occurred within the RAF, SPK and even the '2 June Movement' in that, rather than using their aggression as a protest against the Federal Republic and the United States governments, their terrorist activities were instead increasingly tied to the release of their comrades and to their hatred of the judicial system. With practically all of the RAF's main players in prison, those left behind became known as second-generation terrorists – men and women who weren't active during the late 1960s, but who were nonetheless determined to carry on the fight. And one subject exercised their minds more than any other – what they saw as the systematic mistreatment of their imprisoned colleagues.

For much of the time the detainees were kept in solitary confinement – a policy that took its toll on many prisoners, including Astrid Proll, who had been arrested in May 1971. Proll spent nearly five months in almost complete isolation in the Women's Psychiatric Section of the prison. Starved of any kind of mental stimulation, confined to a bare white room with no pictures on the walls, with no one to talk to and with barely any outside noise to listen to, her treatment was likened to shock therapy.

Meinhof was also kept under similar conditions, for a period of eight long months, during which she wrote a poem, 'From the Dead Tract' ('Aus dem Toten Trakt') that put into words the extreme torture such a punishment exacted. 'You can no longer identify the meaning of words,' she wrote. 'Visits leave behind no trace.'

Margrit Schiller, who was serving out a long stretch in Lübeck prison, believed she too was in the 'dead tract' and if there was any doubt as to how severe this punishment truly was, one only has to refer to an account by Heinz Brandt, (a survivor of Auschwitz) who in addition to his time in a concentration camp had also suffered long periods of solitary confinement in East Germany where he was imprisoned over a period of some years.

> As crass and paradoxical as it may sound, my experiences with strict, radical isolation were worse than my time...in a Nazi concentration camp . . . [in] the camp, I still had the basis for human life, namely communication with my fellow inmates . . . We were able in the camps to see, not only outrageously fascistic and sadistic mistreatment, but also the possibilities for resistance and collective life among the prisoners, and, with this, for the fulfillment of the fundamental need of a human being: social existence.[7]

So severe was the treatment that the inmates' only recourse was to stage a series of hunger strikes, starting in January 1973. These were extremely tough times for the detainees, but in respect of their mistreatment and their fight to improve prison conditions they were at least supported by their respective attorneys, and by legal organizations such as the 'Committees Against Isolation Torture in the Prisons of the FRG.'

Now a new fight began – trying to forcefeed those prisoners who were refusing to eat. Doctors strapped inmates to their beds, clamped their mouths open and pushed tubes down their throats and nostrils into their stomachs. Again, SPK member Margrit Schiller was subjected to this institutionalized violence, stating that some doctors and prison guards were deliberately brutal in their technique, often leaving her and her fellow protestors bruised and bloodied.

Meanwhile, outside the prisons, ex-SPK members who had now fully integrated with the Red Army Faction mounted further guerrilla activities, most of which were designed to bring about the release of their comrades.

On November 10, 1974, the Federal Republic's Supreme Court President, Günter von Drenkmann, was killed in a botched kidnap attempt. Then, on April 24, 1975, several former SPK members stormed the West German Embassy in

Stockholm, Sweden, taking twelve hostages. Among the terrorists were: Siegfried Hauser, Hanne-Elise Krabbe, Karl-Heinz Dellwo, Lutz Taufer, Bernhard-Maria Rossner and Ullrich Wessel. They ushered their hostages – who included the Ambassador and the economics, military, cultural and press attachés to the embassy – into the library, then searched the rest of the building for remaining staff members, completely missing one of the secretaries who had hidden in a cupboard inside Room 306.

While all this was occurring, Swedish police, having been alerted to the situation, immediately moved into the ground floor of the embassy where they set up an operational center. This angered the terrorists to the point that they demanded the police withdraw otherwise they would shoot one of the hostages – the military attaché, Lieutenant Colonel Baron Andreas von Mirbach. The police refused and the terrorists bound Mirbach's hands before leading him towards the top of the upper-floor stairwell, where they shot him, first in the leg, then in the head and chest, throwing him towards the police who dragged the dying man away. The authorities quickly evacuated the ground floor and took up a less antagonistic position outside the building.

With the police out of the way, the terrorists decided to place massive amounts of TNT explosive in the embassy's basement. They then made contact with a German press agency and informed them of their demands. First and foremost, they wanted twenty-six of the Baader-Meinhof terrorists (including Gudrun Ensslin, Andreas Baader and Ulrike Meinhof) released. Back in Germany, however, the government, led by Chancellor Helmut Schmidt, was not prepared to be blackmailed by the terrorists and made it clear that they would not negotiate. This attitude prompted the terrorists to state that they would begin to execute one hostage every hour until the government started to release their friends. One hour passed by and nothing happened, but then Doctor Heinz Hillegart, the embassy's economic attaché, was taken to a window and shot in the back. The attaché's body was left hanging out of the window, a sign for everyone watching not to take the terrorists' threats lightly.

What happened next was a freak accident. A short-circuit in the electrical wiring of the detonators caused some of the TNT in the basement to explode and two of the terrorists died. The others survived the explosion but in the ensuing mayhem were swiftly captured by the police. Terrorist Siegfried Hausner, who had suffered terrible burns after the TNT explosion, was flown directly to Stammheim Prison's hospital wing, but died a few days later from his injuries.

In total the siege had lasted ten days, during which time two hostages had been killed and three terrorists had died. Some of the hostages later claimed that they had formed 'friendships' with their captors and even felt a certain sympathy for their cause. This was not an emotion shared by the majority of people living in Germany where, on May 21, 1975, the trial of Baader, Ensslin, and Jan-Carl Raspe began.

Spelling the beginning of the end of the Baader-Meinhof SPK movement, this trial ran for nearly two years, ending in April 1977 when the defendants were collectively found guilty of four murders and twenty-seven attempted murders, and of establishing an illegal criminal organization – for which they were each given life sentences. Shortly afterwards, Baader, Raspe and Ensslin all committed suicide in their cells in Stammheim prison, although controversy continues to surround the exact circumstances of their deaths, with some preferring to believe that the suicides were somehow 'staged' to cover up the unlawful killing of the prisoners. Ulrike Meinhof, who had been tried in 1974 for her part in the freeing of Baader and who had received an eight-year sentence, hadn't fared much better, for on May 9, 1976 she was found hanging in her cell, also the apparent victim of suicide.

Although terrorist activities continued for several years after their deaths, the heart had been ripped out of the beast. Support for the movement gradually petered out. Ironically, given both the SPK and the RAF's left-wing agendas, the effect their actions had on West Germany as a whole was quite the opposite to that which they had intended, with the electorate taking an increasingly conservative stance. Today, with East and West Germany reunited, for many the idea of following any kind of left-wing or communist philosophy would be simply unthinkable.

[1] *Bringing the War Home*, Jeremy Varon, University of California Press, 2004.

[2] *Der Baader Meinhof Komplex* (*The Baader Meinhof Group*), Stefan Aust, Hoffman & Campe (Germany), 1985.

[3] *Hitler's Children: The Story of the Baader-Meinhof Gang*, Jillian Becker, Lippincott, 1977.

[4] Ibid.

[5] Ibid.

[6] 'Die Rote Armee aufbauen,' *833*.

[7] *Bringing the War Home*, op. cit.

THE THUGS – WORSHIPERS OF KALI

I have never heard of such atrocities, or presided over such
trials, such cold-blooded murders, such heart-rending scenes of
distress, and misery; such base ingratitude; such a total
abandonment of the very principle which binds man to man;
which softens the heart and elevates mankind above the brute
creation . . . mercy to such wretches would be the extreme of
cruelty to mankind . . . blood for blood.

F. C. SMITH,
Agent to the Governor-General of India, Calcutta, 1832

In the year 1839, Queen Victoria, who had always been fascinated by the more
Oriental reaches of her empire, received information that a novel was to be
published, the main subject of which concerned an horrific account of an
Indian secret society whose aim was the ritual murder and robbery of unwitting
travelers. Summoning the publisher, Richard Bentley, to the palace, Queen Victoria
demanded that page proofs be sent her immediately. Bentley acquiesced and the
first few chapters of what would later become known as *Confessions of a Thug* by
Colonel Philip Meadows Taylor – a colonial officer stationed in Hyderabad at the
time of the Thuggee killings – were dispatched.

The story revolved around a character called Ameer Ali (said to be based upon
a real-life criminal called Feringheea) who strangles his way to fame and fortune by
killing a large number of women, a few of whom he falls in love with, a few of whom
he doesn't, but all of whom end up dead. Naturally, given the sensational subject
matter and the exotic cruelty, from the moment the book was published it became
a bestseller, enthralling the British reading public within the first few lurid pages.
The book also catapulted the word 'thug' – from the Hindi word *t'ag* meaning
deceiver – into the English language.

Although Queen Victoria might not have been aware of this group prior to
publication of the novel, the Thugs, or Thuggee, had been mentioned in literature
before, the earliest authenticated case being around 1356 in a passage from Ziya'-
ud-Din Baran's *History of Firuz Shah*:

> In the reign of that sultan, some Thugs were taken in Delhi, and a man
> belonging to that fraternity was the means of about a thousand being
> captured. But not one of these did the sultan have killed. He gave
> orders for them to be put into boats and to be conveyed into the lower

country, to the neighborhood of Lakhnauti, where they were to be set
free. The Thugs would thus have to dwell about Lakhnauti and would
not trouble the neighborhood of Delhi any more.[1]

Before 1839 several mentions of the Thugs had also been made in England. John
Fryer wrote of their existence towards the end of the seventeenth century and in
1833 George Swinton, the Chief Secretary to the Government of India, sent seven
severed heads to Edinburgh for forensic examination. It was thought the heads all
belonged to Thug members and after extensive tests were carried out the examiners
concluded that each of the skulls revealed remarkable characteristics usually seen
only in criminals. 'The mass of the posterior and basilar regions is large,' stated the
report, 'the coronal region is too small to enable the moral faculties to exercise
sufficient restraint over the propensities; and hence the natural tendencies of the
individuals were to selfish and immoral courses of action.'[2] All of this guaranteed
that the Thugs continued to fascinate Victorian England, particularly with stories of
human sacrifices being made to the Hindu goddess of destruction, Kali. Popular
publications such as *Blackwood's Magazine* and the *Quarterly Review* printed stories
outlining everything then known about the cult of the Thugs, while the author Jules
Verne mentioned the Thugs in his book *Around the World in Eighty Days*,[2] but if
anyone was in any doubt as to how far-reaching the news of this notorious sect was,
the following account by Mark Twain should set the record straight:

> Fifty years ago, when I was a boy in the then remote and sparsely
> peopled Mississippi valley, vague tales and rumors of a mysterious
> body of professional murderers came wandering in from a country
> which was constructively as far from us as the constellations blinking
> in space – India; vague tales and rumors of a sect called Thugs, who
> waylaid travelers in lonely places and killed them for the contentment
> of a god whom they worshiped; tales which everybody liked to listen to
> and nobody believed, except with reservations.[3]

Yet, though it seemed that 'nobody believed' in these tales, the exoticism of the
stories nevertheless complemented the West's romantic, overblown vision of
Oriental life and what it meant to live on such a dark and terrible continent where
an abundance of gods were worshiped, all of whom were, according to the politician
and anti-slavery campaigner, William Wilberforce, in 1813, 'absolute monsters of
lust, injustice, wickedness and cruelty.' A little less than a decade later, Captain
William Sleeman began making the first of his enquiries into the murder of several
travelers whose bodies had been located in a series of shallow graves. They had all
been strangled. It was Sleeman, in fact, who first alerted the Western world to the
existence of India's Thug cult, although his very staid and factual reports were soon
reworked by the general press in order to satisfy their readers' taste for the
sensational. Victorian England thirsted for tales of dark and terrible deeds –
especially those committed in the far-flung reaches of Empire. They thrilled to
stories of Indian widows practicing suttee; the ritual of burning themselves to death

This striking depiction of the goddess Kali clearly shows her famous necklace of skulls and girdle of severed arms, embellished here with a few recently-severed heads, but looking far more vigorous than the corpse-like creature often used to represent her.

on their husbands' funeral pyres. In literature, stretching as far back as the sixteenth and seventeenth centuries, and nearly every inclusion of an Oriental character made mention of their criminal and sexually aberrant nature. The Oriental was to be mistrusted, treated with scepticism, kept at arm's length, although in the same breath he was also painted as being highly alluring and mysterious – the type of person who, while plotting your murder, would simultaneously befriend you. Nowhere is this more apparent than in Captain Philip Meadows Taylor's novel which Queen Victoria had been so eager to read:

> Gradually my band arranged themselves around their new victims. All were at their places, and I eagerly looked out for the first scout who should give us intelligence that the *bhil* was ready. A strange feeling it is, Sahib, that comes over us Thugs at such moments: not a feeling of interest or pity for our victims, or compunction for the deed we are about to do, as perhaps you might expect to hear, but an all-absorbing anxiety for the issue of the adventure, an intense longing for its consummation, and a dread of interruption from passing travelers; and though I had become now callous in a great measure, still my heart was throbbing with anxiety and apprehension, and my replies to the Sahoukar's witty and jolly remarks were vague and abstracted; my whole thoughts were concentrated upon the affair in hand, and it was not to be wondered at. He remarked on my altered behavior, and I rallied myself, and was soon able to amuse him as I had done before.

But at what point did fiction separate from fact? How much of Meadows Taylor's sensational novel was based on truth? The answer is, quite a substantial part, for although the more exotic side of his story owes a fair amount to the novelist's vivid imagination, nothing can really prepare one for the enormity of the Thug crimes. Setting aside the lurid nature of the murders themselves, the sheer number of Thuggee victims is astonishing – estimated at anything between one and three million over a period of 100 years – and underlines the fact that what was taking place in India during this period was a 'religion of murder,' a deep-rooted belief system that demanded blood be shed. At its center sat the Hindu goddess Kali.[4]

The name Kali derives from the Sanskrit word for 'time' or 'dark'; but it is also supposed to mean Black Female, which is quite appropriate considering the nature of her influence. Cemeteries, blood and skulls are all associated with her worship, while in paintings she is represented as a black woman with an azure face, often streaked with yellow. Frequently her hair is braided with green serpents and she wears a long necklace of human skulls, a girdle of severed arms and worst of all, sometimes babies' corpses as earrings (although these are supposed to represent infant mortality as opposed to the murder of infants.) In nearly all representations of Kali, her mouth is shown to be bleeding and her tongue is often poking out as if in some gesture of defiance. Kali's eight arms normally brandish weapons or sometimes the severed head of a demon. Despite all this gruesomeness however, in southern India and in Kashmiri tradition, Kali is not an evil deity, but a curious kind of life force. Indeed her law-abiding devotees (as opposed to her murderous ones) have built a vast amount of beautiful poetry around her, often depicting the goddess as a tender, loving mother. To this end she has had temples built in her name, in particular in Kolkata, west Bengal, and in Kamakhya in Assam. All of the above is well documented, but in his book *Thug, Or a Million Murders*, William Sleeman's grandson, Colonel James L. Sleeman, reveals how it was that Kali became linked with the Thuggee to the extent that she did.

> According to Thug legend, there was a time when the world was pestered by a terrible demon whose main aim was to devour mankind. As fast as children were born so the demon ate them. Kali tried to put a stop to this murder by killing the demon with a sword, but every time she struck it and blood was spilt, up sprang a new demon, [. . .] until the hellish brood multiplied to such a degree that she realised the impossibility of completing her task unaided. In this dilemma Bhowani [Kali] brushed the sweat from her arm and from it created two men, to each of whom she gave a strip of cloth, torn from the hem of her garment, and commanded them to strangle the demons, thus overcoming the blood difficulty. These legendary progenitors of Thuggee worked with such skill and vigor that soon all the demons were slain, and the goddess gave the *ruhmal*, or strip of cloth, as a reward for their assistance, bidding them transmit it to their posterity with the injunction to destroy all men who were not of their kindred.[5]

James L. Sleeman then goes on to explain that although this perpetrated a 'cult of murder,' there were certain rules which had to be adhered to; for instance, it was unlawful to kill women or those suffering from leprosy. Fakirs were also off limits as were religious mendicants, goldsmiths, potters, dancers and musicians. Nevertheless, over a period of time, the Thugs slowly began to ignore these laws and soon any traveler, be they female or otherwise, was a potential Thug victim.

By the nineteenth century, nearly 40,000 deaths were being recorded each year as a result of Thug activity, although by this time the religious significance of the slaughter had all but disappeared. Straightforward robbery was now the motive, clear-cut murder with the intention of stripping the victim of his or her valuables. Many Thugs grew rich on their spoils and became influential citizens whose veneer of respectability deflected suspicion. Indeed, when they weren't committing murder the Thugs were model citizens who, Sleeman Jnr. points out, were more often than not, committed to their families, to the rearing of their children and to the supporting of their wives. To illustrate this, Sleeman Snr. recorded the case of an Englishman, Dr. Cheek, who employed a young Indian bearer to look after his children. The man was exceptionally good at his job, gentle and kind to the children and every year took one month's holiday in order to visit his elderly mother. Later however, it was discovered that this man was a Thug and that while he was an

An unnamed artist created this image of Thugs in captivity in a prison in Aurungabad for the Illustrated Travels *journal around 1860.*

exemplary employee for eleven months of the year, during the twelfth he devoted his time to strangulation.

William Henry Sleeman made meticulous investigations into crimes such as this, becoming an expert in the cult. Much of the information to which we are privy stems directly from his involvement with the hunting down and subsequent trial and execution of these villains. It was Sleeman Snr. who calculated the figure of 40,000 murders per year by patiently interviewing all the captured Thugs whom he quickly discovered belonged to several generations of the cult and of whose crimes his present-day prisoners were extremely proud.

It was family tradition and therefore this made it possible for Sleeman to calculate the number of murders which had been committed by the fathers, grandfathers and great-grandfathers of his prisoners. One Thug in particular, by the name of Gholam Hossyn, believed his lineage stretched as far back as Alexander the Great and Sleeman recorded in some detail the type of rituals his prisoners' ancestors performed before and after each killing.

A typical Thug murder, according to Sleeman, would have run thus: first of all a gang of Thugs (anywhere between 10 to 200 men) would befriend their prospective victim or victims by pretending to be merchants or soldiers traveling without weaponry in order to waylay any suspicions the target might harbor. The Thugs would then travel alongside their victims, cooking for them, assisting with campsite chores, telling them stories and generally acting in as courteous a manner as possible, until everyone felt at their ease. The journeys could take as long as two weeks or more for, as Sleeman Jnr. explains, 'Sometimes they traveled long distances together before a suitable opportunity for treachery occurred; a case is on record where a gang journeyed with a family of eleven persons for twenty days, covering 200 miles, before they succeeded in murdering the whole party without detection.'[6] The next step would normally take place at night, around the campfires while everyone was mingling together, telling each other stories, smoking, drinking and singing. This was the time when the Thugs would drug their targets and once the drugs had taken effect and at a pre-arranged signal – normally a code phrase such as 'bring the tobacco' – they would then whip out their *ruhmals* (handkerchiefs weighted with stones) and strangle their prey. The murders would be very swift, with the stones in the *ruhmals* breaking the victims' necks. Afterwards the Thugs would dedicate the corpses to Kali and more often than not hold a sacrificial feast of consecrated *gur* (an unrefined sugar believed to increase the desire for Thuggee) which, or so legend would have it, once tasted would ensure a Thug's dedication to murder for the rest of his life. The feast would carry on late into the night after which the bodies would be gathered together and buried before the thieves made off with their spoils.

The Thugs were also, according to Sleeman, highly superstitious, believing that Kali could communicate and express her wishes to them through the cries of wild animals. Lizards, jackals, crows, cranes and especially baby owls, were those to which they paid particular attention.

Sleeman goes on to describe how members of the group would often be given specialized roles. According to him, new recruits to the cult would be given the role of scouts, or *bykureeas*, and once they had mastered this role they rose to the position of buriers of the dead, or *lughas*. Both roles were very important, but the top two jobs were as the holders of limbs (while the victim was being strangled) otherwise known as *shumseeas*, and finally the stranglers, or *bhurtotes*, the most highly regarded position of all. In fact belonging to the Thugs was like being part of an army in that it was a highly disciplined organization where everyone knew their place and role.

Fascinated by the nature of Thuggee, Sleeman interviewed hundreds of the Thugs in an attempt to understand their cult more deeply. In one interview, he asked the detainee how he could murder innocent men, women and children and then speak of these crimes with such nonchalance?

> Sahib Khan: From the time that the omens have been favorable, we
> consider them as victims thrown into our hands by the deity to be

killed, and that we are the mere instruments in her hands to destroy them; that if we do not kill them she will never be again propitious to us, and our families will be involved in misery and want.

Sleeman: And you can sleep as soundly by the bodies, or over the graves of those you have murdered, and eat your meals with as much appetite as ever?

Sahib Khan: Just the same, unless we are afraid of being discovered.

Sleeman, however, wasn't the only Englishman fascinated by Thuggee. On April 28, 1810, Major-General St. Leger issued a directive from HQ Cawnpore to the effect that, 'Several Sepoys [an Indian soldier in European service] proceeding to visit their families on leave of absence from their Corps have been robbed and murdered by a description of persons denominated Thugs . . . these murderers contrive to fall in with him [the traveler] on the road or in the Sarais . . . they first use some deleterious substance, commonly the seeds of the plant Duttora, which they contrive to administer in tobacco, pawn, the hookah, food or drink of the Traveler. As soon as the poison begins to take effect, by inducing a stupor or languor, they strangle him.'[7]

In the same year that St. Leger wrote this report, another mass murder also took place, this time on the road between Nagpur and Nerbudda. A large group of approximately 350 Thugs befriended a party of travelers, joining them on their journey between the locations mentioned above. Regaling their companions with stories and other entertainments, the Thugs easily manipulated their new friends into believing them to be nothing more than fellow travelers. With their defences down the travelers made easy prey. One night having eaten and drunk around the campfires, the Thugs rose up as one at a given signal and strangled their companions en masse. Rather than ritual murder for the purposes of religious worship, it was most certainly money that lay at the heart of this crime, for the Thugs made away with 17,000 rupees, a small fortune in those days and far and away a large enough sum to guarantee this crime stood out from numerous others. Twenty years later, the murder was still at the forefront of public consciousness, making it one of the very first that Captain William Henry Sleeman decided to investigate.

Born on August 8, 1788 in Stratton, Cornwall, to a military father, from a very young age William Henry Sleeman had always wanted to join the army. An able student, he had studied both Arabic and Hindustani in England before he went to work for the army of the Honorable East India Company in 1809. Initially Sleeman was posted to the 12th Native Infantry at Awadh before being appointed in 1819 as Junior Assistant to the Government Agent in the Saugor and Nerbudda Territories, during which time he continued to study Oriental languages and made it his duty to familiarize himself with the often confusing complexities of the numerous sects and cults of India. Sleeman became fascinated with the Hindu practice of worshiping the goddess Kali, Shiva's consort, who it was said haunted burial grounds and fed off human blood.

In 1816, following the accounts given by Major-General St. Leger (of which Sleeman must have been well aware,) there appeared an article in the *Madras Literary Gazette* written by a Dr. Robert C. Sherwood who had also grown increasingly fascinated by tales of a mysterious society of assassins murdering travelers in the name of Kali. Sleeman's resolve was set: his life's work was to be the eradication of the Thuggee and despite initial reservations of his superiors, Sleeman was eventually appointed magistrate in charge of the Nursingpore District. Now he had the power to realize his dreams.

The work, however, was very slow. Sleeman had to travel from one small town to the next hearing cases while at the same time methodically gathering information from those willing to talk. Not an easy task when the majority of people were far too frightened of the Thugs to stand as witnesses against them. Even then, as Sleeman wrote, he was still not convinced that the secret society of Thuggee even existed.

> While I was in charge of the district of Nursingpore in the years 1822, 1823 and 1824, no ordinary robbery or theft could be committed without my being acquainted with it; nor was there a robber or thief of the ordinary kind in the district with whose character I had not become acquainted in the discharge of my duty as magistrate; and if any man had then told me that a gang of assassins by profession resided in the village of Kundelee – not four hundred yards from my court – and that the extensive groves of Mundesur – only one stage from me – was one of the greatest *beles* or places of murder in all India . . . I should have thought him a fool or madman.

As time passed, however, Sleeman began to assemble a detailed picture of Thuggee and its practitioners. Thuggee, he discovered, was primarily a hereditary system associated with Hindus and Muslims that transcended both religion and caste. Although the cult revolved around the fanatical worship of the goddess Kali, not all Kali devotees were Thugs. Sleeman estimated that there were at least 5,000 Thugs in India. The cult was obviously ancient, and Sleeman suggested that a cryptic mention by Herodotus of a people (the Sagartians) in central Asia proficient in strangling with a cord might possibly refer to a source of Thuggee more than two millennia earlier. The Thugs themselves believed that their activities were depicted in eighth-century cave temple carvings at Ellora, Maharashtra, but such carvings have never been found. What has been established is that during the Sultan of Delhi's (Jalal-ud-din-Khilji) reign in the thirteenth century, approximately one thousand so-called Thugs were detained and afterwards deported from Delhi to Bengal. Sleeman worked tirelessly, gathering historical facts, interviewing suspects, and traveling from town to town listening to stories; yet it wasn't until 1826 that he first had the opportunity to bring any of the Thugs to justice.

One day a group of thieves suspected of possessing a large number of stolen items were brought to the courthouse where Sleeman was working. Sadly for the prosecution, it was decided that there wasn't enough evidence to hold the men and

Ram Luckum Sein, a hereditary Thug of Bengal, is depicted here with his bodyguard in an illustration for the Illustrated News of the World *magazine in 1858.*

later that same day the group was released. Nevertheless, following an argument between two of the arrested men, one of them by the name of Kalyan Singh went to Sleeman begging for protection. In the ensuing interview Singh confessed that the group were Thugs and that they were planning yet another murderous escapade. Without hesitation Sleeman, together with a guard of mounted Sepoys, set off in search of their prey. Nor was it long before they found the men and put them under arrest. Once in custody Sleeman then interrogated one of the group, a man known only as Moti (Pearl) who finally confessed to having buried four victims in a spot near to where the group had been arrested. On returning to this location Sleeman found the bodies of three men and a young boy, all of whom had had their necks broken and their bodies pierced with knives so that the corpses wouldn't bloat up. The following morning, more bodies were discovered, some of which were identified by neighboring villagers. But more appalling even than this – when the arrested Thugs were later interviewed it quickly became apparent that among their number were a government messenger and a police inspector. Sleeman realized to his shock that the Thug cult could count among its members not only ruffians and vagabonds, but also a fair quota of otherwise respectable citizens.

The Thug, Moti, also gave a highly detailed account of further crimes he had committed, in particular the murder of a high-ranking clerk and his family during 1823. The clerk had been traveling the Nagpur road when Moti and his gang befriended him. For a time the group all traveled together until one evening while everyone was drowsing off to sleep Moti wrapped his *ruhmal* round the clerk's throat. The clerk struggled with his attacker and managed to shout out the word 'Murder!' before Moti killed him. Alerted by her husband's cry, his wife ran from her tent, but was attacked by one of Moti's gang and killed, as was her oldest child, while the youngest one, who was still just a baby, was thrown into its parents' grave and buried alive. Horrific as this murder seems, it was only one of numerous such incidents. James Paton, an officer who also worked in India during this period, produced many startling watercolours depicting Thug crimes, pictures that included Thugs gouging out the eyes of their victims, and strangling and dismembering bodies before throwing them into graves. Paton was not, of course, present at any of the incidents he illustrated and his pictures must, therefore, be viewed as 'imaginings', but they do stand as strong testimony to the fear that Thuggee culture produced.

Sleeman was the antidote, a one-man Victorian crusade, battling against overwhelming odds although in 1828, with the appointment of Lord William Cavendish Bentinck as Governor-General of British India, he was finally afforded some moral support. Despite his exhaustive endeavors against the Thuggee, Sleeman still found time for a little romance in his life and in 1829 he married Amélie de Fontenne whom he had first met on Mauritius.

Aside from his private life, week after week Sleeman aggressively pursued his mission of arresting Thug members, initially incarcerating them in Saugor Jail, until he began to find 'approvers' among them; men who would act as informers and point Sleeman in the direction of their victims' graves. In exchange, these approvers would have their death sentences commuted to life imprisonment. Suddenly, Sleeman was receiving a flood of information and every week more and more trials were held, with more and more executions for those found guilty.

Doctor Spry, the governor of Saugor Jail, relates the fate of one group of convicts, who were to be put to death on the following morning:

> The night was passed by these men in displays of coarse and disgusting levity. Trusting in the assurance that, dying in the cause of their calling, Bhawani would provide for them in Paradise, they evinced neither penitence nor remorse. Stifling their alarm with boisterous reveling, they hoped to establish in the minds of their comrades, who could hear them through the wall, a reputation for courage, by means which at once proved their insincerity and belied their fortitude. Imagine such men on the last night of their existence on earth, not penitent for their individual errors, or impressed with a sense of the public mischiefs to which they had contributed, not even rendered serious by the dismal ordeal which in a few hours was to usher them into an unknown world, but singing, singing in the condemned cell, and repeating their unhallowed carols while jolting along in the carts that conveyed them to their gibbets!

The above account is just one of many detailing the numerous executions resulting from William Sleeman's arrests. It is believed that during the 1830s and 1840s Sleeman, together with seventeen loyal assistants and over 100 sepoys, captured and subsequently prosecuted approximately 3,000 Thugs of whom 470 were put to death by hanging. The others were either transported to different provinces or were imprisoned for life. But there was one name which kept cropping up in interviews with the 'approvers' that both fascinated and concerned Sleeman above all others: the name of Feringeea.

Feringeea was said to be the Prince of Thuggee, the jewel in the tainted crown of Kali's bloodthirsty cult. Knowing that in order to eradicate Thuggee altogether, Feringeea had to be arrested, Sleeman sent out a large party of sepoys to track him down only to be disappointed when they returned without their quarry. Instead, they arrested Feringeea's mother, wife and child. This was a clever move, for a few days later Feringeea turned himself in and immediately begged to turn 'approver.' His offer was accepted and for long days and nights Sleeman interviewed this chief of Thugs, eliciting huge amounts of information on the nature of his crimes. But even Sleeman had his limits and, although he had proved to be stalwart in his campaign against terror, eventually either the pace of the work, or the nature of it, began to take its toll. In 1849 he was moved to a different post; this time as Resident in Awadh. Even here, however, Sleeman's health suffered until, in 1854 he was told that if he didn't leave India, he would undoubtedly die. Taking his doctor's advice, he and his wife set sail on board the *Monarch* in January 1856, but as the ship approached the coast of Ceylon, Sleeman's health deteriorated and on February 10 he died.

Almost as a tribute to the massive effort he had expended in pursuit of the Thugs, others stepped forward to carry on Sleeman's work until, having been more or less suppressed, the 600-year-old cult (possibly with far older links) of Thuggee eventually disappeared altogether. It was not a sad downfall, although given that one man was almost single-handedly responsible for it, it was perhaps a surprising one. In many ways Captain William Sleeman should be regarded as a true Victorian hero, battling as he did against one of the most evil secret societies ever known.

[1] *The History of India as told by its own historians*, Sir H. M. Elliot, New Delhi, 1996.

[2] *Children of Kali*, Kevin Rushby, Constable & Robinson, 2002.

[3] *Following the Equator: A Journey Around the World*, Mark Twain (1897), Dover Publications, 1989.

[4] Although Kali is a Hindu deity, there were also Muslim Thugs roaming the country, committing murder as well.

[5] *Thug, or A Million Murders*, Colonel James L. Sleeman, Sampson Low, Marston & Co., 1933.

[6] Ibid.

[7] *Children of Kali*, op. cit.

THE CAMORRA –
A SHADOW OVER
NAPLES

Naples is a Third World city with Third World politics. It's super-
rich surrounded by a miserable hinterland sprawling back from
the volcano and the bay, a dilapidated jungle of violence, half-
finished buildings, motorways that lead nowhere, cocaine,
primitive Catholicism and stinking dumped rubbish [. . .] There is
vast private wealth in the city – at night the downtown streets are
crammed with new cars, mobile phones and fur coats – but this is
illegal wealth, the result of the most important ingredient of the
Neapolitan scandal: the Camorra.

ED VULLIAMY, the *Guardian*, March 29, 1993

Pre-dating the Mafia by several decades, some historians have argued that the Camorra is a direct descendent of an obscure, fifteenth-century Spanish secret society called the Garduna. A more convincing theory is that the Camorra first began operating some time between the end of the eighteenth and beginning of the nineteenth centuries, mainly in Naples, amongst the poorest sections of society who were nearly all illiterate, hence there being very few written documents recording the origins of this largely criminal organization. What isn't in doubt is that Naples, because it was one of Europe's largest cities during this period, was also one of its most over-populated. There wasn't enough work to ensure everyone enjoyed a living wage, a situation which in turn bred extreme poverty and hardship for large sections of the Neapolitan population. But whereas the middle classes during this period banded together to form some of the most powerful secret societies known to history, such as the Freemasons and the Carboneria, for the majority of Neapolitans there was no such help at hand. Instead the rich grew richer, while the poor remained penniless; an economic reality exacerbated by the actions of the king of the region, Ferdinand II, who reigned from 1830 to 1859. However, Ferdinand was not a man of the people, particularly the poor whom he regarded as being the lowest of the low. Contemporary historian Marco Monnier wrote:

> He never considered for a moment raising the people up from their level
> of degradation; on the contrary, he wanted to keep them there until the
> end of time as he knew very well that, given the nature of the period we
> live in, an absolute monarchy is only possible if it rules over a degraded
> and exhausted populace.[1]

Conditions were rife, therefore, for the emergence of an organization specifically tailored to the needs of the downtrodden, although the Camorra's name doesn't appear on any official documentation until 1820, when a written statute of a Camorra organization was made. This revealed a structured society complete with initiation rites, rules, regulations and funds, operating at the heart of the Neapolitan underworld.

Initially the Camorra appears to have made its greatest inroads into society through small monopolies, which it set up within the prison system. Once again the historian Marco Monnier is invaluable by giving us a marvelous portrait of an inmate's complicated relationship with the Camorra. Monnier states that the inmate would not be allowed either to eat, drink or gamble without the permission of a camorrista (a Camorra member), while a tenth of all the money an inmate received in jail – with which he could buy food and tobacco – had to be given to the camorrista. Failure to abide by these rules could result in the 'risk of being clubbed to death.' On top of this, the prison authorities would also pay the Camorra a fee for keeping the prisoners under control.

It was all very lucrative and within the space of only a few years the Camorra's influence grew to include money from gambling and theft as well as a substantial rake-off from all the goods being exported and imported through Naples. The Camorra also set itself up in the role of the police. This was especially true in the less salubrious neighborhoods of Naples where they wielded the greatest influence. In short, during King Ferdinand's reign the Camorra made itself an integral part of city life, the only true representative of the city's poor. It was, of course, in no way a political organization, simply one that existed to make money.

All this was to change, however, when in 1860 Giuseppe Garibaldi landed in Sicily with one aim in mind; the unification of Italy under one ruler. As he moved from Sicily to southern Italy and onwards up the country, chaos broke out in Naples as the Bourbon king (by this time Francis II had taken on the role) attempted to quell the public's enthusiasm for Garibaldi's success, but to little avail. Soon, what few policemen there were left began breaking their ranks and joining the mob. The old order was collapsing, and on June 26 a state of siege was declared. A new Prefect of Police was elected, Liborio Romano, who immediately turned to the Camorra – one of whom, Salvatore De Crescenzo, had been convicted six times – to reinstate some sort of order over the masses. Crescenzo's former crimes (which included murder) didn't seem to matter to Romano, as long as he and his colleagues could keep control over the city. The plan worked; order was brought to the streets and the king fled Naples prior to the arrival of Garibaldi.

The Camorra were now in a semi-official position, acting as the city's main police force, a position they quickly turned into a lucrative enterprise by moving into the contraband industry, often forcing shopkeepers to buy smuggled goods, albeit at incredibly low prices. This meant that the city's tax revenue took a substantial plunge, but the shopkeepers were too frightened to refuse the Camorra's offers.

They chose the lesser of two evils. If they paid a tax to the sect [the Camorra] they only ran the risk of being discovered by tax inspectors and receiving a minor conviction; but if they paid the tax inspectors then they were certain of being caught by camorristi and given a good beating. So they paid a tax to the sect.'[2]

Despite this, the new authorities in Naples did recognize that the Camorra had grown too strong, which was something they were determined to remedy, although by this point the organization was so deeply entrenched in Neopolitan society that it was impossible to destroy altogether. Nevertheless, in the summer of 1862 approximately 1,000 camorristi were rounded up and either placed under house arrest or imprisoned in the city's jail. Over the next forty years the Camorra did experience a general decline as a secret society, mainly due to the city's intolerance of corruption, but also because, at the beginning of the nineteenth century, mass migration took place that deprived the Camorra of their main power base – the urban poor.

By the outbreak of the First World War, the Camorra had been all but wiped out and later, around 1922, with the arrival of Fascism in Italy, those Camorra operatives still working in Naples were quickly quashed. Benito Mussolini's regime was not one that would tolerate organized crime. While stamping out what they saw as insurgents, the Fascists did invite certain sections of the Camorra to join their cause, but this was mainly so that they could monitor the more rural areas of southern Italy and keep them under control. Prior to Mussolini's rise to power, one could almost have divided the country into two separate parts – the industrialized areas and cities to the north such as Milan and Genoa, and the south which still depended largely on agriculture for its main source of income. The gap widened even further after the war, with the south preferring to re-elect old politicians and stick to old ways, one consequence of which was that political corruption reasserted itself very quickly.

In 1943, when the Allies first invaded Sicily during the Second World War, British and American undercover agents set out to make contact with certain 'pro-allied' forces through an intermediary known to most as Lucky Luciano – one of America's leading Mafiosi, who at this time was serving a lengthy prison sentence back in the States for running a prostitution racket. The Allies – through Luciano – appointed several Mafiosi as mayors of a selected number of Sicilian towns, quickly allowing the Mafia to re-establish its stranglehold over Sicily as a whole. Around the same time another Mafiosi operative by the name of Vito Genovese, who had earlier left America to evade an outstanding murder charge against him, settled in Naples from where he began to operate several illegal, but highly lucrative, businesses. One such involved the misappropriation of the Allies' supplies (particularly food), which was later sold on the black market.

But Genovese's crimes weren't the only ones haunting Naples and its environs during this period, for although there were no actual Camorra gangs operating within the city, the fact that the Mafia were making huge profits from their illegal activities

During this trial of a Camorra group in Viterbo in March 1911, the thirty-four accused men were seated in a steel cage to keep them in order. The informer sat in a separate cage for his own safety.

meant that in very small ways new crime organizations began to establish themselves. The Camorra saw to it that the surrounding region of Campania, which comprised mainly farming land, fell under their direct control.

Their influence was particularly strong in rural areas to the north and east of Naples, especially in the rich cattle area around Nola. Sometimes gangs would shoot it out for dominance in a given market; for example, sixty-one murders were committed in the Nola area during 1954-6 alone. They also intimidated farmers who refused their services or protection, normally by burning their crops.[3]

By the mid-1950s the Camorra's influence pervaded all agricultural areas, including that of milk production – a move that in real terms meant huge profits for the organization. Enjoying the steady rise in their influence, camorristi then began laying plans to extend their business practices back into Naples itself. After all, most of the produce they were handling passed through the city at one point or another, so it made perfect sense. Politically, too, the Camorra were once again making huge inroads into the fabric of Neapolitan life. One only has to look to the funeral in 1955 of one of the Camorra's major players, Pascalone 'e Nola, to see this at work, for no less than twelve Neapolitan MPs sent wreaths. But perhaps the area in which the Camorra were going to make their biggest impression over the next several years was in the Mafia-dominated contraband industry.

Cigarette smuggling was big business in the 1950s, as there were huge profits to be made. Initially, the main center for these operations was the free port of Tangiers in northern Africa. When this was closed in 1961, most of the warehouse operations selling cigarettes moved to the Yugoslavian coast, and Naples quickly became one of the world's biggest cigarette-smuggling cities. Naturally, the Mafia controlled a large part of this lucrative pie, but the Camorra weren't far behind, and soon they also became involved in the increasingly popular drug-trafficking industry. Given the large profits to be gained, this latter area inevitably resulted in a great deal of violence and internecine warfare. A notorious example of this was the slaughter of Gennaro Ferrigno (an importer of Peruvian cocaine) by Camorra boss Antonio Spavone in 1971 and, later the following year, the killing of an ex-policeman, Emilio Palamara.

Perhaps one of the most notorious camorrista to emerge from the pile was a man by the name of Michele Zaza (often referred to by the sobriquet 'Mad Mike'). As the son of a fisherman, Zaza came from very humble beginnings, but by dealing in illegal arms and contraband cigarettes (somewhere in the region of 5,000 tons of the stuff per year) he soon made inroads into the Neapolitan underworld, becoming one of the Camorra's most feared leaders. He once boasted to an investigating magistrate:

> I used to load fifty thousand cases [of cigarettes] a month. I could load a hundred thousand cases, $10 million on trust, all I had to do was make a phone call [. . .] I'd buy $24 million worth of Philip Morris in three months, my lawyer will show you the receipts. I'm proud of that $24 million.[4]

For all his wealth and bravado, Zaza was part of the old-style Camorra, a secret society that was soon to be overtaken by the *nuovo camorra organizzata* (NCO), or New Organized Camorra, of Raffaele Cutolo. Cutolo had, for most of his adult life, lived in jail and it was from there that he built up his organization, initially befriending young inmates who were unfamiliar with, and therefore scared of, the prison system. By winning these men's trust, Cutolo soon had a loyal following. He also befriended many inmates who were too poor to buy regular food. Another strategy Cutolo implemented was to organize payments to be made to families of those who were loyal to him inside the prison. Soon Cutolo's NCO had hundreds, if not thousands, of members, not only within the jail where he was incarcerated, but also in other prisons dotted throughout the country. He also had groups of men and women who worked for him on the outside, in towns and cities to the east of Naples such as Ottaviano. Cutolo further distinguished himself from other Camorra leaders by harboring a fierce dislike of the Mafia and any Neapolitans whom he felt were collaborating with these Sicilian thugs. In this manner, he created an extremely loyal following, all of whom identified themselves strongly with Naples and Campania. Cutolo also established a fairly traditional set of values and rules (some of which harked back to the eighteenth-century Camorra), including one that stated children should not, under any circumstances, be kidnapped or abused. This new-style Camorra began to appeal to increasing numbers of disillusioned young men. This testimony from an NCO member describes how he first became aware of the organization:

> I was in Novara jail, and my relatives had come to see me [. . .] when I went back to my cell and sat down on my bed I started to think that everything I had done in my life had been wrong 'cause I had never done anything which was important to me personally. Every single thing I've done was somebody else's idea. I ain't done nothing in my life. I was a peasant, and in 1978 I got arrested for extortion by mistake, but I was innocent. I went to the old Avellino jail, where I got to know certain camorristi. I thought that the Camorra was just.[5]

The time and effort Cutolo spent on his young recruits paid enormous dividends, and he saw to it that large numbers of unemployed, disillusioned, directionless youngsters felt they had something to work towards. By the late 1970s, the NCO was the most active criminal organization in the Neapolitan district. Extortion was their main source of income, followed by cocaine. However, Cutolo was not without rivals and one such competitor proved to be the cause of his eventual downfall. The NF (*nuovo famiglia* or new family) was an alliance built up of all the other Camorra groups to fight against the dominance of Cutolo's NCO, whom everyone agreed had grown too powerful. Frequent battles broke out between the two factions, although it wasn't until the early 1980s that Cutolo's organization really began to suffer, eventually dying out altogether. This was not only down to the in-fighting, but also to the authorities who began cracking down hard on the NCO (who were more infamous and more conspicuous than the NF). Other reasons for the organization's demise included the relative youth and inexperience of its members, which in turn meant that internal disputes usually met with one NCO killing another. Cutolo himself was also debilitated when President Sandro Pertini personally ordered that he be removed from his mainland prison and sent to a maximum-security jail on an island near to Sardinia. This was the last nail in Cutolo's coffin, but if it spelt the end of the NCO, it certainly didn't deter other Camorra groups from expanding their

In 1985 the football field of the Poggioreale Prison was turned into a giant court room when 640 Camorra members went on trial. Also in attendance were 300 lawyers and more than 1,000 policemen.

businesses and growing in influence. An earthquake that devastated the Naples area on November 23, 1980 handed the Camorra a huge opportunity to make money and further inveigle itself into Neapolitan politics and society.

Causing almost 3,000 deaths and 9,000 injuries, the estimated number of people who were made homeless by the earthquake was between 200,000 and 300,000. Massive building programmes were required and the Camorra, who had for decades been positioning themselves within local government, were now in the ideal situation to win construction contracts, siphoning off large amounts of government money in the process. One group involved in the building scams was the Nuvoletta gang, led by the notorious Camorra boss, Lorenzo Nuvoletta, aided by his three brothers, Angelo, Ciro and Gaetano.

Born and brought up within a farming community to the north of Naples, the young Nuvoletta boys soon joined a Camorra group led by Luigi and Enrico Maisto. In the early 1960s, however, bored with being bit-players, they decided to branch out on their own and established themselves as landowners, supplying foodstuffs to both military and government-run establishments such as hospitals. The Nuvolettas made vast amounts of money during this period, not least because they swindled several insurance companies over a variety of false claims. The money they made from this was then ploughed into the setting up of several money-lending establishments, which soon engaged most local businesses as their clients. Heroin was next on the Nuvoletta brothers' agenda; drug smuggling being the easiest way to make vast amounts of money over a relatively short period of time.

Building up their crime empire, of course, was not without its risks. On more than one occasion the brothers were arrested by police and charged with a variety of offences including extortion. It was also believed that, unlike many Camorra groups, the Nuvoletta gang also enjoyed strong ties with the Sicilian Mafia – often providing safe havens for those Mafiosi who were on the run from the authorities. This testament by Camorra supergrass Pasquale Galasso details how meetings were often held at the Nuvoletta brothers' villas, at which the Mafia were frequently present:

> Our worries arose from the possibility that the police would arrive during our meetings and cause a bloodbath, yet Nuvoletta always managed to calm us down. Sometimes when Carmine Alfieri and I looked out at his farmhouse when leaving Vallesana, we saw some police cars parked outside Nuvoletta's house. That proved to us he was well protected [. . .] in the course of these meetings we had to sort out once and for all the tensions Cutolo had created. I can recall that Riina, Provenzano and Bagarella [all Mafiosi] were in Nuvoletta's farmhouse at the same time.[6]

Being connected to the Mafia had enormous benefits for the Nuvoletta brothers, not least because the Mafia also afforded the Nuvoletta gang protection both politically and from other Camorra organizations.

Reaping the rewards from their many businesses, the Nuvolettas now decided to invest their capital in the ever-burgeoning construction industry, with cement factories their particular choice. After setting up their first operation in April 1979, two years later the company made almost 500 percent profit. Extraordinary as this was, the massive gains were mostly due to the 1980 earthquake. Cement was necessary in all areas of reconstruction. It was almost a licence to print money, particularly after such a major disaster. But not everything was plain sailing, for in the same year that the earthquake struck, workers in the shipyards of Castellammare, who were angered by the Camorra's demands for protection money, mounted demonstrations throughout the summer.

The Nuvolettas didn't allow such a minor matter as social unrest to stand in the way of progress, and throughout the 1980s they made significant inroads into Neapolitan public life, not least when Vincenzo Agizza – a Nuvoletta gang member – was made a Christian Democrat councilor in 1980. This was just the tip of the iceberg. Many other council members and politicians were also connected to the Camorra, if not directly, then indirectly through family members. This meant that the

Nuvolettas were soon in control of an international corporation with fingers in such diverse pies as the construction industry, the entertainment business, drugs, fraud, stud farming, real estate and agriculture. Still, as powerful and rich as they undoubtedly were, the Nuvolettas were not immune to attack, as was proved in 1984 when Ciro Nuvoletta was murdered by a rival Camorra group, the Bardellinos. This began a war between the two factions, which saw eight people killed and twenty-four seriously wounded. Perhaps the most notorious Camorra-related event during this turbulent period, one that illustrated the extent to which the Camorra worked hand-in-hand with some of Italy's most prominent politicians, was the Cirillo affair.

On April 27, 1981, a terrorist organization called the Red Brigade (not to be confused with the German Red Army Faction) kidnapped Ciro Cirillo (a Christian Democrat politician), killing two of his security guards and injuring his secretary. The Christian Democrats had, three years earlier, suffered the loss of another of their members, Aldo Moro, who was also kidnapped and later murdered by the Red Brigade. Knowing what was at stake, therefore, the Christian Democrats (CDs) immediately wanted to negotiate for Cirillo's release. This brought the Camorra squarely into the picture.

One day after Cirillo's capture, the Italian Secret Services were granted permission to visit Raffaele Cutolo in the Ascoli Piceno prison. Present at this meeting was the Christian Democrat Mayor of Giugliano, Giuliano Granata, which indicated just how far the CDs were willing to work alongside the Camorra to negotiate the release of their colleague. In fact, the government was fully complicit in the whole affair, with the Italian Minister of the Interior, Virginio Rognoni, declaring that, 'The Camorra could have an interest in helping to free Councilor Cirillo. Sometimes the relations between organized crime and terrorism are intertwined, other times they are separate. All possible channels must therefore be opened.'[7]

The Camorra's own willingness to become involved in negotiations must, as Tom Behan points out in his book on the group, have something to do with the fact that the police had deployed so many officers in the area to form checkpoints and roadblocks that the Camorra's illegal activities were severely curtailed. The sooner the Cirillo affair ended, the sooner 'business as normal' could resume. To this end, Cutolo, through the prison network, made contact with his opposite number within the Red Brigade who was also serving out a long prison term, though not in the same jail. But what was Cutolo's asking price for his involvement? How far was the government willing to go in order to secure Cirillo's release? Cutolo himself has said (though naturally this cannot be verified) that the Christian Democrat minister, Vincenzo Scotti, allegedly arranged for Cutolo's faction to be 'gifted' a substantial number of machine guns as payment.[8] Cutolo was, no doubt, also hoping for an early release from prison, as well as perhaps 'winning' a larger share of construction contracts than his organization was managing to secure at the time. Negotiations continued until it was agreed that both the Red Brigade and Cutolo's New Camorra were to receive large financial pay-offs garnered from a variety of construction

In a protest against a Camorra turf war that had seen dozens killed in Naples during 2004, people lay spreadeagled in the street covered in white sheets marked with fake bloodstains to represent those who had lost their lives.

companies who all supported the Christian Democrats. Three months after he was kidnapped, Cirillo was released from captivity unharmed. Yet this was only the beginning of the story, for afterwards countless questions were asked (particularly by the newspapers) about the extent of the Democrats' collusion with organized crime to secure Cirillo's release – not to mention how much money had changed hands during their meetings.

More disturbing than this, however, was the fact that several key players in the affair were subsequently murdered, including Antonio Ammaturo (head of the Naples Flying Squad) who was killed on July 15, 1982, Vincenzo Casillo (one of Cutolo's chief negotiators in the affair) who was killed by a car bomb in 1983, and his partner of several years who was found dead a few months later, her body dumped in a motorway ditch.

Eventually, a judicial enquiry was ordered to investigate exactly what had occurred both during and after the kidnapping. In conclusion the enquiry stated the following:

> In judgement it seems clear that the evidence points to an attitude on the part of leading Christian Democrats that was markedly different from that of the party's 'official line'; which was that of reacting with firmness to all Red Brigade blackmails and refusing all hypotheses of a negotiation or a compromise. In reality, there were members of the party who did not follow this official line but were active in various ways to obtain Cirillo's release, turning above all to the mediation of Raffaele Cutolo and accepting negotiations with the Red Brigade.[9]

With a good number of Italian politicians willing to work alongside the Camorra, this secret organization established a firm hold on Italian politics and society as a whole. Yet, unlike its Sicilian counterpart (the Mafia), which prides itself on secrecy, the Camorra's activities are frequently not entirely covert. For the most part this is probably due to the nature of their business dealings. With contraband cigarettes, for example, the trade requires a relatively large number of people to operate smoothly, many of them in clearly visible roles.

A second way in which the Camorra and Mafia operate differently is the way in which the Camorra either shun, or do not wish to encourage, a clear sense of hierarchy within its different organizations. This makes it very difficult for opposition groups to eradicate any particular Camorra 'family', for without a recognizable head of operations and subordinate chiefs, there are no targets. Virtually anyone joining the Camorra can rise to the top of his chosen 'profession', thus making the Camorra an ideal recruiting ground for youngsters wishing to make vast amounts of money in extremely short periods of time. Indeed, the Camorra indirectly employs huge numbers of teenagers, all eager to sell their goods, pedal drugs or extort money, while also encouraging them (those who are under eighteen years of age) to rob and commit murder, because if they are caught they cannot be tried or punished as adults.

Nor, these days, do the youngsters joining the Camorra have to undergo any type of initiation ceremony or prove their 'family credentials' like most Mafiosi recruits do. Family ties are important to the Camorra, but they are not essential. What is necessary is a willingness to engage in any or all of the Camorra-style businesses such as money laundering, drug dealing, usury, intimidation or extortion, the latter apparently constituting a huge business in the Naples area of Italy. In 1992 a shop owner's forum stated that an estimated 46 percent of shops in Naples were paying extortion money to the Camorra (whereas the national average was only 12 percent).

Usury is also frequently employed by Camorra organizations as a means of bringing in revenue. In an area that boasts notoriously high levels of unemployment, where credit is difficult to acquire for people without any regular income, private money-lending has almost become a way of life. Again, in Tom Bean's book on the Camorra, he states that the Association of Italian Bank and Finance customers has estimated that the practice of usury accounts for a national total of US$10 billion business. Illegal gambling is another huge Camorra-run enterprise with large numbers of illicit gaming houses set up throughout Naples and the region of Campania. The Camorra also operates several illegal betting systems, the revenue from which in 1989 was estimated to have been in the region of US$4 billion, resulting in a clear $16 million profit.

Huge profits are also to be made from the construction industry. In this respect politicians in the Camorra's pay were of vital importance in securing the contracts, sub-contracts and authorizations. 'The relationship between politicians and bureaucrats, businessmen, and then camorristi,' said a senior member of the Alfieri Camorra gang, Pasquale Galasso, during an Anti-Mafia Commission enquiry, 'is ultimately realized and achieves total fusion in the mechanism of public sector contracts. On the basis of all that I have noticed personally in my legitimate business activities and my work with Carmine Alfieri and other camorristi and businessmen, it is clear to me that the politician who manages the financing of a contract, is a mediator between the Camorra and a large company, which is nearly always from northern or central Italy. Such mediation takes the form of demanding a bribe from the company for himself or his representatives, and the awarding of sub-contracts to companies directly controlled by Camorra groups.'[10]

So, with the Camorra so deeply entrenched in the socio-economic fabric of Italian life, is there any chance that this secretive organization can ever be brought to account or eradicated?

In short, the answer is 'no', although the reasons for this are manifold. First and foremost, with so many politicians, policemen and judges in the Camorra's pocket, it would hardly be in the government's interest to crack down hard on them. Institutionalized corruption runs rife in Italy. Numerous politicians have been accused of serious crimes only to avoid being either arrested or tried on these charges. In the late 1990s, the Italian Prime Minister Silvio Berlusconi tried to facilitate a law which allowed for the freeing of all politicians facing trial. Due to a huge public outcry the bill was eventually dropped, but in 2001 Berlusconi announced he wanted the crime of false accounting struck off the statute books – the Prime Minister was at the time facing three separate trials for this crime. Neither are the police immune from criticism, with one government report in 1997 showing that any effort to stamp out Camorra-related crimes was impossible when several senior police officers were being paid monthly 'salaries' by the Camorra.

In direct contrast, the general public seems far more willing to stamp out organized crime, and are far more effective in doing so, because they are the ones who ultimately vote politicians, governments and judges in and out of office. Large groups of students, particularly in the Naples area, have mounted mass demonstrations against the presence of the Camorra in their city, often with the backing of Neapolitan shopkeepers, who close their premises as a sign of solidarity with the students and as a demonstration of their disgust at having to pay protection money. The church has also, to a certain extent, made a stand against the Camorra, organizing marches and distributing anti-Camorra literature.

Yet, despite all of this – the arrest of several senior Camorra players in the mid-1990s and the death of several others, the rise in the number of super-grasses willing to talk to the authorities, and the groundswell of public opinion against organized crime – no political strategy that leaves the foundations of the existing system untouched will ultimately work, and may even give rise to a far stronger Camorra in the future.

[1] *La Camorra: Notizie storiche raccolte e documentate per cura di Marco Monnier*, Marco Monnier, G. Barbera (Florence), 1863.

[2] Ibid.

[3] *See Naples and Die: The Camorra and Organized Crime*, Tom Behan, I. B. Tauris, 2002.

[4] Ibid.

[5] Ibid.

[6] Ibid.

[7] *Rapporto sulla camorra della Commisione antimafia*, L'Unità (Rome), 1994.

[8] *Il Manifesto* (Rome), 22 September 1994.

[9] *See Naples and Die: The Camorra and Organized Crime*, op. cit.

[10] Commissione Parlamentare di inchiesta sul fenomeno della mafia e sulle associazioni criminalis similari, *Audizione di Pasquale Galasso 17 settembre 1993*, Camera dei Deputati (Rome) 1993.

THE HELL FIRE CLUB – DEVILRY, DEBAUCHERY AND POLITICS

Franklin knew Le Despencer very well. He was fully aware of an
enterprise which the Englishman had been conducting for some
years more or less surreptitiously, known as the Hell Fire Club.
Its activities were familiar to Franklin and he occasionally
joined in them.

CECIL B. CURREY, *Road to Revolution:*
Benjamin Franklin in England

The eighteenth century in England was a strange and exciting period, one in
which the concept of democracy constantly battled against ever-threatening
tyranny, where the divide between rich and poor was monumental and over
which, towards the end of the era, hovered the terrible cloud of the Napoleonic Wars
(1799-1815). Great men of letters jostled for acclaim with painters, philosophers and
architects, the like of which few previous centuries had ever witnessed. Laurence
Sterne was writing *Tristram Shandy* (published 1760), Jonathan Swift published
Gulliver's Travels (1726), Dr. Johnson was compiling his dictionary, while Sir Joshua
Reynolds produced some of his greatest paintings. Other artists of the period
included Thomas Gainsborough, Sir Thomas Lawrence and of course, William
Hogarth. Architects such as Sir Christopher Wren and Robert Adam were designing
some of that century's most noteworthy buildings, including St. Paul's Cathedral,
and Capability Brown quietly revolutionized garden design to the extent that we can
still see his influence in landscaped gardens and parks today. This, then, was an
innovative, turbulent period, aptly described by Charles Dickens as being, 'the best
of times and the worst of times,' during which one of the most colorful, not to
mention bizarre, secret societies was first established in Britain.

There had been other secretive British groups, clubs such as the Hectors, the
Mohawks and the Blasters, but unlike these organizations, the Hell Fire Club's
membership included some of the most influential men of the day; men who
included a Prime Minister, a Lord Mayor of London, a Chancellor of the Exchequer,
a son of the Archbishop of Canterbury, as well as a handful of some of the country's
finest artists. So who was it that first conceived the idea of this highly secretive,
positively influential club?

Sir Francis Dashwood, baronet and heir to one of the greatest of all eighteenth-century fortunes, was born at the turn of the century in 1708. His father was an extremely wealthy businessman who had married into the aristocracy. Dashwood Senior pushed his son hard, and, as was the vogue in those days, when young Francis reached the age of twenty, he was sent on a Grand Tour of Europe with a tutor in tow to complete his education. The pair traveled through many countries, but it was while in Italy that young Dashwood's spirits soared and his curiosity became aroused when he fell in love with the country's classical architecture, the Renaissance paintings and sculptures and the romantic myths and legends of Italian history. Francis also became intrigued by the Catholic Church, although he later developed a deep hatred for this institution, but the greatest influence upon Dashwood while sojourning in Italy came when he was introduced to Prince Charles Edward Stuart, the pretender to the British throne. Following their meeting, or so it is claimed, Sir Francis became a Jacobite secret agent and his fascination with intrigue and secrecy might explain his later involvement with the Rosicrucian movement and the Freemasons.

By 1746 Dashwood was ready to form his own secret society, which would be known by a variety of names, such as the Order of the Knights of St. Francis, the Monks of Medmenham and the Order of the Knights of West Wycombe. Initial meetings were held at an old inn called the George and Vulture (later immortalized by Charles Dickens in *Pickwick Papers*) in Cornhill in the City of London.

Sir Francis's knights, of whom there were thirteen in total, each named after one of the twelve apostles with Sir Francis taking the role of Christ, were loyal servants,

Sir Francis Dashwood, founder of the Hell Fire Club, is depicted here by Hogarth in a symbolic, quasi-religious pose with a halo above his head but his crucifix set aside. The open book may be a Bible, or may be something far more sinister. The mask at his elbow represents the secrecy of his society and the near-naked nymph with which he is toying the magic and debauchery in which he indulged. The spilled wine and ruined fruit again symbolize the Hell Fire Club's drunken debauchery.

all of whom appreciated meeting at the George and Vulture. But while the inn was at first suitable for the society's purposes, by 1752 Dashwood decided to move his club to a ruined medieval abbey, Medmenham, on the banks of the Thames near Marlow, a mere six miles from his ancestral home at West Wycombe.

Originally the abbey had been a twelfth-century Cistercian monastery, before falling into secular hands and being converted into a Tudor manor house. Dashwood, far from wishing to preserve the abbey, instead planned that most eighteenth-century of changes, converting the building in the trend-setting style of the 'Gothic revival'. This, after all, was the era that would later produce Walpole's *Castle of Otranto* and M.G. Lewis's *The Monk*, both of which were packed full of ghostly happenings, apparitions, murders and vampires. Dashwood spent vast sums of money installing stained-glass windows picturing the twelve apostles in often extremely indecent poses, ornate stone carvings, frescoes and a motto engraved about the main door stating, 'Do As Thou Wilt.' Other changes to the abbey included a room devoted to Roman mythology, the walls of which were reputedly painted with copies of indecent frescoes from that period. Adjacent to this room was the library, said to contain the finest collection of pornographic books in the country. There was also a small Robing Room and a Withdrawing Room. In the main dining hall stood a statue of the Egyptian god of silence, Harpocrates, with a finger to his lips, no doubt reminding everyone who entered the abbey that what occurred within its walls was not to be spoken of on the outside. Nor was statuary confined to the abbey building, for the extensive gardens were replete with little temples in the Grecian style and hundreds of stone and marble figures of nymphs, gods and goddesses scattered everywhere one cared to look.

Yet if the house and gardens were impressive, the arrival of the monks themselves at the abbey, which always took place at night, was a truly awesome sight to behold. Journeying by gondola up the Thames, dressed in snow-white robes with hoods lined with scarlet silk and holding lighted torches, they made some onlookers imagine that they were watching the spirits of the original monks returning to haunt them.

Once inside the abbey, however, there were no outside spectators for the ceremonies and rituals played out within the abbey walls. The group's antics involved debauchery, black magic and Satanism. Satanism has, over the centuries, attracted people from all walks of life, due no doubt in part to the theory that Satan was an heroic figure who refused to bow down to any higher authority. Milton reflected on just this attitude in his greatest work, *Paradise Lost* (1667), in which Satan (who is arguably the most charismatic figure in the whole piece) states, 'Better to reign in hell, than serve in heaven.' A rebel to the last, so it is easy to see why Satanism appealed to the members of what was now called the Hell Fire Club, who also prided themselves on their own rebelliousness. What cannot be so easily documented is the extent to which the club practiced this black art, or how seriously they took it. The artist William Hogarth, who was a member of the club, did make a now very famous print showing Sir Francis partaking of his rather dubious devotions, dressed in the

Sir Francis Dashwood's Hell Fire Club was also known as the Order of the Knights of St. Francis (or Knights of West Wycombe) and the Monks of Medmenham. The original twelve members took the names of the apostles with Sir Francis assuming the title of Jesus.

habit of a Franciscan monk, kneeling before a naked nymph. It was also common knowledge that a large part of belonging to the Hell Fire group consisted of partaking of licentious pleasures, normally with prostitutes. Despite this, most members had wives, including Sir Francis, who married a woman called Sara Gould (known to everyone as 'Lady Mary') in 1745. The prostitutes, however, and the games they played with Hell Fire members, usually while dressed up as nuns, were the mainstay of these men's earthly pleasures. During the eighteenth century there were countless brothels catering to the gentry's every need. One of the most famous was Charlotte Hayes's establishment in London and, due to her having kept a ledger recording the comings and goings of her girls, we have been left documentary evidence that she provided 'nuns' for the abbey. 'June 18, 1759. Twelve vestals for the Abbey. Something discreet and Cyprian for the friars.'[1] The kind of antics in which they indulged involved pretty much every kind of sexual fantasy imaginable. The 'Abbot of the Day' would get first pick of the ladies, who wore nun's costumes and masks, after which everyone else would pair off. Normally couples then retired to single cells in the Withdrawing Room. Alternatively, they could use the abbey's extensive gardens, or if they preferred they could stay in the Roman Room, where they could practice the type of voyeurism so favored by John Cleland in his pornographic novel *Fanny Hill*, written in 1749. Brothels of the period also encouraged this type of behavior, positioning couches round the walls of the main 'play' area so that onlookers could be accommodated.

The sexual shenanigans enjoyed in the abbey, and the pomp and ceremony surrounding their rituals, encouraged membership of the club to blossom throughout the 1750s, to such an extent that Dashwood was eventually forced to split the members into two different categories. The first were known as the Superior Members and comprised of the twelve apostles plus Sir Francis. The second group were Inferior Members, of whom there may have been in the region of forty to fifty. When one of the Superior Members died, the remaining apostles would select a replacement from the Inferior group, among whom there was a great deal of competition to be granted the honor.

There was, of course, an initiation ceremony that everyone who wanted to join the Hell Fire Club, in any capacity, had to endure.

At midnight the candidate, clothed in a milk-white robe that flowed loosely around him, walked alone to the entrance of the chapel and knocked on the door. As it opened, he prostrated himself, then rose to walk slowly to the altar rails where he fell on his knees. The apostles sat in carved chairs along the wall, and Sir Francis, in his priestly robes, conducted the ceremony, attended by the poet Paul Whitehead, who kept records of the society's meetings, which he destroyed shortly before he died, years later, to try to keep secret the exact nature of the monks' rituals. (Whitehead's attempts at secrecy were only partially successful, for a good deal has been written by others about the Hell Fire Club ceremonies.) When the initiate sank to his knees before Sir Francis, the narcotic herbs burning in the braziers filled the chapel with fumes that dimmed the light of the candles. The candidate was called upon to abjure his faith and then to recite after Dashwood a perversion of the Apostles' Creed and the Articles of Faith. Next he was sprinkled with a mixture of salt and sulphur and baptized in a black font. He was then given some mystical name by which, in future, the brotherhood would always refer to him during meetings. After receiving the blood-red triangular Host, the candidate was finally admitted into full membership.[2]

Unlike today, where there is rigorous scrutiny and general abhorrence of politicians who dabble in anything regarded as being even slightly outside what is considered 'normal behavior,' there were no such constraints in Sir Francis's time. Members of the twelve apostles were frequently drawn from the highest echelons of social and political life. Dashwood's second-in-command was none other than the Earl of Sandwich, who became First Lord of the Admiralty in 1748 and served in this capacity again in 1763 and 1771, in control of the Royal Navy and, therefore, one of the most powerful men of the period, despite being described as being all but incompetent.

Next in the Hell Fire Club's chain of command was the Earl of Bute. Like Sandwich, the Earl was a close friend of King George III, and in 1762 he became Prime Minister – the most powerful man in the country. Other members of the twelve apostles included the Archbishop of Canterbury's son, Thomas Potter, who was later made Vice-Treasurer for Ireland by Prime Minister William Pitt; the poet Charles Churchill who, although not well-known today, was regarded by contemporaries as one of England's greatest men of letters; the novelist Laurence Sterne; Lord Melcombe; and the politician George Selwyn. Joining this worthy crowd, William Hogarth frequently attended Hell Fire meetings to sketch the participants, sketches that would later appear in some of the artist's series of prints.

Given the high-society status of its membership, there is little doubt that the Hell Fire Club wielded huge influence in England's corridors of power. It can even be contended that Sir Francis Dashwood (who was appointed Chancellor of the Exchequer by King George III) and his fellows were effectively running the country. Yet there was one man who, although he dabbled with the Hell Fire Club, ultimately found its antics so distasteful that he almost destroyed the group.

Introduced to the club by Thomas Potter, John Wilkes was not an immediately likeable man, but Sir Francis Dashwood apparently felt fondly toward him and he was begrudgingly accepted into the fold.

Born in 1727, Wilkes, a staunch Whig, was elected to Parliament as the Member for the Borough of Aylesbury, for which it is said he worked most diligently. His membership of the Hell Fire Club was not, however, quite so successful, for shortly after he gained entry he was expelled, following a prank he played on his fellow members. During one of their black masses, Wilkes, who had grown irritated by the anti-religious pretensions of the ceremonies, released a baboon dressed up as the Devil into the congregation. The result was pandemonium, with the Earl of Sandwich shouting aloud that the Devil was upon him, while other members collapsed in fright.

The Hell Fire Club 'monks' traveled up the River Thames in gondolas for their ceremonies at Medmenham Abbey, arriving at night wearing white robes and carrying candles, looking for all the world like the ghosts of the Cistercian abbey's original twelfth-century inhabitants.

Finally, the poor animal escaped through a window and order was restored, but not before the twelve apostles demanded of Sir Francis that Wilkes be excommunicated.

Wilkes felt little dismay or remorse at having been thrown out of the group; instead, he expressed his intense relief. He was glad to be shot of the Hell Fire Club and concentrated his energies on his blossoming political career, involving himself in one of the main debates of the time, about whether to give American Colonists representation in Parliament. As a Whig, Wilkes was all for it, but in this he was strongly opposed not only by the King, but also by 'the King's Friends' – a powerful group that included Bute, Sandwich, Dashwood *et al*. Whenever Wilkes attempted to make a speech in Parliament, the Hell Fire members combined to shout him down in rowdy exchanges.

In retaliation, Wilkes decided to use the pen rather than debate, employing the pages of a magazine that he had founded with Charles Churchill. The *North Briton* was a political pamphlet and, therefore, the best possible vehicle for the campaign Wilkes had in mind. Casting aside all caution, in the forty-fifth issue of the magazine he published a blistering attack on the government during which he included a choice piece of gossip (gleaned from his time with the Hell Fire Club) to the effect that Bute had had an affair with the King's mother. The result was extraordinary, for no sooner did Number 45 (as it soon became known) hit the streets than furious mobs began to hold demonstrations against both the government and the King. Neither Bute nor the King could move without being barracked, and the latter eventually invoked what was then known as a 'general warrant'. This allowed for the arrest of anyone thought to be associated with a criminal act, and the subject of the warrant was Wilkes.

The hapless Wilkes was duly arrested and incarcerated in the Tower of London. Yet far from calming the mood of the populace, by locking Wilkes up the King only provoked further rioting. Mobs ran amok, smashing windows and looting property until the King had to order Wilkes's release. Even then the mob wasn't satisfied and there remained a grave feeling of dissent among the general public. The King's Friends decided, therefore, to retaliate 'in kind' by publishing a bawdy poem Wilkes had written during his time with the Hell Fire Club; a poem which, when released, was pretty much guaranteed to shock and appall the general public. Called *An Essay on Woman*, the piece was actually a parody of Alexander Pope's *An Essay on Man* beginning with the line, 'Awake, my Sandwich' in imitation of Pope's 'Awake, my St. John.' By this time the King's Friends among the Hell Fire Club had nothing to lose, for George III had become a laughing stock, Bute was discredited and Sandwich, whose reputation had never been good, was now universally loathed.

On November 15, 1763, the Earl of Sandwich stood up in Parliament and recited the entire poem to his fellow politicians. The result was astounding. There was much hilarity with, for instance, Lord Chesterfield standing to announce: 'Thank God, gentlemen, that we have a Wilkes to defend our liberties and a Sandwich to protect our morals,' after which there erupted a now very famous exchange between Sandwich and Wilkes, with the former shouting out, 'Sir, you will either die on the gallows or of the pox!' and the latter replying calmly, 'That, my Lord, depends on whether I embrace your principles or your mistress.'

After many heated exchanges, Parliament decided to delay any action against Wilkes (such as charging him on the grounds of indecency or blasphemy), but while the government hesitated, the King's Friends were not so tardy. They saw to it that the poem was distributed throughout London to a shocked public, whose support for Wilkes dramatically changed. Wilkes's friends, meanwhile, tried to help him by explaining that they still supported his policies, if not his private life. But Wilkes was in an incredibly difficult position for, unlike many of the Hell Fire Club members, he did not have a title or limitless funds at his disposal. Although he might have fought like with like and revealed more about the club's less salubrious practices, he could not afford a lengthy battle with the Hell Fire Club, especially since, having been branded a Satanist and a writer of obscene literature, his political career was in ruins. No one wanted to be seen consorting with such a man, certainly not members of his own party. Even Pitt, who had always been a staunch supporter of Wilkes, rose in

Parliament and before everyone present stated that his fellow politician was 'a blasphemer who did not deserve to be ranked among the human species.'

Even so, members of the Hell Fire Club, not satisfied that they had dragged Wilkes so low that his political career could never be revived, together hatched an even more wicked plan. They hired a lowly member of the House of Commons by the name of Samuel Martin to denounce Wilkes in front of everyone as a coward and a scoundrel. The insult called for nothing less than a duel. A time and place was arranged and on November 16, 1763, the pair faced each other with pistols. Although a first round of the duel was declared void, during the second Martin, who had put in a great deal of target practice prior to denouncing Wilkes in Parliament, wounded his opponent in the groin. The injury was not, however, fatal.

Having failed to have Wilkes killed, the Hell Fire Club now relied on the Commons to force a bill through Parliament declaring their former friend an outlaw for high treason against the King, as well as for producing indecent literature. In this, at least, they were successful and a warrant was put out for Wilkes's arrest, but he, wary of the Hell Fire Club's powers, had already fled to France.

Despite their success in the matter of John Wilkes, the repercussions of Number 45 meant that Bute's and Dashwood's political careers were effectively shattered, while Sandwich was forced to resign from the Admiralty (although he was later reinstated). The antics of the Hell Fire Club, on the other hand, continued unabated. Holding black masses, invoking the Devil to appear, enjoying orgies and drinking to excess, all carried on as normal. A few glitches were experienced along the way, such as the one caused by the publication of a novel entitled *Chrysal, or The Adventures of a Guinea* by Charles Johnson. The novel was a 'confidential,' with the golden guinea coin playing the main role, describing everything it saw on its strange journey through life from the time of its origin in a Peruvian gold mine. Part of its journey included a brief sojourn with a member of the Hell Fire Club where the guinea 'witnessed' a black mass and an orgy. Suddenly everyone wanted to visit Medmenham Abbey which, although not named in the book, was soon singled out as the most likely site. Crowds began to turn up to watch the 'monks' arriving by night, while others attempted to break into the gardens, sometimes even into the abbey itself. For a secret society this was a distinctly undesirable turn of events. Something had to be done and, as ever, Sir Francis Dashwood was just the man to do it.

Sir Francis's own house at West Wycombe was large enough to accommodate any number of clubs and it was decided to move the Hell Fire Club to this location. But while the building was large enough and private enough, it sadly lacked that most of elusive of things – 'atmosphere'. Undeterred, Sir Francis came up with the extraordinary idea of excavating a vast network of caves under West Wycombe Hill. The caves had originally been created as part of a mining operation to provide material for road building and the spoil produced in extending them was used in one of Sir Francis's own philanthropic road-building schemes. Extending the caves, however, also had a far more sinister purpose and it was an undertaking in which Sir Francis reveled, personally designing each room, each twist and turn of these underground caverns. The entrance was surrounded by dark yew trees (trees normally associated with graveyards), beyond which lay a passageway leading downwards to join a whole system of caves and catacombs. On the walls of the corridors were carved grotesque faces (thought to be images of the Devil) while beyond the catacombs lay a Banqueting Hall from the ceiling of which hung a huge Rosicrucian lamp. Beyond this room was the Triangle (so named because of the shape of the chamber) and after that a river which the apostles named the River Styx, beside which stood a well called 'The Cursing Well' that was filled with 'unholy' water. In the very deepest part of the caves lay the Inner Temple, a circular room in which the black mass was practiced. The caves suited the Hell Fire Club's purposes perfectly. Hidden from view, no prying eyes could see what the Hell Fire members were doing or how many prostitutes were being hustled into the place. Normal service was resumed and continued discretly.

Around this time, Benjamin Franklin redoubled his efforts to persuade the British government that unless the American Colonists' demands to have proper representation in Parliament were met, a revolution was likely. Sir Francis Dashwood immediately invited Franklin down to his country estate where the two became firm friends (later devising the Franklin Prayer Book together, a revision of the Book of Common Prayer), although it is difficult to say whether Franklin ever became a member of the Hell Fire Club itself. It would seem likely, however, that he did, as membership meant instant access to several senior politicians and statesmen who would have been invaluable to Franklin in attempting to place American MPs in the House of Commons. Sir Francis certainly did everything he could to help Franklin achieve some kind of compromise with the King's Friends over the American Colonist question, and would even go so far as to invite the Prime Minister, Lord North, who served his country in this role from 1770-82, down to West Wycombe in order to meet Franklin. But for all the help Franklin was given, his pleas would ultimately fall on deaf ears; the British government was not to be moved.

Meanwhile, a ghost from the past had reappeared in the shape of the notorious John Wilkes who, having spent several years in France, returned to London in 1768. Despite there still being several arrest warrants out for him, Wilkes decided to take a calculated risk and once again run for Parliament, this time as the MP for the Middlesex constituency. This move must have impressed Dashwood, who had always respected anyone willing to flout authority, for on hearing of it he decided to give Wilkes his support. The news of Wilkes's return and parliamentary candidacy spread fast, setting off a series of highly public demonstrations. Benjamin Franklin described one such:

> I went last week to Winchester and observed that for fifteen miles out of town there was scarce a door or a window-shutter next to the road unmarked with 'No. 45' or 'Wilkes and Liberty' and this continued here and there to Winchester which is 64 miles. London was illuminated for

two nights at the command of the mob who made their rounds at intervals during the whole night and obliged those who had extinguished the candles to light them again, their windows being smashed if they refused.[3]

The King was not merely unamused, but terrified that Wilkes's re-election might bring about the downfall of the monarchy. But the latter's involvement with the Hell Fire Club still counted against him, particularly with the more staid elements of society. He did, of course, command strong support among a certain element of society who saw him as a symbol of liberty, a man who had opposed the King and the arrogant King's Friends. With a warrant for his arrest still outstanding, Wilkes's next move was to force George III's hand by marching to the King's Bench Prison, where he demanded to be given a cell. It was all highly embarrassing for the monarch, but Wilkes remained where he was, corresponding from his prison cell with Franklin, whose cause for the Colonists he supported wholeheartedly.

Meanwhile, every day saw a crowd of supporters gathering beneath Wilkes's cell, until the King put a stop even to this by mounting an armed guard underneath the window. This could only spell disaster and, sure enough, shortly after the guard arrived, a riot broke out, resulting in the shooting of seven people. Several of the victims were women. The incident ignited further rioting together with a countrywide march on London, with the demonstrators demanding the release of Wilkes. Something urgent had to be done so the King's Friends held a meeting at which they declared Wilkes's original arrest warrant invalid due to faulty wording. Wilkes was immediately released, much to the mob's delight, and Sir Francis whisked his erstwhile friend down to West Wycombe.

During Wilkes's sojourn in France and his spell in the King's Bench Prison, Dashwood had built a church on the hill above the caves. St. Lawrence's was (and is) a beautiful, if somewhat mystifying, structure, given that Sir Francis espoused Satanism. Some people believe it was built in order to make up for all Sir Francis's misdeeds, while others prefer the theory that it was built simply to improve the view from West Wycombe Hall. Wilkes certainly appreciated being shown the building, although his stay at West Wycombe was not to last long as he was compelled to rush back to London, where the elections were about to take place. This was an election that Wilkes had had to fight several times over. The King's Friends had first fielded a candidate by the name of Dingley, but sadly he died before the election took place. Searching round for a replacement candidate, the King's Friends then chose a Colonel Luttrel, but to no avail. Wilkes won a resounding victory, yet even so his path to Parliament was not without hitches for the King, infuriated that such a man could be re-elected, issued an order that Wilkes not be allowed to enter Parliament. It seemed that Wilkes had failed in his bid and the King's Friends had once again managed to scupper his political dreams by forcing a resolution through Parliament refusing to allow him to be seated due to his being a blasphemer, a traitor and a writer of salacious poetry. It was as if time had stood still; once again riots broke out, Lord North, the Prime Minister, was dragged from his carriage by an angry mob and nearly killed, and men from all over the country marched on London, until finally Parliament backed down. At long last John Wilkes, sworn enemy of the King, took his seat in Parliament for the second time in his life.

Unfortunately, for several members of the Hell Fire Club life had not been so kind. Thomas Potter, the Archbishop of Canterbury's son, died in 1759 at the age of forty, while the poet Charles Churchill met his end in France at the tender age of thirty-three. Meanwhile, Lord Melcombe developed dropsy, but instead of going to a doctor, sought out a charlatan quack who prescribed all kinds of strange remedies. Finally, in 1762, Melcombe suffered a major fit and fell downstairs, killing himself. The death toll continued; the club's secretary, Paul Whitehead, died in 1774. In his will he left his heart to Sir Francis, who had it placed in an urn which was later secured inside a mausoleum built on top of the caves at West Wycombe (though the heart was later stolen by a souvenir hunter in 1839). Nor did the Earl of Sandwich fare much better. The public never forgave him for his attack on Wilkes or his reading aloud of Wilkes's poem in Parliament. Sandwich did his public image further damage when, as an elderly man, he took up with a young girl called Martha Ray. Martha had already caught the eye of a curate, who fell in love with her and offered her marriage, but Martha turned him down, preferring instead the rich pickings she enjoyed with Sandwich. One night while Sandwich and his young mistress were stepping into their carriage, the curate rushed up to them, put a pistol to Martha's head and killed her. The curate was later hanged for her murder, but the public saved its vilification for Sandwich who, they claimed, had prevented the girl from marrying and was thus as guilty of Martha's death as the curate had been. Sandwich could no longer enjoy respectable society and eventually retired to the country, where he died in 1792, unloved and unmourned.

Lord Bute, the ex-Prime Minister and third in command at the Hell Fire Club, denounced the new government, particularly with reference to their handling of the American Colonists, after which he retired to Italy a bitter and disappointed man. He, like the Earl of Sandwich, died in 1792.

In old age Sir Francis Dashwood lived the life of a quiet country gentleman. He often reminisced about the 'good old days' when he and his companions pleasured themselves with orgies and passed the rest of the time playing at politics. Sir Francis died on December 11, 1781, and with his passing there slipped away one of the most curious of all secret societies – a group of men who, to every intent and purpose, ran the country, but whose real passion lay deep underground, in caverns beneath the quiet West Wycombe countryside.

---

[1] *The Hell Fire Club*, Daniel P. Mannix, Four Square, 1961.

[2] Ibid.

[3] Ibid.

PICTURE ACKNOWLEDGMENTS

© Boating Images Photo Library / Alamy: page 186

Courtesy of The Bancroft Library, University of California, Berkeley:
  BANC PIC 1996.003--fALB : 266, page 63;
  BANC PIC 1996.003--fALB : 110a, page 66

Reuters / CORBIS: page 130

Tony Gentile / Reuters / CORBIS: page 176

Gianni Giansanti / Sygma / CORBIS: page 173

PA / EMPICS: pages 33, 50

Getty Images: pages 24, 40, 43, 52, 94, 102, 110, 114, 133, 138, 144, 149

AFP / Getty Images: pages 85, 86, 91, 118, 121, 126

Time Life Pictures / Getty Images: pages 55, 60, 72

Illustrated London News Picture Library: page 75

Mary Evans Picture Library: pages 13, 159, 163, 183

Mary Evans Picture Library / Harry Price: page 27

www.TopFoto.co.uk: pages 97, 105, 156, 170, 180